Manchester Medieval Sources Series

series advisers Rosemary Horrox and Simon MacLean

This series aims to meet a growing need amongst students and teachers of medieval history for translations of key sources that are directly usable in students' own work. It provides texts central to medieval studies courses and focuses upon the diverse cultural and social as well as political conditions that affected the functioning of all levels of medieval society. The basic premise of the series is that translations must be accompanied by sufficient introductory and explanatory material and each volume therefore includes a comprehensive guide to the sources' interpretation, including discussion of critical linguistic problems and an assessment of the most recent research on the topics being covered.

NOBLE SOCIETY

Manchester University Press

Medieval Sources*online*

Complementing the printed editions of the Medieval Sources series, Manchester University Press has developed a web-based learning resource which is now available on a yearly subscription basis.

Medieval Sources*online* brings quality history source material to the desktops of students and teachers and allows them open and unrestricted access throughout the entire college or university campus. Designed to be fully integrated with academic courses, this is a one-stop answer for many medieval history students, academics and researchers keeping thousands of pages of source material 'in print' over the Internet for research and teaching.

titles available now at Medieval Sources*online include*

Trevor Dean *The towns of Italy in the later Middle Ages*

John Edwards *The Jews in Western Europe, 1400–1600*

Paul Fouracre and Richard A. Gerberding *Late Merovingian France: History and hagiography 640–720*

Chris Given-Wilson *Chronicles of the Revolution 1397–1400: The reign of Richard II*

P. J. P. Goldberg *Women in England, c. 1275–1525*

Janet Hamilton and Bernard Hamilton *Christian dualist heresies in the Byzantine world, c. 650–c. 1450*

Rosemary Horrox *The Black Death*

David Jones *Friars' Tales: Thirteenth-century exempla from the British Isles*

Graham A. Loud and Thomas Wiedemann *The history of the tyrants of Sicily by 'Hugo Falcandus', 1153–69*

A. K. McHardy *The reign of Richard II: From minority to tyranny 1377–97*

Simon MacLean *History and politics in late Carolingian and Ottonian Europe: The* Chronicle *of Regino of Prüm and Adalbert of Magdeburg*

Anthony Musson with Edward Powell *Crime, law and society in the later Middle Ages*

Janet L. Nelson *The Annals of St-Bertin: Ninth-century histories, volume I*

Timothy Reuter *The Annals of Fulda: Ninth-century histories, volume II*

R. N. Swanson *Catholic England: Faith, religion and observance before the Reformation*

Elisabeth van Houts *The Normans in Europe*

Jennifer Ward *Women of the English nobility and gentry 1066–1500*

For further information and subscription prices, see *www.manchesteruniversitypress.co.uk/ manchester-medieval-sources-online*

NOBLE SOCIETY

Five lives from twelfth-century Germany

selected sources translated and annotated
by Jonathan R. Lyon

Manchester University Press

The right of Jonathan R. Lyon to be identified as the author of this work has been asserted by him in accordance with the Copyright, Designs and Patents Act 1988.

Published by Manchester University Press
Altrincham Street, Manchester M1 7JA

www.manchesteruniversitypress.co.uk

British Library Cataloguing-in-Publication Data
A catalogue record for this book is available from the British Library

Library of Congress Cataloging-in-Publication Data applied for

ISBN 978 0 71909 102 5 hardback
ISBN 978 0 71909 103 2 paperback

First published 2017

The publisher has no responsibility for the persistence or accuracy of URLs for any external or third-party internet websites referred to in this book, and does not guarantee that any content on such websites is, or will remain, accurate or appropriate.

Typeset
by Toppan Best-set Premedia Limited
Printed in Great Britain
by CPI Group (UK) Ltd, Croydon, CR0 4YY

For John Van Engen

CONTENTS

LIST OF MAPS AND GENEALOGIES

Maps

Genealogies

ACKNOWLEDGEMENTS

A translation project of this sort inevitably requires more time and energy than one initially anticipates, but I have been immensely fortunate to receive support from numerous people, without whom this project never would have come to fruition so quickly. First and foremost, I thank Lisa Wolverton for agreeing to join me in translating, annotating and introducing one of the five texts in this volume, *The deeds of Margrave Wiprecht of Groitzsch*. This proved to be a complicated text – and a difficult one to translate; I cannot imagine producing such a polished translation without our partnership. Just as importantly, translating the text together gave us the opportunity to discuss a wide range of issues about the German–Slav frontier and eleventh- and twelfth-century history more generally, and I have learned a great deal from Lisa throughout this process. I look forward to our future collaborations.

Christina Lutter at the University of Vienna first called my attention to another of the texts that I have translated here, *The life of an unnamed* magistra *of Admont*, and I am grateful for our many conversations about the text and Admont more generally. The participants at the Chicago area's Saturday afternoon medieval intellectual history seminar read an early draft of my translation of *The deeds of Count Ludwig of Arnstein* and offered many helpful suggestions for how to improve the text. Two of my colleagues at the University of Chicago, Michael I. Allen and Rachel Fulton Brown, also provided guidance on translating passages of the texts that proved especially challenging. I thank my two graduate assistants for their support as well; Christopher Fletcher determinedly tracked down source citations for me, and Tristan Sharp read the translations one final time to note inconsistencies. Chieko Maene, a GIS specialist in the University of Chicago's Social Sciences Division, made the maps, for which I thank her. I am also grateful to Simon MacLean for inviting me to contribute to the Manchester Medieval Sources Series, the Manchester University Press staff for their friendly guidance, and the Press's anonymous reviewer for suggested improvements. Lastly, I would be remiss if I failed to acknowledge the graduate students in my Newberry Library Seminar on medieval biography; our conversations were not only great fun but were also invaluable in helping me write the introductions to the texts translated here.

My *Doktorvater*, mentor and friend, John Van Engen, first taught me that being a good medievalist meant working at multiple levels within the historical discipline. Having original ideas and clear theses – and knowing how to answer the dreaded 'so what?' question – are essential to a successful career. Learning how to read critically and engage the secondary scholarship in the field is equally important. And alongside these 'big picture' lessons, John has routinely reminded me – and demonstrated throughout his own career – that it all starts by getting your hands dirty and knowing your sources. This means going back to the original manuscripts and charters as often as possible, and it means taking the time to read, translate and *understand* the medieval evidence. Having spent the better part of the last four years living and breathing the five texts I have translated here, I appreciate now, more than ever before, the wisdom of his words.

ABBREVIATIONS

CDSR I A 2	*Codex Diplomaticus Saxoniae Regiae*, part I, section A, vol. 2
MGH DD F. I	*Die Urkunden Friedrichs I.*
MGH DD H. IV	*Die Urkunden Heinrichs IV.*
MGH DD K. III	*Die Urkunden Konrads III. und seines Sohnes Heinrich*
MGH DD L. III	*Die Urkunden Lothars III. und der Kaiserin Richenza*
MGH SS	*Monumenta Germaniae Historica, Scriptores*
MGH SSrG	*Monumenta Germaniae Historica, Scriptores rerum germanicarum in usum scholarum separatim editi*

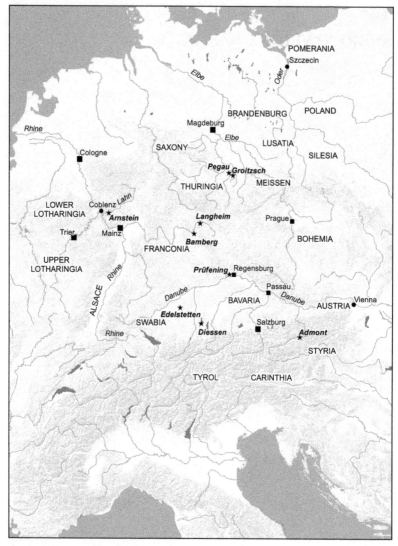

Key (applies to Maps 1–5):
★ key location in text
■ archbishopric
■ bishopric
▲ monastery
● other town, castle or village

1 The German kingdom and its eastern neighbours in the twelfth century

INTRODUCTION

Noble society in the twelfth-century German kingdom was vibrant and multi-faceted. Many of the men born into aristocratic families spent their lives in the violent pursuit of land and power, building castles and fighting for their lords, their relatives and themselves. Many of the women born into these families managed households as wives, mothers and widows and acted as leading patronesses of the religious life. Other nobles, both male and female, dedicated themselves to prayer and spiritual improvement in a monastic community, while others walked a middle course between the lay and religious spheres as influential prelates who oversaw both their Christian flocks and their churches' extensive political and territorial interests. Regardless of which roles individual noblemen and noblewomen played in society, the members of this elite are the people whose words and actions have been preserved in the vast majority of sources that survive from the German kingdom in the central Middle Ages. Noble culture, in both its secular and ecclesiastical forms (if it is appropriate to draw a distinction between the two), permeates our extant evidence.

This volume aims to illuminate the diversity of the aristocratic experience by providing five texts, translated into English for the first time, that show how noblemen and women from across the German kingdom lived and died between approximately 1075 and 1200. The subjects of these works – a margrave, a bishop, a *magistra*,[1] an abbess and a count – were all prominent figures in the German kingdom. To read these five sources together is to appreciate how interconnected political, military, economic, religious and spiritual interests could be for

---

1 In the two texts translated here, in which the title *magistra* appears, it refers to the leader of the women's side of a double monastic community; the *magistra* was under the authority of the abbot or provost who was the head of the male side of the community. For more on this term, see the introduction to *The life of an unnamed magistra of Admont.*

some of the leading members of the twelfth-century nobility – and for
the authors who wrote about them. Whether fighting for the emperor
in Italy, bringing Christianity to pagans in what is today northern
Poland, or founding, reforming and governing monastic communities in
the heartland of the German kingdom, the subjects of these texts call
attention to some of the many ways that elite culture shaped European
society in the central Middle Ages.

In the twelfth- and thirteenth-century manuscripts that preserve
these five Latin sources, scribes employed the terms *vita* ('life') and *gesta*
('deeds') to describe the texts and their contents. Both terms reflect the
biographical character of these sources; a single person is the subject
of each text. Both terms also embed these works within rich literary
traditions in the medieval West. The word *gesta* is a common one in
biographical writing from the period, well known to historians of the
medieval German kingdom through a variety of important texts, including
Wipo's *Deeds* of Emperor Conrad II (d. 1039) and Otto of Freising's
Deeds of Emperor Frederick I Barbarossa (d. 1190).[2] In addition, *gesta*
is a term used to label biographical sources about many other leading
members of European society more generally, including popes, dukes,
bishops and abbots.[3] On rare occasions, medieval authors wrote about
the 'deeds' of lords of lesser rank as well, and two of the texts translated
here belong to this category.[4] The term *vita*, in contrast, tends to be
associated most commonly in modern scholarship with hagiography,
that enormous body of sources that preserves accounts of the lives and
miracles of saints – or at least of people thought to be saintly, regardless
of whether or not they had been formally canonized.[5]

---

2 Wipo, *The deeds of Conrad II* and Otto of Freising and Rahewin, *The deeds of Frederick
Barbarossa.* For secular biographies in this period, see Morrison's introduction to
Imperial lives and letters of the eleventh century, 40–2.

3 See, for example, *The deeds of Pope Innocent III; The 'Gesta Normannorum ducum'
[The deeds of the dukes of the Normans*]; *A warrior bishop of the twelfth century: The
deeds of Archbishop Albero of Trier;* and William of Malmesbury, *The deeds of the
bishops of England.* For more on *gesta,* see Sot, *Gesta episcoporum, gesta abbatum* and
the brief but excellent discussion of one *gesta* tradition in Nicholas Paul, *To follow
in their footsteps,* 21–4.

4 For the rarity of such works, see Vogtherr, 'Wiprecht von Groitzsch und das
Jakobspatrozinium', 39–40.

5 For hagiography, see the classic treatment in Delehaye, *Legends of the saints* and,
more recently, Bartlett, *Why can the dead do such great things?* For some examples
of important hagiographical *vitae* in English translation, see *Soldiers of Christ: saints
and saints' lives from Late Antiquity and the early Middle Ages* and *Medieval hagiography:
an anthology.*

However, modern scholars must be careful not to draw too sharp a distinction between the terms *vita* and *gesta*. In the medieval period, they could have very similar connotations. There are, for example, *vitae* of non-saintly rulers. The Roman author Suetonius's *Lives of the Caesars* was a model for Einhard's *Life* of Charlemagne (d. 814), and there is a *vita* of the decidedly un-saintly German ruler Henry IV (d. 1106) as well.[6] There are also *vitae* for other leading secular nobles – Donizo of Canossa's *Life* of Margravine Matilda of Tuscany (d. 1115), for example – as well as for popes and bishops who were never canonized or associated with large numbers of miracles.[7] As several of the sources translated here attest, medieval authors seem to have used the words *vita* and *gesta* interchangeably without any sense that they represented two distinct literary genres.[8] All five of these works can therefore be read together fruitfully as a cohesive set of sources for elite society in the twelfth-century German kingdom.

Medieval forms of biography – whether labelled 'lives' or 'deeds' – rarely if ever align neatly with modern conceptions of how one ought to write the life of another person.[9] The hagiographical baggage attached to the term *vita*, in particular, tends to give medieval biographies an air of fiction. Unbelievable miracle stories, repetitive *topoi* that seek to embed the text's subject in long traditions of saintliness, and unreliable historical details fill some of the best-known saints' lives.[10] While all of the texts translated here contain these hagiographical features in varying amounts, none is completely overwhelmed by them, because of the five men and women who are the subjects of these texts, only one was ever formally canonized: Bishop Otto I of Bamberg (d. 1139). He became a saint approximately forty years after the composition of the *vita* translated here. Only one of the other texts, *The life of*

---

6 Suetonius, *Lives of the Caesars*; Einhard, *The life of Charlemagne*; and *The life of Emperor Henry IV*. See also *Charlemagne and Louis the Pious: the lives by Einhard, Notker, Ermoldus, Thegan, and the Astronomer.*

7 Donizo of Canossa, *Donizonis Vita Mathildis*. See also the papal lives translated in *The papal reform of the eleventh century* and the *Vita Burchardi* about Bishop Burchard of Worms.

8 For example, in the opening poem of the *The life of an unnamed* magistra *of Admont*, the phrases *fulgida vita* and *pia gesta* both appear in the first three lines. For a different perspective on the genre question, see Sot, *Gesta episcoporum, gesta abbatum*, 18.

9 Cf. Bartlett, *Why can the dead do such great things?*, 519.

10 See *Saints and cities in medieval Italy*, 4–7, for a good recent overview of some of the challenges of using hagiographical sources.

Mechthild of Diessen (d. 1160) by Engelhard of Langheim, may have had
the canonization of its subject as one – but certainly not its only – goal.
The authors of *The deeds of Margrave Wiprecht of Groitzsch* (d. 1124),
The life of an unnamed magistra *of Admont* (d. mid-twelfth century),
and *The deeds of Count Ludwig of Arnstein* (d. 1185) showed little if any
interest in recording their subjects' miraculous or wondrous activities.
In other words, none of these texts was written about someone who
had already been canonized, and the authors of three of the five had
no intention of asserting the saintliness of their subjects. As a result,
although the collection of *vitae* and *gesta* translated here may not offer
readers the types of biographical information they expect to find in
modern biographies, these works do illuminate the lives and times of their
subjects in ways that few other surviving sources from this period can.

Thus, this volume seeks to provide scholars and students alike with a
set of texts that can deepen their understanding of elite society within
the German kingdom of the twelfth century. Since the year 2000, there
has been an impressive surge in the number of Latin sources available
in English translation for earlier periods of German history.[11] Scholars
have been especially interested in translating works of *Reichsgeschichte*,
or imperial history, meaning that numerous accounts of high politics
are now available in English for the centuries prior to the twelfth. For
example, many of the most important narrative sources for the Ottonian
period (918–1024) have been translated.[12] The Salian century (1024–1125),
which includes what is quite possibly the most famous event in all of
medieval German history, the Investiture Controversy (1075–1122), has
also seen a new round of translations of important chronicles.[13] Most
of the twelfth century, in contrast, is not as fortunate. The greatest
historian of the period, Bishop Otto of Freising (d. 1158), has had both
of his narrative works of history – *The two cities* and *The deeds of Frederick*

11 See the Bibliography for an extensive list of sources from the medieval German
kingdom in English translation.

12 *Ottonian Germany: the chronicon of Thietmar of Merseburg*; Widukind of Corvey, *Deeds
of the Saxons*; Liudprand of Cremona, *The complete works*; *Queenship and sanctity: the
lives of Mathilda and the epitaph of Adelheid*; *History and politics in late Carolingian
and Ottonian Europe: the chronicle of Regino of Prüm and Adalbert of Magdeburg*; and
*Warfare and politics in medieval Germany, ca. 1000: on the variety of our times by Alpert
of Metz*.

13 *The annals of Lampert of Hersfeld*; *Chronicles of the Investiture Contest*; *Eleventh-Century
Germany: the Swabian chronicles*; and for Bohemia in this period, Cosmas of Prague,
The chronicle of the Czechs. Older translations for this century include *Imperial lives
and letters of the eleventh century* and Adam of Bremen, *History of the archbishops of
Hamburg-Bremen*.

Barbarossa – translated into English, but these translations are now more than sixty years old.[14] More recently, scholars have produced translations of a small number of other texts for the reign of Emperor Frederick I Barbarossa, making him the twelfth-century German ruler with the most source material available in English.[15] Popular interest in the woman who may be the best known figure from this period in German medieval history, Hildegard of Bingen (d. 1179), has also generated a variety of good translations, not only of her own works but of works about her as well.[16] However, the remaining source material available in English for the twelfth-century German kingdom is scattered across a wide range of publications, some of them decades old.[17] As a result, there is no other cohesive body of works in translation comparable to this one for the lived experience of twelfth-century German noblemen and women.

The five people who are the subjects of the texts translated here cut across many of the strata of German elite society. Wiprecht of Groitzsch, though he had no noble title for much of his life, moved in prominent circles at the imperial court and in Saxony during the late eleventh and early twelfth centuries. He eventually obtained the title of margrave, giving him authority over part of the border region along the Elbe River in the north-east of the German kingdom. Thus, his life highlights some of the opportunities that were available to ambitious lords, especially in the decades around 1100, to rise from relatively obscure beginnings into the uppermost levels of the German nobility. The subject of the second text, Bishop Otto I of Bamberg, was born into the Swabian nobility in the south-west of the kingdom; though little is known about his family background, he became a leading figure at the imperial court before obtaining the bishopric of Bamberg. Like Wiprecht, therefore, his career points to the possibilities for upward mobility that some nobles enjoyed in the early twelfth century. In contrast, both Ludwig of Arnstein and Mechthild of Diessen came from families of comital

---

14 Otto of Freising, *The two cities*; and Otto of Freising and Rahewin, *The deeds of Frederick Barbarossa*.

15 See also *Barbarossa in Italy* and *The crusade of Frederick Barbarossa*. This ruler is also the subject of a monumental new biography in English: Freed, *Frederick Barbarossa*.

16 See, for example, Hildegard of Bingen, *The letters of Hildegard of Bingen*; Hildegard of Bingen, *Scivias*; and *Jutta and Hildegard: the biographical sources*.

17 See, for example, *The life of Godfrey of Cappenberg*; *The life of Otto, apostle of Pomerania*; *A warrior bishop of the twelfth century*; *Vita sancti Eckenberti*; *Elisabeth of Schönau: the complete works*; Helmold of Bosau, *The chronicle of the Slavs*; *The chronicle of Henry of Livonia*; and Eidelberg, ed. and trans., *The Jews and the crusaders*.

rank that were already, at the time these two were born, leading lineages in the Rhine River valley and in western Bavaria respectively. Both of them, in other words, belonged from birth to the regional elites that dominated local life in the twelfth century. The unnamed *magistra* of Admont, on the other hand, came from a ministerial family, meaning she was of unfree status; she was therefore not a member of the free nobility. Nevertheless, as her rise into a leadership position at the prominent monastic house of Admont attests, ministerials in many regions were becoming the de facto lower nobility during the twelfth century, giving them a significant role to play in elite society.[18] These five sources, when read together, thus offer a rich picture of multiple levels of German elite society, from some of the leading families of the nobility to people whose lives were lived in the ambiguous zone between free and unfree status.

German noble society in the central Middle Ages

The sources translated here span the reigns of the German kings and emperors Henry IV (1056–1106), Henry V (1106–25), Lothar III (1125–37), Conrad III (1138–52) and Frederick I Barbarossa (1152–90). All five of these rulers have roles to play in the texts, and their courts are important centres of patronage at key moments for some of the men and women discussed in these works. Nevertheless, imperial court politics are not the principal subject of any of the sources in this volume. Instead, much of the action in these texts unfolds on a much smaller scale at the level of local societies: in castles, small towns and religious communities. Because noblemen and women were central figures in these societies, situating the nobility within the local landscape of the twelfth-century German kingdom is essential background for introducing these sources.

As scholars have long argued, the period c. 1075 to 1200, covered in this book, was an important one in the history of the medieval German nobility.[19] The significance of this period is partially the product

---

18 For more on this point, see below.

19 Good discussions of this subject in English can be found in Reuter, 'The medieval nobility'; Arnold, *Princes and territories in medieval Germany*; Freed, 'Reflections on the medieval German nobility'; and Fuhrmann, *Germany in the high middle ages*. For a recent German overview of the scholarship in this field, see Hechberger, *Adel im fränkisch-deutschen Mittelalter*.

of the dramatic increase over the course of this century and a quarter in the source material available to study elite society. There is relatively little extant evidence for the structure of the nobility and for individual noble families prior to the year 1050; in contrast, many of the lineages that would come to dominate aristocratic society during the twelfth, thirteenth and fourteenth centuries first emerge from obscurity in the decades around the year 1100.[20] This increase in sources is particularly striking in the case of charters: archival documents that record property donations and exchanges as well as confirmations of rights and privileges. These survive in far greater numbers for the twelfth century than the eleventh. Issued by kings, bishops, monastic communities and nobles, charters have traditionally been the most valuable sources for studying the German nobility. They make it possible to reconstruct the genealogies of many noble lineages and also provide evidence for some of the ways aristocratic lordship functioned on the ground: how nobles acquired territory, built and maintained networks of relatives and friends, protected their rights and privileges, divided their inheritances and preserved their memories after death.[21] Other types of sources, including the *vitae* and *gesta* translated here, are also much more common from the later 1000s onwards. Thus, the decades between 1075 and 1200 are a key transition period in the study of the medieval German nobility, because it is possible for historians to study many more aspects of elite society during these years than during the preceding ones.

However, the increase in surviving sources is not the only reason why scholars have identified this period as a critical one. There were also significant changes occurring within noble society itself that would have far-reaching consequences for the German kingdom in subsequent centuries. Three of these changes in particular will be highlighted here, because they provide important context necessary for understanding the five texts translated in this volume. First, the Investiture Controversy and its aftermath saw a decline in royal authority that created opportunities for nobles – many of them from relatively obscure backgrounds – to acquire more power and influence at the local level. A second change, closely connected to the first, was a transformation in the nature of lordship; from dukes to counts to unfree ministerials, members of all the strata of elite society in the German kingdom exercised their rights and authority in very different ways in the mid-twelfth century

---

20 Lyon, *Princely brothers and sisters*, 16–32.

21 For charters as sources for medieval German history, see Freed, 'German source collections' and Freed, 'Medieval German social history'.

than their predecessors had a hundred years earlier. Finally, this transformation of lordship was tied to the emergence of new aristocratic
lineages that would come to play a pivotal role in promoting and
supporting the new calls for monastic renewal and reform in the decades
around 1100. The wave of monastic foundations during this period
would have been unimaginable without the changes taking place
simultaneously within the nobility. All five of the texts translated here
were written at religious communities founded between the 1070s and
1130s, at the height of this surge in interest in the spiritual life, and
all of them describe in various ways the noble culture that was taking
shape during the same decades.

The Investiture Controversy and its aftermath

'The Investiture Controversy' has become a useful – if admittedly
misleading – term for explaining a wide range of different aspects of
German history during the late eleventh and early twelfth centuries.
At its core, it refers to the dispute initiated by Pope Gregory VII
(1073–85) over whether or not the German ruler Henry IV – and
eventually other Christian kings as well – had the right to appoint
bishops in his own territories and to invest them with their episcopal
authority.[22] German kings and emperors had routinely chosen the prelates
in their lands for over a century prior to the 1070s, but Gregory VII
sought to put an end to the practice. His dramatic excommunication
of Henry IV in 1076 – and Henry's subsequent pleas for forgiveness
in the snows outside Canossa – were the famous beginning of a long-
running conflict over the nature of secular and spiritual authority in
medieval Europe. As *The life of Bishop Otto of Bamberg* translated here
attests, Henry IV was still appointing members of his own court to
German bishoprics in the years after Gregory's death. The 1122 agreement known as the Concordat of Worms, which was arranged by Emperor
Henry V and Pope Calixtus II (1119–24), was a compromise solution.[23]
The German rulers agreed to intervene in episcopal appointments only
in cases where there was a disputed election, and they were to invest
bishops only with the *regalia* – those elements of episcopal authority
that derived from the king (including lands and other forms of income)

---

22 For more detailed discussions of the Investiture Controversy in English, see Robinson,
   'Reform and the church, 1073–1122'; Weinfurter, *The Salian century*; Blumenthal,
   The Investiture Controversy; and Haverkamp, *Medieval Germany 1056–1273*.

23 For an English translation of this agreement, see Miller, *Power and the holy in the
   age of the Investiture Conflict*, 120–1.

– but not the spiritual elements of the bishop's office. This was certainly not the end of questions about the limits of secular and spiritual authority; there was not a sharp line dividing 'Church' and 'State' in the German kingdom after 1122.[24] As *The life of Mechthild of Diessen* and *The deeds of Count Ludwig of Arnstein* both show, though in strikingly different ways, the two spheres continued to overlap during later decades of the twelfth century.

The clash between emperors and popes at the centre of the Investiture Controversy was only one feature of the shifting political and social landscape of the German kingdom in the period between 1075 and 1200. Prior to the outbreak of the conflict, Henry IV had already faced an uprising by discontented members of the secular and ecclesiastical elite in Saxony. Pope Gregory VII's excommunication of Henry IV in 1076 added fuel to the fire, and the Saxons soon joined with other nobles from the south of the German kingdom in their opposition to Henry's rule. With Gregory's support, they denied Henry's claim to the kingship and elected the duke of Swabia, Rudolf of Rheinfelden, as the new German king (or anti-king, as he is more commonly known). Henry IV survived this threat to his rule, but Rudolf's death in 1080 did not put an end to his troubles in Saxony.[25] As *The deeds of Margrave Wiprecht of Groitzsch* describe at length, both Henry IV and his son Henry V would continue to face significant Saxon opposition throughout the late eleventh and early twelfth centuries.

Pope Gregory VII's and his successors' assertion of papal authority over the Church and all spiritual matters – in combination with the Saxons' and other nobles' challenges to German royal authority – undermined the rule of both Henry IV and Henry V. All of this had ramifications for later rulers as well. After Henry V's childless death in 1125, the German secular and ecclesiastical princes asserted their right to elect his successor, and a majority chose the Saxon duke Lothar rather than Henry V's closest male relative, the Swabian duke Frederick II from the Staufen lineage. The electoral nature of German kingship would become stronger in subsequent years, and the imperial court increasingly came to be a place where the rulers were expected to make decisions with the consent of the princes. The kings and emperors were conceived of, at least in noble circles, as the first among equals, and the princes in later centuries maintained the right to depose the German

24 Dale, 'Inauguration and political liturgy' and Benson, *The bishop-elect*, 303–15.

25 For a more detailed discussion in English of events in Saxony in the later eleventh century, See Robinson, *Henry IV*.

king and elect another if they deemed it necessary.[26] The five texts in
this volume all reveal various aspects of this distinctive political culture
during and after the Investiture Controversy. The German kings and
emperors do not dominate the action in these sources; they are sometimes
present, typically at the edges, only occasionally at the centre. Members
of the secular and ecclesiastical elite are the ones who drive the action
in these texts, and their decisions can be seen shaping life inside and
outside the Church, from one end of the German kingdom to the other
– and sometimes even beyond its frontiers.

The transformation of noble lordship

The decline of German royal authority during the period of the Investiture
Controversy elevated the power and influence of the nobility; in the
process, the nature of noble authority and lordship underwent a series
of transformations at all strata of elite society. This was evident even
at the uppermost levels of the nobility, with the princes who held the
title of duke (*dux*). There had been only five dukes in the German kingdom
in the tenth century: the dukes of the Swabians, Bavarians, Saxons,
Franconians and Lotharingians. Beginning in the later eleventh century,
the number of dukes increased significantly as the German rulers divided
the older duchies and created new ducal titles to reward loyal followers.
In the process, the title lost much of its original meaning. Instead of
being the leaders of the various peoples of the kingdom, the dukes
increasingly became linked to territories, especially to the landed holdings
of individual noble lineages.[27] Thus, in Swabia during the early twelfth
century, the Staufen lineage possessed the title of duke of Swabia, but
two other lineages – the Welfs and Zähringens – also held ducal titles
and exercised lordship over their lands in Swabia independently from
Staufen ducal authority. Further east, Emperor Frederick I separated
the march of Austria from the duchy of Bavaria and elevated it into a
new duchy in 1156; the new ducal title was based first and foremost on
the family holdings of the Babenberger lineage, which had controlled
Austria since the later tenth century.[28] In those marches that did not
become duchies during this period, the title of margrave (*marchio*)
underwent a comparable transformation to that of duke; increasingly, it

---

26 Weiler, 'Suitability and right'; Schneidmüller, 'Rule by consensus'; and Weinfurter,
      The Salian century, 159–79.

27 For this process, see Arnold, *Medieval Germany, 500–1300*, 68–74.

28 For all of these lineages, see Lyon, *Princely brothers and sisters*, 16–32.

became hereditary in noble lineages, meaning that important territories in border regions began to move further outside of royal control.[29]

This change in the meaning and significance of noble titles is even more striking in the case of counts. In the Carolingian period, *comes* referred to a royal official, appointed by the rulers, who possessed judicial and military authority within a specific region of the Carolingian empire; the office was not hereditary, and the counts sometimes did not even possess their own properties and rights in the counties where they exercised their authority.[30] During the Ottonian and Salian periods, this gradually changed, and by the early twelfth century, the holders of the comital title bore little if any resemblance to their Carolingian predecessors. Noble lords increasingly considered the title hereditary and used it – regardless of whether it had been given to them by a ruler or not – to indicate their regional prominence. Many of these lords were from lesser noble families, but in the absence of effective royal authority in the decades around 1100, they were able to dominate society at the local level by building new stone castles, clearing new lands and consolidating their lineage's rights and properties.[31] They also acquired the advocacies over local monasteries, giving them responsibility for defending and exercising judicial authority on the extensive estates of monastic communities.[32] *The deeds of Count Ludwig of Arnstein* is an excellent source for understanding the nature of this new form of comital lordship in the twelfth century. Wiprecht of Groitzsch, who appears sporadically in extant sources with the title of count before he became margrave, is another local lord who spent much of his life strengthening his control over the territories around his castle of Groitzsch on the north-east frontier of the kingdom. As *The deeds of Margrave Wiprecht of Groitzsch* attest, the German kings and emperors had a very limited role to play in regulating how these lords exercised their authority.

Below the level of the counts, the societal transformations of the eleventh and twelfth centuries are not always as easy to observe. In general, it appears that the lowest strata of nobles and other freemen (*liberi*) were in the process of contracting. There were various factors behind this decline, but the most significant was the rise of the unfree

---

29 Arnold, *Princes and territories in medieval Germany*, 121–5 and more recently Stieldorf, *Marken und Markgrafen*, 587–97.

30 Goldberg, *Struggle for empire*, 215–7.

31 For a good example of this type of lordship, see Freed, *The counts of Falkenstein*.

32 For monastic advocacies in this period, see Lyon, 'Noble lineages, *Hausklöster*, and monastic advocacy in the twelfth century'.

ministerials (*ministeriales*) in many parts of the German kingdom. During
the violent upheaval of the period of the Investiture Controversy, secular
and ecclesiastical princes increasingly began to rely on unfree members
of their own households to fulfil military and administrative functions
in their territories. Because these ministerials were of servile origin,
they could not marry without their lord's permission and could not
alienate most forms of property; in other words, they did not have the
same kinds of rights that freemen had. By turning to these unfree
ministerials as their key base of support, rulers, bishops, abbots and
abbesses, dukes, margraves and counts were able to depend upon
households of reliable fighters and administrators who were firmly
under their control. In return, as these ministerials took on more and
more responsibilities, they essentially absorbed and replaced the lower
strata of freemen at the local level. Over the course of the twelfth
century, these ministerials even competed with the lesser nobility in
some regions of the German kingdom, and their unfree status did not
diminish the prominent part they were able to play in elite society.[33]
The life of an unnamed magistra *of Admont* demonstrates this very well;
Admont in the mid-twelfth century was a well-respected double monastic
house to which many of the leading noble families of the south-east of
the German kingdom sent their sons and daughters, yet this woman
of servile origin was able to attain the highest position of authority
within the female community. Other ministerials also appear in important
roles in some of the other texts translated here.

Finally, another significant transformation within the society that
is the setting for this volume concerns the term *miles*. The most
straightforward translation of this word is 'knight', and by the close
of the twelfth century – by which time chivalric culture had begun to
influence German noble society – this is an appropriate English rendering
of the term. For the period before 1150, however, the issue is more
complicated, and scholars have spilled a significant amount of ink debating
what a *miles* was during these decades.[34] Most important to emphasize
for the texts translated here are the term's military connotations; a
miles was a member of a lord's household who fought on horseback and

33 The most detailed discussions of German ministerials in English include Freed,
    Noble bondsmen; Arnold, *German knighthood*; and Freed, 'Nobles, ministerials and
    knights'. See also Althoff, *Family, friends and followers*, 133–4.

34 See, for example, Bachrach, '*Milites* and warfare in pre-crusade Germany'; Mortimer,
    'Knights and knighthood in Germany'; Freed, 'Nobles, ministerials, and knights';
    Arnold, *German knighthood*; and more generally, Kaeuper, *Medieval chivalry*, 71–7.

thus performed a key function in medieval warfare. In most cases, they were probably unfree during the late eleventh and early twelfth centuries, meaning they overlapped to a certain extent with the ministerials. However, regional variations make it impossible to generalize for the whole German kingdom; in those places where *milites* tended to be freemen, 'vassals' may be an appropriate translation.[35] Because of the complexity of the problem, the term *miles/ milites* has been left untranslated in this volume – as is common in some other recent translations – in order to avoid romantic notions of chivalric knights or, on the other hand, too generic a rendering like 'warrior', which does not quite capture the specific functions of these men in the texts translated here.[36]

Because of all the changes affecting the nature of noble power and authority over the course of the twelfth century, readers of the five *vitae* and *gesta* in this volume should come to the texts expecting to encounter a flexible social and political order. German elite society in this period was not rigidly hierarchical – and it certainly was not 'feudal' in the classic sense of the term.[37] Personal ability and personal initiative enabled some men and women in this society to have remarkably successful careers, despite relatively obscure family origins. Other nobles, even those born into prominent lineages, were not forced to fulfil roles in elite society that they did not want to play; they had choices about how to live their lives. For example, Bishop Otto of Bamberg's dedication to missionary work in Pomerania, as detailed at length in the *Life* translated here, was highly unusual for an imperial prelate of his generation. And as *The deeds of Count Ludwig of Arnstein* show, Ludwig's decision to convert his castle into a religious house and abandon the violent lifestyle of the secular nobility was very much a personal choice. This was a noble society in flux, open to numerous different trends and developments, and all five sources reveal the broad range of opportunities and possibilities available to its members.

Noblemen, noblewomen and monastic reform

The texts translated here provide rich evidence for the character of monastic life between 1075 and 1200, a pivotal period for the development

---

35 Freed, 'Nobles, ministerials, and knights', 581–4.

36 *Ottonian Germany*, 64; Cosmas of Prague, *The chronicle of the Czechs*, 23; and *The histories of a medieval German city, Worms c.1000–c.1300*, 28.

37 See Brown, 'Tyranny of a construct'; Reynolds, *Fiefs and vassals*; and more recently for Germany, Dendorfer and Deutinger, eds., *Das Lehnswesen* and Patzold, *Das Lehnswesen*.

of many religious orders in Latin Christendom. Scholars have long recognized that the late eleventh and early twelfth centuries were a time when a chorus of voices inside and outside the Church denounced the divisions, disorder and decline in the religious life of their day. They called for change, for a *reformatio*, a renewal of the monastic and spiritual life.[38] This was a far-reaching call, for religion was embedded deeply in this society. Monastic communities, for example, were not just spiritual centres: they were also economic hubs, because of the vast landed estates many of them controlled; they were nodes in political and social networks at the regional level and sometimes beyond; and they were places of memory and commemoration for the nobles who founded and endowed so many of them. 'Reform' is therefore a concept that touches on numerous aspects of medieval European life.

It is also a concept that has come under increasingly intense scrutiny and critique, because too many scholars have used it unthinkingly as a catch-all term and as a simplistic explanatory model for a whole range of discrete eleventh- and twelfth-century phenomena.[39] Recent scholarship has argued that the monasteries of the late eleventh and early twelfth centuries were not necessarily in a state of physical or spiritual decline; instead, they simply did not conform to the expectations of younger generations of secular and ecclesiastical leaders who had developed new ideas – and new rhetoric – for how to institute the ideal monastic lifestyle. Viewed from this perspective, reform becomes a fluid and multi-faceted process – not a single moment or event – that followed a different course in each community rather than a standardised blueprint. In other words, reform was implemented idiosyncratically by individuals and informal networks of churchmen, founders and patrons, often over multiple generations; it was not a coherent institution directed from the top down.[40] Historians have also critiqued older arguments about reform that tended to exclude women from their discussions, or to cast women in a negative light, rather than taking seriously the medieval sources that show women's enthusiasm for reforming the Church and

---

38 Constable, *The reformation of the twelfth century*, 3; Robinson, 'Reform and the church, 1073–1122'; Blumenthal, *The Investiture Controversy*, 1–27; and Van Engen, *Rupert of Deutz*, 262–98.

39 See Howe, *Before the Gregorian Reform*, 6–7 and Tellenbach, *The church in western Europe*, 157–8 for especially pointed remarks about this problem.

40 See especially Vanderputten, *Monastic reform as process* and, more generally, Melville, *The world of medieval monasticism*, 180–5. For an excellent study of the complexities of reform in a German setting, see Eldevik, 'Driving the chariot of the Lord'.

their active engagement in reform processes.[41] The sources translated here lend support to both of these recent trends in the secondary literature; they describe lay and religious leaders founding new monasteries – and 'reforming' older ones – in the rhetorical language of monastic improvement and spiritual renewal that is so commonplace in surviving twelfth-century works.

While current historiography is pressing for new perspectives on 'church reform', it is nevertheless an older scholarly argument that helps to explain why issues of monastic renewal are so prevalent in the texts in this volume. For more than half a century, historians have stressed that the medieval German nobility was not antagonistic to monastic reform movements, as earlier generations of scholars had assumed, but was in fact pivotal to the spread of reformist ideals.[42] Secular noblemen and noblewomen founded and endowed many of the religious communities that were central to implementing ideas of reform and to promoting a more rigorous monastic lifestyle; the new lineages of counts and other lords rising to prominence in the decades around 1100 liked to support these reformed houses to show their piety and their concern for the spiritual well-being of their families. *The deeds of Margrave Wiprecht of Groitzsch* and *The deeds of Count Ludwig of Arnstein* are both rich sources for the close relationship between secular lords and reformers. Monastic houses like Wipecht's foundation at Pegau and Ludwig's at Arnstein offer some of the most tangible evidence for the nobility's interest in reform, but evidence can be found in numerous other places as well. Across the German kingdom, noblemen and noblewomen often placed their younger sons in monasteries, or sent them to be educated at cathedral schools; they frequently offered their daughters to convents as well. Many of these children later attained prominent positions in the Church – as bishops and abbots or abbesses – meaning that these men and women of noble birth also led the way in implementing reform agendas. *The life of Bishop Otto of Bamberg* describes Otto as working tirelessly to improve the monasteries controlled by the bishopric of Bamberg, as well as those he founded or acquired. And *The life of Mechthild of Diessen* discusses how Mechthild, the daughter of a count, was elected abbess of the women's community at Edelstetten in order to reform the women's conduct and their commitment to the religious life.

---

41 See especially Griffiths, 'Women and reform in the central Middle Ages'.

42 For a classic treatment of this topic, see Schmid, 'Adel und Reform in Schwaben'. For an overview of the subject in English, see Howe, 'The nobility's reform of the medieval church'.

The rich variety of different monastic reform movements that developed during the period 1075 to 1200 is also evident in the sources in this volume. The Rule of St Benedict had been one of the most important guides for the monastic life in medieval Europe since the sixth century, and many of the reformers of the eleventh and early twelfth centuries called for a return to the tenets of this Rule. While Cluny in France is unquestionably the most famous Benedictine centre of reform during this period, there were Benedictine houses in the German kingdom that also became focal points for spreading reform ideas. One of the earliest and most influential of these in the territories east of the Rhine was Hirsau in the Black Forest, which borrowed heavily from the Cluniac way of life.[43] Hirsau's influence spread through the monastery of Corvey to Margrave Wiprecht of Groitzsch's foundation at Pegau, as his *Deeds* describe. Further to the south and east, the Benedictine community at Admont was founded in 1074 by Archbishop Gebhard of Salzburg (1060–88), a prelate who was deeply committed to promoting spiritual reform in his archdiocese.[44] As *The life of an unnamed* magistra *of Admont* explains, Admont's reputation as a community that followed an especially exemplary form of the monastic life led to the *magistra* frequently travelling to other religious houses to be a model for nuns in those convents.

Two other religious groups that were of great significance for the twelfth-century German kingdom also have important roles to play in some of the texts translated here. During the late eleventh century, there developed alongside the orders of cloistered monks a group known as regular canons; these were clerics who embraced many reform ideas, including clerical celibacy, and dedicated themselves with renewed zeal to the apostolic life and performing the divine office. They also adopted a rule, the Rule of St Augustine, which emphasized communal living for these canons along similar lines to the monastic lifestyle. This Augustinian Rule became especially popular in cathedral chapters, where many canons desired to follow a regulated, communal way of life while carrying out their duties of pastoral care.[45] Numerous secular nobles

---

43 The classic treatment in German is Jakobs, *Die Hirsauer*. For more recent overviews of the Hirsau reform in English, see Melville, *The world of medieval monasticism*, 85–7 and Cowdrey, *The Cluniacs and the Gregorian Reform*, 196–210.

44 Melville, *The world of medieval monasticism*, 130. For more detailed discussions in English of Admont's significance, see various articles in Beach, ed., *Manuscripts and monastic culture*.

45 Melville, *The world of medieval monasticism*, 125–35 and Constable, *The reformation of the twelfth century*, 54–6.

also found this group attractive and chose to establish Augustinian communities on their own lands. Double houses, which included both a men's community of canons and a separate women's community of canonesses, were common in this group, and Bavaria – the setting for much of *The life of Mechthild of Diessen* – was a region where the Augustinians were especially well-entrenched by the later twelfth century.[46]

The Premonstratensians, a religious group with origins in the early 1100s, also followed the Rule of St Augustine, but they were more rigid in some of their practices than other Augustinian communities and came closer to living a strict monastic lifestyle. Following the Cistercian model, the Premonstratensian houses organized themselves into an order, with common statutes and a general chapter, in order to bind their separate communities together more tightly.[47] The group's founder, Norbert of Xanten (d. 1134), was a larger-than-life figure: a wandering preacher, the founder of the religious community at Prémontré from which the order gets its name, and – in the final years of his life – archbishop of Magdeburg.[48] Norbert makes appearances in two of the texts translated here, *The deeds of Count Ludwig of Arnstein* (which concerns the foundation of a Premonstratensian house at Arnstein) and *The life of Bishop Otto of Bamberg*. His presence in both these texts is just one of the many ways in which ideas of reform and monastic renewal can be seen running like a thread through the sources in this volume, weaving them together into an intricate, cohesive whole.

Reading the texts

Each of the five sources translated in this volume is preceded by a brief introduction, which is designed to provide the necessary background specific to the individual texts. As a result, the five sources can each be read separately as a stand-alone work. However, as this general introduction has emphasized, they have also been selected with the intention that they be read together, so that scholars and students alike

---

46 Backmund, *Die Chorherrenorden und ihre Stifter in Bayern*, 29–46 and more recently Crusius, ed., *Studien zum Kanonissenstift*.

47 Melville, *The world of medieval monasticism*, 158–63 and Crusius and Flachenecker, eds, *Studien zum Prämonstratenserorden*.

48 *Norbert and early Norbertine spirituality*, 7–15 and Melville, *The world of medieval monasticism*, 115–20.

can gain a fuller picture of German noble society in the period between 1075 and 1200.

For any reader, there are several issues that should be kept in mind when considering the five sources together. As noted above, all of these texts were written inside monastic communities and reflect, to varying degrees, the interests of the monastic authors and/or their monastic audiences. *The deeds of Margrave Wiprecht of Groitzsch* survives in a manuscript from the monastery at Pegau, a male community Wiprecht founded near his castle of Groitzsch and chose as his burial place. A monk at the house of Prüfening in Bavaria wrote *The life of Bishop Otto of Bamberg*; as the text describes in some detail, Otto was the founder of Prüfening. *The life of an unnamed* magistra *of Admont* was written inside the female community at Admont by someone who probably knew the *magistra* personally. The Cistercian monk Engelhard of Langheim composed *The life of Mechthild of Diessen*, and one of the dedicatory letters makes it clear that the provost and canons at Diessen were part of the intended audience. Finally, *The deeds of Count Ludwig of Arnstein* is extant in a manuscript from the Premonstratensian house at Arnstein, which Ludwig had not only founded but had also joined while still a young lord.

The monastic agendas of the texts' authors and compilers can be quite explicit at times. For example, both *The deeds of Margrave Wiprecht of Groitzsch* and *The deeds of Count Ludwig of Arnstein* contain detailed lists of the property holdings of the religious houses where the texts were written. Along similar lines, *The deeds of Margrave Wiprecht of Groitzsch* and *The life of Bishop Otto of Bamberg* both include copies of important privileges for the monasteries that produced these works. Here, in other words, is clear evidence that the monastic authors intended these texts to preserve not only Wiprecht and Otto's memories but also key sources for their own communities' histories. Even the short text of *The life of an unnamed* magistra *of Admont* includes brief passages praising the archbishops of Salzburg, under whose authority the community at Admont lay, in order to link the religious house to its most important patrons. *The life of Mechthild of Diessen*, in contrast, is more subtle in raising concerns specific to the canons and canonesses at Diessen in some of the later chapters of the work. Thus, while working with all of these texts, the reader must remember that the lives and deeds of the subjects of the individual works are being filtered through the lens of monastic perspectives and monastic self-interest.

The monastic milieu in which these texts were produced is also evident in the source material the authors used in the construction of their works. Both monasteries and houses of canons were important centres of education in the twelfth-century German kingdom, and their libraries held not only Christian texts but also famous works from pagan antiquity. The *vitae* and *gesta* translated here rely to varying degrees on references to other sources, but all of these citations – from Virgil, Horace, Sallust, the Bible, Boethius, Gregory the Great and a host of other works – reflect monastic forms of education during the twelfth and early thirteenth centuries. Of the five texts, *The deeds of Margrave Wiprecht of Groitzsch* is the one that is least reliant on outside material; citations from the Bible and classical works are few and far between, though it does borrow in some places from other medieval narrative sources. On the other end of the spectrum is *The life of Mechthild of Diessen*, which frequently interweaves biblical citations and allusions into many of its chapters; its author, Engelhard of Langheim, assumed an audience very familiar with a wide range of stories from both the Old and New Testaments. Admittedly, the numerous references to other sources can be distracting at times in some of the texts translated here. For example, the second and third books of *The life of Bishop Otto of Bamberg* are modelled on Sulpicius Severus's fourth-century *Life of Saint Martin of Tours* to such an extent that some readers might grow suspicious of the veracity of the account of Bishop Otto's missionary work in Pomerania. This is a common problem in the *vita* and *gesta* source material from the medieval period, which is one reason why earlier generations of scholars dismissed these works as historically unreliable.

Nevertheless, more recent generations have shown how these works can be read against the grain to recover cultural attitudes and social practices.[49] For example, one fruitful approach to the texts translated here is to consider their differing perspectives on women inside and outside monastic communities. *The life of an unnamed* magistra *of Admont* and *The life of Mechthild of Diessen* are not the only texts in which women play prominent roles. Margrave Wiprecht of Groitzsch's first wife, Judith of Bohemia, is a central figure in his *Deeds*, and the text frequently portrays her as one of the most generous supporters of the fledgling monastic foundation of Pegau. Likewise, Count Ludwig of Arnstein's wife, Guda, has an important place in his *Deeds*, since, according to the text's author, it was her inability to bear children that first prompted Ludwig to consider joining the religious life. Combining the

---

49 See, for example, Schulenburg, 'Saints' lives as a source for the history of women, 500–1100' and more recently Webb's introduction to her *Saints and cities in medieval Italy*.

depictions of these two noblewomen with the depictions of Mechthild
of Diessen and the unnamed *magistra* of Admont therefore offers the
opportunity to explore numerous aspects of the role of noblewomen
in the culture and society of the German kingdom.

Other cultural attitudes and social practices that readers will find
discussed in multiple sources in this volume include those surrounding
dying and death. With the exception of *The life of Otto of Bamberg*,
which has very little to say about the bishop's passing, the other four
texts translated here all offer detailed descriptions of their subjects'
final days. *The deeds of Margrave Wiprecht of Groitzsch, The life of Mechthild
of Diessen* and *The deeds of Count Ludwig of Arnstein* also give accounts
of their subjects' burials. Such rich depictions of individuals' deaths are
rare in other types of sources from the twelfth century.[50] Additional
topics worth exploring across these sources include material culture
– there are lengthy descriptions of numerous valuable objects, especially
in *The deeds of Margrave Wiprecht of Groitzsch* and *The life of Otto of
Bamberg* – and the differences between society in the heartland of the
German kingdom and society along its frontiers. In short, these are all
sources that reward close reading.

Notes on the translations

I have sought to balance readability with due respect for the original
Latin texts throughout the translations included in this volume. Thus,
while I have preferred English grammatical structures to Latin ones
in most places, I have tried to maintain the medieval authors' writing
styles as much as possible without making sentences unnecessarily
confusing or complicated. These are not quite word-for-word translations,
but they try to capture the feel of the Latin originals without sacrificing
the accessibility of the texts. With that in mind, I have tried to limit
the number of words I have kept untranslated to a minimum; *miles/
milites* is one of the few exceptions, as noted above, and other exceptions
are explained in the notes to the individual texts. In keeping with
common practice, direct citations from other sources are italicized in
the texts, while indirect references are indicated in the footnotes.

---

50 The death scenes here can be read fruitfully alongside the description of Elisabeth
    of Schönau's death in *Elisabeth of Schönau*, 255–73. For the significance of death
    scenes in the hagiographical tradition, see Bartlett, *Why can the dead do such great
    things?*, 529–35.

Only two of the five texts translated here – namely *The deeds of Margrave Wiprecht of Groitzsch* and *The life of Bishop Otto of Bamberg* – can be found in the *Monumenta Germaniae Historica*, the enormous and invaluable compendium of edited primary sources for German medieval history. Similarly, only one of the five – namely *The life of Bishop Otto of Bamberg* – exists in a modern German translation. This is not to suggest that the other sources in this volume are not well known to scholars; nineteenth-century German and Austrian historians were familiar with all of them, and every one of them has also attracted the attention of more recent scholars.[51] Nevertheless, most of these sources lack modern German translations and are not included in the *Monumenta Germaniae Historica*, because the German-speaking scholarly community continues to hold a rather narrow view of what constitutes a historically significant and valuable primary source. By choosing to include here several texts that do not belong to the traditional canon of medieval German historical sources, my aim has been to introduce an English-reading audience to the rich material that survives for the twelfth-century German kingdom – even if much of this material has never been central to the grand narratives of medieval German history and *Reichsgeschichte* that have shaped scholarly traditions in the German and Austrian academic communities.

---

51 Wattenbach, *Deutschlands Geschichtsquellen* discusses four of the five texts translated here, omitting only *The life of an unnamed* magistra *of Admont*, which was first published in 1893. See the introductions to the individual texts below for more detailed discussions of the secondary scholarship concerning each work.

THE DEEDS OF MARGRAVE WIPRECHT OF GROITZSCH (D. 1124)

Translated, annotated and introduced by Jonathan R. Lyon and Lisa Wolverton

INTRODUCTION

The vivid description of the life of the noble lord Wiprecht of Groitzsch translated here is in many ways exceptional. The surviving sources from the twelfth-century German kingdom rarely include lengthy accounts of the activities of secular lords; most of the writers of this period were monks who had little interest in recording so many details about the violent, sinful lifestyle enjoyed by successful nobles. The monastic authors and compilers of this text, who wrote at Wiprecht's own monastic foundation of Pegau, were not so reticent. Wiprecht emerges from these pages as a ruthless and cunning lord, one whose fortunes fluctuated dramatically as he played the games of court politics and local lordship with varying degrees of success during a career that spanned almost half a century. Through conflicts with his rivals and service to both Emperor Henry IV and the Czech king Vratislav, Wiprecht gradually established a prominent position for himself in the frontier region between Saxony and Bohemia, where he acquired, cleared and developed more and more territories around his castle of Groitzsch. His marriage to Vratislav's daughter, Judith, further elevated his social status and supplied him with the necessary income to establish and endow the religious community at Pegau. In the closing years of his life, Wiprecht experienced both victory and defeat in the violent conflicts between Emperor Henry V and the Saxon nobles. He completed his ascent into the upper echelons of the imperial elite when Henry appointed him margrave, probably of Lusatia, but his success was short-lived; badly injured soon thereafter, he himself became a monk at Pegau, where he died and was buried.

This text offers a very different perspective on Henry IV and Henry V's reigns than the typical pro-Salian or pro-Saxon narrative sources: a single nobleman stands squarely at the centre of the political action at key moments – in Italy, at the imperial court, and in eastern Saxony.

At the same time, for understanding political, social, religious and economic developments in the region between Saxony and Bohemia during the early twelfth century, it is a rich, almost unparalleled source. Nationalist historians of the late nineteenth and early twentieth centuries envisioned a state of permanent enmity between Germans and Slavs, but this text compels a more nuanced approach to frontier society and the many different forms that interactions among peoples could take.

Context

Wiprecht of Groitzsch has earned a reputation in modern scholarship as the social climber par excellence of the late Salian period.[1] Although the work begins by linking him genealogically to legendary kings of Germany and Denmark, he seems to have been born into a more modest family of successful frontier lords along the Elbe River. To label him German would be misleading; as his *Deeds* attest, his place of origin was a region where Scandinavians, Slavs and Saxons mixed freely. The year of his birth is unknown, but it was probably in the decade or so after 1050. According to the text, his mother gave him to Margrave Udo of Stade for his early education and military training. Later, when Wiprecht began to play a more active role in eastern Saxony – presumably in the period of the Saxon rebellion against King Henry IV, though the text is silent about his role in this conflict – he came into contact with Vratislav of Bohemia, who would become a pivotal figure in his life and also his father-in-law. The turning point in Wiprecht's career seems to have been Henry IV's first Italian campaign during the early 1080s; according to the *Deeds*, Wiprecht led the Czech contingent alongside Vratislav's young son, Bořivoj. Thereafter, Wiprecht of Groitzsch would be an increasingly prominent player in Saxon and imperial politics until his death.

---

1 Patze, 'Die Pegauer Annalen'; Vogtherr, 'Wiprecht von Groitzsch: Bemerkungen zur Figur des sozialen Aufsteigers im hohen Mittelalter'; and Haverkamp, *Medieval Germany, 1056–1273*, 203–4. It appears that Timothy Reuter also intended to publish an article about the 'self-made man' Wiprecht, but to our knowledge it never appeared. See his own reference to it in Reuter, 'Past, present and no future in the twelfth-century Regnum Teutonicum', 29, n. 60.

Wiprecht is named in numerous other sources from the late eleventh and early twelfth centuries. He is first mentioned, if only briefly, in Bruno of Merseburg's pro-Saxon account of the uprising against Henry IV.[2] Not surprisingly, given Wiprecht's marriage to a member of Bohemia's ruling Přemyslid dynasty, he and his eldest son appear in Cosmas of Prague's *Chronicle of the Czechs* – which can be read fruitfully alongside the text here.[3] Together with his first-born son, Wiprecht is also named as witness to a pair of diplomas issued by Henry IV in 1104,[4] and as evidence of his greater prominence later in life, he appears with more frequency in the charters of Henry V and of other regional magnates in the 1110s and early 1120s.[5] During this later period, he is also named in some other chronicles, including different continuations of Frutolf's universal chronicle, not least because he was a leader of the Saxon rebellion against Henry V in the mid-1110s.[6] However, these materials pale in comparison to the wealth of information offered up in the text here, grounded in local memory and experience – perhaps even first-hand knowledge of the man himself.

The *Deeds* is also a history of the early days of Wiprecht's first religious foundation, the monastic house at Pegau, which was built only a short distance from his castle of Groitzsch. Foundation histories abound from this period, and like this one, they frequently include a combination of fictional and historical elements as well as copies of key privileges inserted directly into the text and detailed lists of the rights, goods and properties donated to the monastery.[7] As a result, this work can also be read for its rich descriptions of the practical requirements and difficulties that attended the foundation of a new monastery. As the

2 Bruno of Merseburg, *Brunonis Saxonicum Bellum*, 380–1, ch. 117.

3 Cosmas of Prague, *Chronicle of the Czechs*.

4 *Die Urkunden Heinrichs IV.* (*MGH DD H. IV*), 658–60, nos 483–4 (both, on related subjects and with identical witness lists, were issued at Regensburg): 'Wicpreht et filius eius de Saxonia'. Father and son likewise both appear in the witness list to a charter of Bishop Walram of Zeitz-Naumburg from the previous year (*Codex Diplomaticus Saxoniae Regiae*, part I, section A, vol. 2 (*CDSR* I A 2, 5, nr. 3)). Wiprecht is also presumably the layman 'Wicbert' mentioned in a royal grant to the church of Meissen in February 1090 (*MGH DD H. IV*, 542–3, nr. 410); if so, this would be his earliest known appearance in a charter.

5 See, for example, *CDSR* I A 2, 15–16, nr. 18; 51–3, nr. 60; and 53–4, nr. 62.

6 Many of these references in other sources have been included in the footnotes to the text.

7 Patze, 'Die Pegauer Annalen', 5.

text makes clear, the monks – and especially their second abbot, Windolf – played a pivotal role alongside Wiprecht in settling and improving the region around Groitzsch and Pegau. They also helped to introduce reforming influences into the area, and this seemingly minor, frontier monastery emerges from the pages below as an important node in a network of monastic communities. The interwoven histories of both Wiprecht and his monastery make clear that the frontier was not an isolated or isolating place.

Text and authorship

The text preserving Wiprecht's deeds is not a stand-alone biography as it has come down to us today, but rather a hybrid work. The first word of the preface is *Gesta*,[8] and indeed the initial sections of the text follow the format of that genre, describing Wiprecht's origins and rise to prominence. However, beginning with an entry copied from Frutolf of Michelsberg's chronicle dated 1079, it adopts the structure typical of monastic annals – if at first unevenly, and with some chronological gaps and repetition – in which events are sequenced as annual reports, each year duly noted. Texts like this, usually anonymous, offer chronological precision at the expense of narrative coherence – the inverse of most *gesta*. Moreover, they are easy to maintain and perpetuate in a monastic environment, where any literate monk might take up the pen. Indeed, this text continues in this annalistic vein into the thirteenth century, sometimes by copying other annals, sometimes with original entries. As a consequence, it is more often known in the literature as the *Annals of Pegau*. Nevertheless, scholars have long recognized that not just the opening sections but also the account of the monastery's early years and the annalistic reports of the events of Henry V's reign all revolve around Wiprecht – until the detailed description of his death in the year 1124. For this reason, we regard the text translated here, namely everything up to and including his death, as his *Deeds* and have titled it as such.

The text is wholly anonymous, but undoubtedly originated within the monastery of Pegau. The issue of authorship has never been analyzed

---

8 For more on this term, see the general introduction to this volume.

closely, but the work has typically been viewed as the product of a single author-scribe working soon after the year 1156.[9] However, we find ample evidence that the text, as it has come down to us today, was assembled by a compiler working from multiple pre-existing texts. This same individual may have authored one or more of the sections. Additional interpolations seem to have been made by others, working after this base text had been assembled. It may even be that a subsequent compiler strove to fuse the work of the first compiler with sources composed later, such as the annalistic entries that comprise the last third of the text. Still later interpolations may have been inserted into this version. Since all but the very last section of the annals (especially the years 1118 to 1123) show evidence of local knowledge and perspective, each of the component parts and insertions but that one likely originated within Pegau. All this – composing, compiling, making insertions – we believe to have occurred in various stages over the course of the first half of the twelfth century. In other words, *The deeds of Margrave Wiprecht of Groitzsch* translated here was a communally, rather than a singly authored text. Viewing it as such explains certain inconsistencies and perplexing repetitions in the text; many of these will be immediately apparent to the reader, while others – indicated in the footnotes – emerge from cross-referencing the information here with dates and additional evidence known from other sources.[10]

Unresolved issues of authorship complicate clear pronouncements about the motivations behind the writing of the text. Wiprecht's foundation of Pegau would have served manifold purposes: to expiate his guilt over his own violent deeds, as the text itself suggests; to memorialize him and his family; to assert a commitment to reform ideals (exemplified by the monastic customs associated with Hirsau);[11] and to deepen his hold on the region by vesting an independent ecclesiastical institution with property over which he would retain the advocacy. So too, it follows, would the monks' commitment to recording their history – linked so closely with their founder, whose fortunes, and theirs, were intertwined with the vicissitudes of local politics at a volatile time – have

9 Patze, 'Die Pegauer Annalen', 3; Vogtherr, 'Pegau', 1195–99; and Vogtherr, 'Wiprecht von Groitzsch und das Jakobspatrozinium'.

10 We have elected not to fully rubricate or annotate the various interwoven component parts, so as not to obscure the narrative. A full analysis and interactive digital presentation is available at the website http://medievalelbe.uoregon.edu.

11 For the monastic reform ideas emanating from Hirsau, see the general introduction.

stemmed from varied impulses. Many of the pressures that would have inspired their writing are plainly evident in the text. Less obvious are the difficulties the monastery faced after the death without heirs of Wiprecht's younger son, Henry, in 1135, and the passing of Groitzsch to the Wettin family through Wiprecht's only daughter, Bertha.[12] For Pegau, a dynastic foundation deeply dependent on Wiprecht, his family and followers for patronage and protection, the mid-twelfth century was a time of great uncertainty and even turmoil. It was therefore also a time when the community's history, rights and privileges needed to be remembered.

Manuscripts and editions

The text translated here is preserved in a single manuscript, which dates from the mid-twelfth century.[13] It is preceded in the codex by a copy of the long chronicle attributed to Frutolf of Michelsberg and his continuators down to the year 1125;[14] this work occupies the majority of the manuscript's pages. *The deeds of Margrave Wiprecht of Groitzsch*, and additional entries in the *Annals of Pegau* down to the 1150s, were written by the same scribe, who plainly considered all these texts as related works of history. A copy of the chronicle from the Saxon monastery of Goseck, made by the same scribe but apparently bound together in the codex later, completes the manuscript.[15] As a whole, the manuscript thus attests to a strong interest in history, especially regional history, at Pegau during the middle decades of the twelfth century. This manuscript formed the basis for the only modern edition of the text, printed in the *Monumenta Germaniae Historica, Scriptores* series under the name *Annales Pegavienses*, or *Annals of Pegau*.[16]

---

12 For this later period, see Patze, 'Die Pegauer Annalen', 40–1.

13 Leipzig, Universitätsbibliothek Leipzig, Ms 1325. Digitized manuscript available at www.manuscripta-mediaevalia.de/#|4 (accessed 13 July 2016).

14 See *Chronicles of the Investiture Contest.*

15 For a discussion of this text, including a detailed description of the entire manuscript, see Ahlfeld, 'Das Chronicon Gozecense'. The manuscript's unusual history is described colourfully in Peter, 'Aufregung und Wirren um die Annales Pegavienses'.

16 *Annales Pegavienses et Bosovienses.* The editor, Pertz, gave this unwieldy title to the text, because he chose to include in his edition a thirteenth-century manuscript from the nearby monastery of Bosau containing the post-1125 entries from the *Annals of Pegau.*

Notes on this translation

This translation is based on the excellent *Monumenta Germaniae Historica* edition of the text, but the digitized version of the twelfth-century manuscript is available online and has also been consulted, when necessary.[17] Although we have chosen to end our translation with Wiprecht's burial and death, it is important to note that no clear break occurs in the text at this point. The entry for the year 1124 continues with a brief comment about what happened after his son, Henry, succeeded him. The scribe who copied the sections about Wiprecht also made or copied the continuation of the annals into the period around 1150, at which point additional hands began adding entries; the final entry included in the manuscript is for the year 1215.

Because of the multiple authors and compilers involved in producing this text, the *Deeds* do not read from start to finish as a smooth, coherent narrative. There are obvious breaks in the work, where different sources were brought together with little effort to connect them logically into a single story. Our translation reproduces all this faithfully, without any editorial intervention to eliminate or soften inconsistencies and repetitions. Although this makes the text difficult to follow in some places, it nevertheless offers an authentic depiction of the work's composite nature as well as a vivid sense of the sometimes messy craft of monastic history writing in the twelfth century.

---

17 We are aware of one modern German translation, that of Hermann Reinhardt Michel, originally published in 1899 and available online at: http://suedraumarchiv.de/index.php?option=com_content&view=category&layout=blog&id=68&Itemid=526 (accessed 13 July 2016). We have not used this translation, written in rather old-fashioned German, in preparing our own. More recently, Thomas Vogtherr, the author of multiple articles on Wiprecht, has indicated his intention to publish a new German translation, but to our knowledge this has yet to appear (see 'Wiprecht von Groitzsch und das Jakobspatrozinium', 35, n. 1).

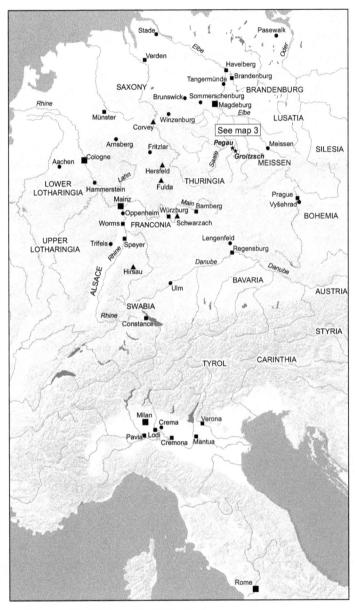

2   The world of Wiprecht of Groitzsch

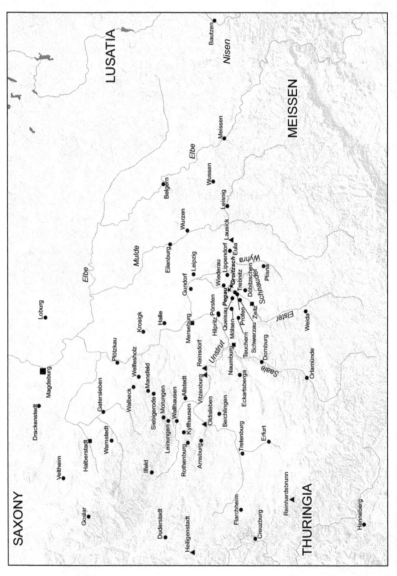

3 Groitzsch and its environs

SAXONY

LUSATIA

MEISSEN

THURINGIA

Goslar
Duderstadt
Heiligenstadt
Veltheim
Halberstadt
Wernstedt
Drackenstedt
Magdeburg
Lobug
Gatersleben
Ilfeld
Plötzkau
Krosigk
Welbeck
Mansfeld
Siebigerode
Morungen
Walhausen
Leinungen
Rothenburg
Kyffhausen
Arnsburg
Oldisleben
Beichlingen
Allstedt
Vitzenburg
Reinsdorf
Halle
Belgern
Eilenburg
Wurzen
Elbe
Mulde
Elbe
Nisen
Bautzen
Meissen
Wussen
Leisnig
Leipzig
Gundorf
Wiederau
Lippendorf
Lausick
Eula
Groitzsch
Wyhra
Trebnitz
Döbitzschen
Plisna
Schnauder
Elster
Pegau
Queisau
Hilpritz
Pörsten
Proten
Zeitz
Mölsen
Teuchern
Schwerzau
Domburg
Saale
Weida
Orlamünde
Merseburg
Unstrut
Naumburg
Eckartsberga
Tretenburg
Erfurt
Piarchheim
Creuzburg
Reinhardsbrunn
Henneberg

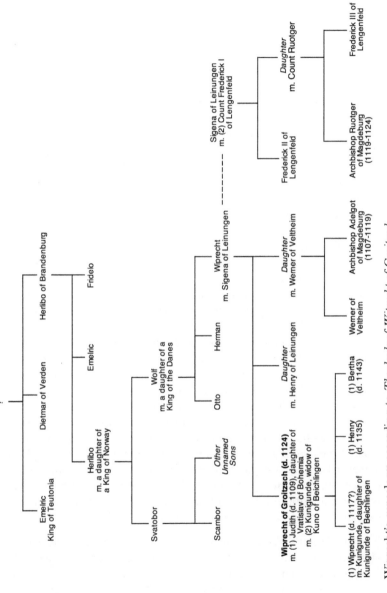

Wiprecht's genealogy, according to *The deeds of Wiprecht of Groitzsch*

TRANSLATION

The Preface begins

The wise foresight of the ancients considered it fitting to commit the deeds of the most excellent men to writing for these reasons: namely, so that through the passing of time their favourable lives might not be lost to the spirits of mortals by the obliteration of old age and forgetfulness; and, preferably, so that, if they should touch on any courageous and honourable actions, the minds of their listeners might delight in them, and they might also profit from imitating them, with their continuous recollection impressed upon them. For pagans and those utterly foreign to the true faith, it was the most important of pursuits to transmit not only their own commendable deeds but also those of their predecessors to posterity in writing, for the sake of perpetual praise and edification (even though a few were invented). Why, then, should we not preferably extol both the honourable and the fortunate deeds of Christ's faithful, by writing and proclaiming all their praiseworthy actions? Their lives are much more commendable, the memory of their deeds is far more delightful, and the performance of their pious works shines more fruitfully.

Therefore, intending to write about the foundation of the monastery of Pegau, we will open our narrative by first starting a little further back with its founder's descent from grandparents and great-grandparents. From there – having offered who was born and from whom as a brief foretaste – we will then disclose with God's help to those wanting to know, plainly and without circumlocution: what cause provided the occasion for the establishment of this place (by divine agency, so we believe); what things its founder, namely Margrave Wiprecht, accomplished generously, vigorously, and fortunately (in the eyes of both God and the world); and how his life ended. We relate it just as we have learned it from the truthful reports of those who either heard from others or saw and were present, many of whom we see still living.

Emelric, king of Teutonia, had two brothers: Dietmar of Verden and Herlibo of Brandenburg. Herlibo fathered three sons, namely Emelric, Fridelo and Herlibo, who were called 'the Harlongi'. Of these sons, Herlibo married a daughter of the king of Norway and extended his lineage with two sons, one of whom was named Svatobor and the other Wolf. Svatobor's sons were Scambor and his brothers.[1]

---

1 This is a fictitious genealogy, but many of the names are drawn from local legends known in this region of Saxony.

Wolf acquired primacy over the Pomeranians[2] but then was expelled from the province and fled to the king of the Danes. The king eagerly received this man of powerful youth, known to him beforehand by his already circulating reputation. Having frequently tested the strength of this man's body and the steadfastness of his spirit thereafter, the king called him forth more familiarly among those especially familiar to him and gave him his daughter in marriage.[3] But a short time later, the girl's brothers became consumed by the taint of envy[4] because of the illustrious man's reputation for strength and prosperous success. They fell upon him to drive him away from their borders and themselves, fearing that Wolf would do the same to them in the future, after the death of their father. Indeed, *gnawing envy, which denies all things* to happy people,[5] provides them, and frequently their authors, the opportunity to lose everything. Therefore, while his father-in-law still lived, Wolf deemed it appropriate to yield to the envy of his sons. A short time later, when he learned that their father had died, he attacked them with a military force and killed them. Since everyone supported him, insofar as he was the son-in-law of the king, he alone obtained the kingdom.

Thereafter, these events followed next for him: from his aforesaid wife he received three sons, namely Otto, Herman and Wiprecht, the father of Margrave Wiprecht.[6] Afterwards, the region of the Balsami surrendered to his rule by a warlike fate.[7]

Finally, old age and frequent battles weakened Wolf. He had earned so much goodwill from the common people, on account of his good fortune, that they thought prosperity could not follow them, either in war or in any other danger, except with him present (even doing nothing). Accordingly, they believed that, with him present, they were always about to attain victory. Having greater confidence in good fortune than, as previously, in his strength, they hoped that – on account of this man in the final stage of life – no adversity would be able to prevail

---

2 Cf. *The life of Bishop Otto of Bamberg*, in which Otto leads two missions to Christianize the Pomeranians during the 1120s.

3 The term *familiaris/es* is common throughout this text in various grammatical forms. We have chosen to translate it simply as 'familiar(s)', because it does not seem to imply any kind of fixed or formal relationship of either kinship, household, or vassalic status. It suggests loyalty, intimacy and physical proximity but only generically.

4 Cf. Wisdom 6:25.

5 Lucan, *The civil war (Pharsalia)*, I.288.

6 i.e., the Wiprecht who is this text's subject.

7 This is probably the region where the Havel River flows into the Elbe, around Havelberg, but there is not general agreement on this. Note that the Latin invokes the 'Balsami' as a people, but we learn nothing about them in the text.

against them. Therefore, since from the weakness of old age he was not strong enough to sit, they tied him on his horse – so that thus he preceded them in battle.

When he submitted to nature, his body was taken away to the temple of the gods by barbarian custom. His familiars ran around the bier by rank, with swords drawn as if in readiness for battle, and performed the funeral rites while making mournful sounds.[8]

With Wolf dead, the uncle of those whom Wolf had killed in the province of the Danes turned his hatred of the father against the sons. Because they despaired of withstanding his invasion, they withdrew from their father's territory. Otto, the eldest of them, departed for Greece and Herman for Russia.

Wiprecht went apart from his other brothers to the region of the Balsami, which had come to him through paternal inheritance. Thereafter, he flourished in arms and in counsel. This eminent *miles* kept busy with many splendid deeds of war.[9] Through his hard work he earned the familiarity of the elder lord Goswin, count of Leinungen.[10] When he saw that Wiprecht's eagerness of spirit corresponded to his nobility, this Goswin gave him his daughter, elegant in appearance, named Sigena. Goswin judged, as was truly the case, that Wiprecht would be an ornament and a monument to his lineage. Goswin allocated to her dowry Morungen and Gatersleben with their lands and allods and other appurtenances. The remaining patrimony – namely Leinungen, Siebigerode and Drackenstedt – he assigned to his two remaining daughters.

Thus was Wiprecht powerful by virtue of a fortunate marriage. From his wife he fathered a son, whom he endowed with both his name and his patrimony, and whom he left behind after his death as a child far more excellent in his father's virtues (as will be clearly evident to those wanting to know).[11] Afterwards, he received two daughters from the lady Sigena. A certain Henry of Leinungen married one of them.[12] The elder Werner of Veltheim married the other.[13] Werner had two sons from her, Werner and Adelgot, later archbishop of Magdeburg.[14]

8 Cf. *Beowulf,* lines 3169–72, for a strikingly similar description of Beowulf's funeral.

9 For the term *miles/milites,* see the general introduction.

10 Today Grossleinungen. Nothing else is known about this Count Goswin.

11 Cf. the description of Ludwig's birth in *The deeds of Count Ludwig of Arnstein,* ch. 2.

12 The identity of this Henry is unknown.

13 The lords of Veltheim were an important noble lineage in eastern Saxony.

14 Archbishop Adelgot [Adelgoz] of Magdeburg (1107–19); see below, p. 82.

Also, the outer road of the village of Pegau had passed to this Werner by hereditary right.

Then, Wiprecht the elder, who possessed the region of the Balsami (as we already said), remembered not only his father's excellence but the injuries he suffered when he and his brothers were driven out. So he frequently harassed the province of the barbarians by military assault, especially the town called Pasewalk – that is, the 'city of Wolf' in the barbarian language.[15] Repeatedly carrying off unbelievable plunder from there, he distributed it to everyone in his province. In this way, he won over to himself, with respect to the grace of loyalty, the favour of both the nobles and the commoners. Then, while still a young man flourishing in the enormity of both his strength and vigour, he came to the end of his life by a premature death, while his son Wiprecht was still a little boy.

The lady Sigena, bereft of the companionship of such a great man, very reluctantly received some degree of consolation after a time, when she allowed herself to be married to Count Frederick of Lengenfeld.[16] From him she received a son of the same name, and also a daughter, whom Count Ruotger took in marriage. He had from her Ruotger, later [arch]bishop of Magdeburg,[17] and Count Frederick. Having taken a wife, this Frederick also fathered a daughter, who married Count-palatine Otto of Wittelsbach and bore two sons, namely Otto, the count-palatine after his father died, and Count Frederick.[18]

These things have been said, as if a digression, not only because the nobility of so great a genealogy compelled us, but also for the sake of praising the lady Sigena, who happily raised her son [i.e., Wiprecht], the founder of the monastery of Pegau. And so, let the reader who desires to know the distinguished nature of her offspring receive these things more indulgently, having relaxed his wrinkled forehead a little bit.

At the same time, the august Emperor Henry [III], the son of that Emperor Conrad [II] who succeeded Henry [II] the Pious, became

---

15 Although the Slavic word for wolf, 'vlk', is reflected in the town's name ('Posduwlc' in *Annales Pegavienses*, 235), the 'barbarians' mentioned as the object of Wiprecht's revenge ought to be Danes.

16 (Burg)Lengenfeld in Bavaria, near Regensburg.

17 Archbishop Ruotger [Rugger] of Magdeburg (1119–24), successor to Archbishop Adelgot, mentioned above. For more on Ruotger, see below, p. 87.

18 Cf. Conrad of Scheyern, *Chronicon*, 621, ch. 19, where Count Frederick III of Lengenfeld's daughter is named Heilica. At least the latter half of this sentence must have been written after the year 1156, which is when Heilica's husband, the Wittelsbach Count-palatine Otto I of Bavaria, died.

master of the highest of affairs.[19] By his hard work, with divine grace cooperating, the *res publica* was enjoying the security of peace.[20] Under him, among the rest of the princes, Margrave Udo of Stade, was ruling.[21] The adolescent Wiprecht, bereft of his father (as we said above), was sent into Udo's service by his venerable mother. Udo raised him honourably until he grew up. Then, since he was one day going to be a colleague of princes, this great prince girded him nobly with the military sword. And he was generously enfeoffed by the same margrave with the town called Tangermünde with its appurtenances.

So the youth went there, growing in abilities and in bodily and spiritual strength, and ever more capable, whether in his counsel or in his deeds. Since he practised much slaughter of his enemies with an armed band for days uninterrupted, he was now to be feared by his acquaintances and familiars no less than by his enemies. And so it was readily wont to happen that at times they guarded against offending him even slightly, because strength begot praise, and praise envy of him. Those who seemed to love his integrity considered his proximity odious. For this reason, many counselled the margrave [i.e., Udo] to send Wiprecht away from himself, to whatever place agreed upon, if it could be done honourably and peacefully, in order to take precautions not only for himself and his men but also for his descendants. The margrave wisely hastened to fulfil what had been prudently suggested. Summoning the youth in a friendly fashion, he handed over into his power – in exchange for the region of the Balsami – his castle by the name of Groitzsch, situated in the Eastern region near the River Elster, with all of the appurtenances that were its by right, in estates and forests, meadows and pastures. In exchange for Tangermünde, he restored to him other benefices pertaining to the Nordmark.[22]

---

19 Henry II (1002–24), the last Ottonian ruler, was canonized as a saint in 1146. He was succeeded by the first two rulers from the Salian dynasty: Conrad II (1024–39) and his son Henry III (1039–56).

20 We have chosen to leave untranslated *res publica*, literally 'public affairs,' rather than rendering it as 'State' or something comparable.

21 Udo I of Stade, margrave of the Saxon Nordmark, lived during the reign of Henry III, dying in 1057. However, his son Udo II of Stade (d. 1082) may be meant here. Udo I and Udo II were both leading nobles in the region along the lower Elbe.

22 Udo seems here to be shifting Wiprecht onto holdings further south along the frontier, away from the centres of Udo's own lordship along the lower Elbe. However, there is no evidence that Wiprecht possessed any rights in the Nordmark, before or after this exchange.

Wiprecht agreed to these things and withdrew to the east, that is, where *the rising sun,* true and rich, *might visit* him *from on high.*[23] And if not immediately, nevertheless willingly, he took himself and his men inside the walls of the same castle [i.e., Groitzsch]. Insofar as he was unable to bear peace and was accustomed to evil deeds, he disturbed whichever nobles were staying in his neighbourhood – not without the ruin of the region. At that time there were many nobles in this province, each one established in his own castle: namely, Betheric from the castle Teuchern, Frederick from *Cutze,* Vicelin from Profen and his brother from [Elster]trebnitz, and Hageno from Döbitzschen.[24] These men came together of one mind, and because *all power* was always *impatient with a partner,*[25] they quickly attempted to remove Wiprecht, who had invaded both the region and their lives.

Unable to oppose them and piecing together how he might not lose his things altogether, Wiprecht judged it the best advice, if, withdrawing from the region for a time, he yielded to their envy. He talked with his men. One of them, his ministerial Hartwig, and another called Peter said that they ought to give themselves to the aforesaid Betheric, together with the town of Groitzsch – as if Wiprecht did not know.[26] Then, having gathered 100 *milites,* Wiprecht took himself to the duke of Bohemia, by the name of Vratislav.[27] Honourably received by him and accepted by everyone on account of the splendour of all of his integrity and hard work, he earned the easy access of familiarity both in the presence of the duke himself and among all his best men.

After some time, just as he was becoming known to everyone – who he was and how great – so also, by contrast with others, he more frequently drew attention to all those things he was wisely considering. Among other conversations with the duke, he said, 'I confess that I cannot wonder enough that you – such a great man, of such great title and power – bear with equanimity the loss and rejection of the royal title and authority.[28] What is apparent enough is this: that counts

---

23 Luke 1:78.

24 *Cutze* has been identified as Kitzen and Kütz, both north-west of Groitzsch, or as Gautzsch to the north-east of Groitzsch.

25 A Latin proverb: *omnis potestas impatiens consortis est.* See Henderson, *Latin proverbs,* 308.

26 For the term 'ministerials', see the general introduction.

27 Vratislav II, duke of Bohemia (1061–92), king after 1086.

28 The Přemyslid rulers of Bohemia and Moravia customarily bore the title 'duke'; in spite of what Wiprecht is made to claim here, Vratislav would be the first to style himself 'king'. His successors, however, reverted to 'duke' immediately after his death.

and magnates, endowed with great power and honour, keeping faith
and homage to your predecessors under oath, refuse to be subjected
to your rule. I will demonstrate how unbecoming and unsuitable this
should seem. I remember that a certain one of your predecessors was
called "Buogo".[29] I would not say counts or others powerful by virtue
of nobility and wealth, but rather dukes and margraves, were fighting
for his principate. He, having attained the rule and royal title, extended
his empire into the province of the Seringi.[30] Thus he shone forth more
famous and more excellent than other princes who were equally powerful.
Wherefore, if you should desire to restore the royal title's loss, consider
now to be the opportune time. The disordered *res publica* will provide a
useful and effective opportunity.[31] To the extent I will be able, I too am
ready with both aid and counsel.'[32] Having followed up on these things
and others, the duke made it known that he judged them advantageous
and promised Wiprecht that he was ready to comply in everything.

At that time, war and the greatest dissension arose between King
Henry [IV], the son of the aforesaid Emperor Henry [III], and the
Saxons, such that people despaired it could not be settled without
bloodshed (perish the thought!). The emperor *had in mind*[33] to make an
expedition into Lombardy and Italy – and to avoid the turbulent faction
of Saxons at the same time.[34]

Wiprecht therefore judged this to be a convenient time to complete
the business that he *had in mind.*[35] He went to the emperor, taking with
him a few of his own men. Wiprecht promised that he was ready to set
out with him for revenge against the enemies of the *res publica* with

---

29 No Czech or other king is known with this name. However, in Slavic 'Bog' means
    'god'.

30 This province has not been identified.

31 The reign of King Henry IV (1056–1106) was marked by a tumultuous early period
    of minority rule, followed by decades of conflict – with the Saxons, other discontented
    magnates, the Papacy, and his own sons.

32 *Consilium et auxilium*, counsel and aid, are the two words typically paired together
    in references to a vassal's obligations to his lord.

33 Sallust, *War with Jugurtha*, 72.

34 The Saxons broke into armed rebellion against Henry IV in the summer of 1073;
    his first Italian expedition began in 1081. The intervening eight years were filled
    with momentous events – including Henry IV's excommunication and its lifting
    at Canossa, as well as Rudolf of Swabia's election as (anti-)king – about which this
    text is silent.

35 Sallust, *War with Jugurtha*, 72.

sixty of his own *milites* and their military equipment – even fighting at their own expense – on this condition, however: if the royal magnificence and the other leading men should judge him indispensable to the *res publica*, the emperor by his munificence would restore to Wiprecht every loss recently incurred by him in the Eastern region and would reward his allegiance.

The princes and the emperor himself joyfully accepted these things. At this, after Wiprecht had obtained everyone's goodwill, he judged the time favourable for him to disclose the reason why he had come. He declared himself ready to do not only these things for the benefit of the *res publica*, but even better things if the emperor and the princes would assent to his advice. Without delay, the emperor declared himself ready to offer his assent. Wiprecht suggested to him that it would do utterly no harm to the imperial dignity, but rather benefit it, if he would allow Duke Vratislav of Bohemia [to be made] into a king and would order him crowned. The duke would also weigh out 4,000 talents for the royal treasury,[36] and moreover would send his son with 300 armed men on the expedition to Italy with the emperor.[37]

But the emperor, because his mind was already wavering about the disorder of the state of the *res publica*, was debating whether to refuse these men and demand those.[38] After Wiprecht gave an oath that he would carry out the expedition with sixty *milites*, all the princes stood forth as sureties of the royal promise: if Wiprecht should match his deeds to his words, he would obtain from the emperor recompense, in dignities and benefices, worthy of him in every way and as might befit

---

36 A talent (*talentum*) was a unit of weight; in Germany in this period it was equivalent to a pound. More typically used for precious metals than for coin, it nonetheless might indicate a measure of monetary wealth. Since the silver penny (*denarius*) was the only coin in circulation during this time in Europe, we presume a talent of silver is meant, here and elsewhere in this text. Gold, of significantly higher value than silver, is usually stipulated explicitly.

37 Bruno of Merseburg names Wiprecht among those Saxons who had switched to Henry's party by January 1080 – before the Battle of Hohenmölsen (see below, p. 53) and the Italian campaign described here (*Brunonis Saxonicum bellum*, 380–1, ch. 117). Although our text suggests Wiprecht was instrumental in bringing Vratislav and Henry together, in fact the latter had been close allies since 1075. The Czech duke regularly fought with and for the German king in his struggle to retain power and, as a reward, received the marks of both Lusatia and Meissen, in early autumn 1075 and August 1076 respectively. Cf. *The annals of Lampert of Hersfeld*, 279 and 329–30.

38 The meaning here is unclear but is perhaps intended to imply that Henry IV was considering accepting Wiprecht's men but not Vratislav's.

imperial magnificence – both for what great labour he might do in his
service (voluntarily and beyond what was owed to him)[39] and as a
reward for the loyalty he was extending verbally.

Dismissed by the king and the princes with this promise and a formal
farewell, Wiprecht then returned to Vratislav in Bohemia. He made
known what things the duke should carry out for the recovery of his
dignity and his title: that he should dispatch four thousand marks of
silver to the emperor and thirty pounds to the empress,[40] and also that
he should send his son Bořivoj with 300 *milites* to Italy. Wiprecht
persuaded him with splendid reasoning.

So Wiprecht came to the court at Würzburg.[41] At this court, after
the princes had solemnly come together from everywhere (except the
Saxons), the duke of Bohemia arrived, surrounded by magnates, the
most excellent he had; Wiprecht led the way with the indicated quantity
of treasure. Then, with the emperor granting it and the princes' judgement agreeing, Vratislav was raised up through royal consecration by
the archbishop of Mainz and the bishops of Constance and Würzburg.[42]

39 i.e., beyond his normal vassalic obligations.

40 Like the talent or pound, the mark (*marca*) was a unit of weight used for precious
metals and as a large denomination of silver coin. The original Scandinavian mark
was equivalent to 2/3 of a Carolingian pound, itself equivalent to 240 pennies. In
the German kingdom in the twelfth century, however, the standard mark of Cologne
was only half of a pound. Later in the twelfth and early thirteenth centuries, pennies
were minted at Friesach at 240 pennies to a mark. As this indicates, the correlation
of coin to units of weight might vary over time and regionally, depending on the
silver content and weight of the pennies issuing from local mints. Extant textual
and numismatic evidence rarely allows modern scholars to define medieval monetary
amounts with precision. Note, however, that the 4,000 *marks* Vratislav is said here to
have contributed was considerably less than the 4,000 *talents* in Wiprecht's original
proposal, even with the empress's additional thirty pounds added on.

41 Berthold of Reichenau, *Chronicle*, 232, reports that Henry IV held court at Würzburg
in August 1079, which seems the most plausible occasion for the events discussed
here to have occurred, if they ever did.

42 No other source suggests that Wiprecht played any role in Vratislav's becoming king; most scholars agree that Vratislav was not crowned until *after* Henry's
return from Italy, at Mainz in spring of 1085. Patze, 'Die Pegauer Annalen', 16–7,
suggests that the events described here may have been a prelude to a more formal
coronation ceremony after the Italian campaign and Henry IV's coronation as
emperor. However, the account given here is problematic, not least because the
churchmen named in the text are unlikely to have been present at Henry's court in
or around 1079. Archbishop Siegfried of Mainz and Bishop Adalbero of Würzburg
had both helped to orchestrate Rudolf of Swabia's election (as anti-king) in 1077
and remained opposed to Henry; only Bishop Otto of Constance supported Henry in
this period.

After that, he swore an oath that he would send 300 *milites* on the expedition, as had been agreed upon. Then the duke[43] turned to Wiprecht and vigorously begged that he travel with his son. Wiprecht responded that this was not at all new to his solemn promise, since, for his own part, he had also sworn it to the emperor. Nevertheless, Vratislav brought it about that, with the king deciding it, Wiprecht would be permitted to always be next to his son's tents. Thus, for certain, Wiprecht would be Bořivoj's inseparable companion and partner. The duke sought this from the king, and it was decided.[44] Then, he obtained permission from the king to return home, not forgetting his promise after the recovery of his honour.

Back home, before everyone, Vratislav summoned Wiprecht, a man loyal and familiar to him, and entrusted his son to Wiprecht's loyalty along with 300 *milites*, generously and suitably readied with all their military equipment, together with money for expenses. He sent Wiprecht with them to augment the royal army. They met up with the army at Ulm, a city in Swabia.

Hurrying more and more – and surpassing the rest of the army on the road – they were the first to cross over the summits of the Alps. Testing their strength, they devastated Lombardy in their barbaric manner; destroyed cities and castles by plunder, slaughter and fire; and violently subjected to their servitude all the strong men they captured. They threatened death to those with local knowledge, if they did not reveal the places that were filled with riches. They forced many fortifications to surrender. Soon they had increased their army to a thousand armed men. When the emperor crossed the Alps after them, he rejoiced with not a little happiness at the things boldly discovered and accomplished by those who had preceded him.

After the multitude of the whole army had come together into one and been duly arranged, from there Henry came to Milan and was received both peacefully and honourably by the consuls and leaders of

---

43 Note that the author quickly reverts to calling Vratislav 'duke' in this passage.

44 No other source attests to the participation of Czech forces on the Italian campaign of 1081–84, whether led by Wiprecht or Bořivoj. However, Cosmas of Prague reports that a contingent of this size (i.e., 300 soldiers) was dispatched by Duke Vladislav I on Henry V's Italian expedition of 1111 (which the Czech chronicler dates to 1112) under the nominal leadership of his young nephew, Břetislav, the son of Duke Břetislav II (Cosmas of Prague, *The chronicle of the Czechs*, 3.38, 227).

the town.[45] With additional help from them, and also from those whom the emperor had joined to himself from diverse provinces, he finally forced to surrender all the other cities, towns and castles situated round about – namely Cremona, Pavia and Lodi, Mantua and Crema, and other fortifications as well (except Verona) – by a four-year campaign and much labour, and not without the loss of his own men.[46]

After he had accomplished these things and commenced along the road, he approached the regions of Italy.[47] And *since high things come crashing down on themselves, for such is the limit of growth in human affairs ordained by heaven*[48] – turbulent Rome, which always either stood open to bad men or bore the attacks of the depraved, was not yet sorry that it had now brought the emperor's displeasure upon itself too.

The emperor, trusting in the size of his Italian and German army, encircled Rome with a tight siege and held out in the same position for about three years.[49] While this was unfolding, because the farmers were absent from their fields, food ran out for the king's army and it suffered savage famine, just as if it were encircled by a great siege. Still there were frequent clashes between the two sides; because an uncertain fate enveloped both sides of the war to their equal detriment, neither side ceased from boldness. Therefore, scouts were sent out to discover whether there might be anywhere where they might be able to recover from their lack of food. It was announced secretly to Wiprecht by his scouts that in the mountains nearby there were provisions, concealed by some people, as well as an abundance of cattle and a flock of sheep. Since Wiprecht was energetic, unconquerable and shrewd, he quickly flew to that place with the men attached to him, both the king's *milites* and the Czechs, and found, as had been reported, that this would help even a large army for some time thereafter.

45 A royal diploma attests that Henry IV was in Milan on 14 April 1081 (*MGH DD H. IV*, 432–3, nr. 330); Bernold of St. Blasien, *Chronicle*, 266–7, reports that Henry IV travelled via Verona (and thus the Brenner Pass), arriving in Verona around Easter (4 April in 1081) before proceeding to Rome.

46 Henry did not spend four years in the early 1080s besieging northern Italian towns; instead, he traveled southward quickly, arriving in Rome less than two months after crossing the Alps.

47 Cf. Otto of Freising, *The deeds of Frederick Barbarossa*, II.13, 125–8, where Otto clearly distinguishes between Lombardy and 'Inner Italy,' where Rome lay.

48 Lucan, *The civil war (Pharsalia)*, I.81–2.

49 Cf. Frutolf of Michelsberg, *Chronicle*, 120. Frutolf reports that Henry besieged the city for two years.

Wiprecht was told, while hastily returning, that the Romans had burst forth [from the city] and challenged the king to a fight. But at that time the Feast of the Ascension[50] was imminent. When the news was reported to Wiprecht, who was already nearby, he immediately seized the war banners. This energetic man flew into battle not sluggishly with all those likewise prepared. In a barbarian manner, three times approaching and retreating from the battle-line of Romans, bursting in to meet them as if cutting the webs of spiders, they raged without control against their adversaries in an excessive slaughter.

Wiprecht saw where the king was hedged about by enemies in a narrow place. With his men, he brought himself toward the king and terrified the Romans so much with his assault that he drove them all the way to the city's gate. The king, likewise pressing upon them manfully, dismounted after his sword was wrested away, and his right hand almost became stiff from the repeated blows. Called by the king, Wiprecht stood by; he handed over his own sword to the complaining man. And because nothing is more warlike than courage in the midst of great need, with the point of his own shield raised up, unarmed against armed men, Wiprecht savagely raved with so strong an attack that they were driven below the circuit of the wall. Thus the victors wished the fight to come to an end. And because on both sides many had been wounded, the emperor kept himself inside his camp for seven days.

Meanwhile, after Wiprecht had given his limbs a rest for a time – although he had not set his mind free from the present business – he summoned one of his men by the name of Raz, who was quite industrious. Wiprecht suggested that, while traversing the circuit of the walls, Raz investigate carefully whether he could discover anywhere an access point for penetrating the walls, so that, having reconnoitred the idling of the watchmen, they might be able to ascend secretly. Raz obeyed, applying his attentiveness shrewdly, and by listening deduced that the walls were without guards. He carefully ascended. After he perceived that no one was present, he returned and secretly informed his lord. He explained that the Romans could be caught by a simple scheme, if he did not disregard it. Reckoning that nothing was to be disregarded – *delay is the bane of preparedness*[51] – Wiprecht took up arms with all of his own men and a few of the Czechs. With two ladders and his *miles*

---

50 A movable feast, forty days after Easter, celebrated on a Thursday.

51 Lucan, *The civil war (Pharsalia)*, 1.281.

Raz leading the way, Wiprecht ascended the walls second after him. Meanwhile, he sent a messenger to the king, [telling him] to hasten to take the gatehouse as soon as possible. Then, fourteen of his *milites* ascended the walls, with the rest also hurrying. The king and a multitude of men also rushed to the gates and cut down the doors with axes. Suddenly, the Romans called out to each other and attacked those who had ascended the walls with a barrage of stones and spears. Finally the king, having taken control of the *urbs*, punished those Romans stoutly charging them with much carnage.[52] Some of his own quite noble and vigorous men also died courageously in this great battle. Nevertheless, they worked a greater slaughter of their enemies.[53]

The pope therefore took flight with his uncle, Peter Leo.[54] They were trying to get to the House of Theodoric[55] through the mother church,[56] but their adversaries anticipated their attempt and intercepted them. Thus, they were confined within the church, where they remained together for three days. After they had repeatedly attempted to break out through the church's doors and to challenge those outside by some kind of a sudden assault, Wiprecht agreed with his standard-bearer that when the doors were thrown open, they two would shove in a timber of astonishing bulk, in order that those inside might not shut the doors so quickly, as they had done before, and retreat back inside. And so, when those men tried to carry out their daring in a similar attempt, Wiprecht and his standard-bearer threw the beam forward and created a gap between the adjoining doors. The Romans were now zealously defending the open doors.[57] First among his men, Wiprecht

---

52 With regard to Rome, '*urbs*' is generally understood to refer to the Leonine City, the fortified section of Rome on the opposite bank of the Tiber from the rest of the city.

53 Cf. Frutolf of Michelsberg, *Chronicle*, 121–3 and *The life of Emperor Henry IV*, 115–17. This account generally accords with both these sources but does not explicitly borrow from them.

54 This must refer to Pietro di Leone, a supporter of Pope Paschal II (though not his uncle); see Wickham, *Medieval Rome*, 223. It suggests that this scene, like the account of Henry's coronation as emperor below, actually describes the confrontation between Paschal and King Henry V in 1111, not Henry IV and Gregory VII; see n. 58 below.

55 A medieval designation for the Castel Sant'Angelo, part of the fortifications of the Leonine City; also known as the 'castle of the Crescentii' (Frutolf of Michelsberg, *Chronicle*, 121).

56 i.e., St Peter's, also in the Leonine City.

57 The author clearly intends the reader to understand that the pope and Peter Leo are accompanied by guards, not themselves fighting alone.

attempted to rush the doors, in order to strike at those resisting for such a long time there. At length, they drove them inside. Wiprecht followed – although, not protected by a shield, he was actually being cut to pieces, little by little, by the enemies' swords. Seizing a swordpoint in each hand, by both voice and example, he encouraged the multitude breaking in after him.

With them thus committing sin – oh the pain! – they engaged in a most violent battle in that same church, and much human blood was shed. To behold it was a frightful mockery of the Christian name, the ruin of a place of the most holy and apostolic honour and authority. Who, reading or hearing about it, does not shudder at so great a sacrilege: that human blood flowed like the Tiber within the sacred confines of the apostles?

Meanwhile, the pope had withdrawn into the sanctuary with Peter Leo. Apprehended there, along with those more distinguished by birth, they were handed over into Wiprecht's custody at the king's order. Afterwards, having considered saner counsel on both sides and after many opinions had been offered on the dispute – as to whether it was an occasion for their release or indictment – the pope was reconciled to the king. The king ordered and carried this out: after three days' labour, the church, venerable to the whole world, was with difficulty finally cleansed of the filth of bloodshed and consecrated anew in his presence; the king was raised up through imperial consecration; and all their captives were released to the pope for free. The slaughter seemed to come to an end and a new life to begin.[58]

At length, the emperor received the most fortified House of Theodoric[59] into his control and stationed in it a garrison of his own supporters. Of the twenty of Wiprecht's *milites* posted there, eleven died, having consumed poison, a trick executed by the Romans' working girls. With

---

58 This author has conflated into a single narrative four separate events occurring over the course of the years 1083 and 1084: Gregory's flight into the Castel Sant'Angelo, Rome's surrender to Henry, Gregory's flight from Rome, and Henry's coronation as emperor (cf. Frutolf of Michelsberg, *Chronicle*, 121–3 and Bernold of St Blasien, *Chronicle*, 273–6). However, Gregory VII was never captured by Henry, they were never reconciled, and Gregory did not crown Henry emperor; rather, Gregory fled before Henry could capture him, and Henry arranged for Wibert of Ravenna to become the anti-pope Clement III (1084–1100) before Wibert crowned him emperor. What is described here accords better with the events that transpired between Henry V and Pope Paschal II during 1111 (cf. *The anonymous imperial chronicle*, 214–15 and William of Malmesbury, *The history of the English kings*, V.420–5, 762–71).

59 Again, Castel Sant'Angelo.

Wiprecht announcing it, their deceit immediately became known to the emperor.[60]

Yet everyone should take note of the active resolve and industrious effort of this man in respect to the king's service. After a period of seven years' time had been completed,[61] only five *milites* from his own sixty and merely nine of the 300 Czechs who had obeyed his will were left to him. With spirits unshaken and fully prepared for whatever danger might approach, they went headlong into death in their barbaric manner.

The emperor, therefore, lest he leave anything unfinished behind their backs, directed his army against the Veronese. At the same time, Peter Leo had confirmed by oath that he himself was ready to come to his aid, having given hostages in the meantime, as well as copious silver as payment to all the troops. While the emperor remained at the House of Theodoric, they set their camps against Verona. The duke of Verona observed (although too late) that he did not have the strength to resist the royal majesty.[62] Sending envoys, he sued for peace. Providing in every way reparations for everything, he deserved to be reconciled by some kind of agreement. He promised that he would show his obedience with gifts and services, so that he might at least be consulted about his power and his city. Wiprecht was therefore directed to Verona on account of the agreement concerning these reparations. The emperor awaited Wiprecht's return at the House of Theodoric.

Standing around the emperor then were the archbishops of Mainz and Cologne, the bishops of Halberstadt and Münster, the abbots of

---

60 Bernold of St. Blasien also tells a story of disaster befalling the garrison left in this castle: *Chronicle*, 269–70.

61 Note that this accords with the author's description of a Lombard campaign lasting four years and a siege of Rome lasting three. However, Henry IV did not spend seven years in Italy at this time, but only three: from April 1081 to June 1084. Henry IV would spend seven years in Italy between 1090 and 1097, but none of the events described here match what we know about this later Italian expedition. Henry V never spent seven years in Italy, so the confusion here cannot be explained by events from his reign either.

62 Securing Verona was crucial to returning to the German kingdom over the Brenner Pass. However, there was no duke of Verona. The doge of Venice is almost certainly meant here, who agreed to a treaty with Henry V on 22 May 1111 in Verona, making this another place where the events of 1084 and 1111 have been conflated. See *Die Urkunden Heinrichs V*: www.mgh.de/ddhv/dhv_79.htm (accessed 2 August 2016).

Fulda and Hersfeld,[63] and the other princes, along with the Czech youth.[64] Meanwhile, men gave a speech about Wiprecht, declaring that he was a man of most extraordinary integrity, and that this had become obvious to everyone on this expedition through sure tests. Then the emperor said that he himself wanted to test this more surely. He ordered him to be recalled with speed, as if he had incompletely indicated the reasoning for his decision [i.e., to send him to Verona].

There was a lion shut up in a certain house there. To test Wiprecht's steadfastness, the emperor ordered it let out. Released, the lion roared. The whole crowd of people present fled to safer places. Wiprecht entered, unaware of what was happening. When the lion was set loose against him, he was warned only by the Czech youth, who put him on guard. Wiprecht, seeing it rushing toward him unexpectedly, strove to take his sword quickly from his sword-bearer. But when Wiprecht seized him by the hand, he threw himself steadfastly toward the lion for the sake of his unarmed lord. However, Wiprecht bore this act indignantly. Trusting more in his own strength than that of another, he restrained the *miles* and – wondrous to say! – approached the lion with his fist. The lion, his mane disordered, soon turned away from him.[65]

In this event, I think, we can discern nothing other than divine providence, which has a care for all. Thus Wiprecht, to whom God's mercy provided such great things in the future, was miraculously snatched away from the present danger. Next, Wiprecht approached the emperor and inquired why he had been recalled. 'For the sake of your salvation,' he said, 'since we just proved by this test that you are blessed.'

But after Wiprecht interrogated him more diligently, the emperor finally revealed to him that he had been recalled to prove his fortitude

---

63 These ecclesiastical princes cannot be identified securely, or plausibly linked, as a group, with the Italian campaigns of either Henry IV or Henry V. Presumably the author has projected this group of donors backwards in time (and conveniently neglected to name the individual prelates) in order to assert that the grants they make to Wiprecht below (p. 49) stemmed from Wiprecht's service in Italy.

64 Implicitly this is meant to be understood as Bořivoj, who would likely have been sixteen or seventeen years old when the Italian campaign began in 1081. This accords with the Latin term *adolescens*, which generally referred to the period from approximately fourteen to twenty-one years of age for boys. However, if this story actually relates to the 1111 campaign, then this youth would instead be Břetislav, the son of Duke Břetislav II, described by Cosmas as a boy (*puer*); Cosmas of Prague, *The chronicle of the Czechs*, 3.38, 227.

65 Cf. Judges 14:5, where Samson confronts a lion.

and steadfastness. Then Wiprecht also sought the truth of the matter from the bishops and the rest of the princes. When they had related the same, he immediately requested permission to return home with his men. But the emperor deferred granting this.

When the emperor, more stubbornly, would not be persuaded by his request, Wiprecht resolved now to part ways from them. 'I judge,' he said, 'that for my labours and my injuries I have merited good compensation from you' – speaking to the king – 'for whom I have endured great dangers. Lo, what sorts of benefices do I receive, I who – for the advantage of the whole kingdom – ran into costs in all my affairs, and especially risks to my own life and my men? I call all these princes to witness that I crossed the summit of the Alps first before everyone; that I stood out among your leading men as a champion in securing the well-being and victory of you and your men; and that I – with my men – am the principal author of everything that you accomplished successfully on this Italian expedition. If it is lawful to be said: I stood out as the one who set the tune. I think it's enough that I uselessly squandered great labour and great expense, and have even lost *milites*. Therefore I will return, ready to serve others now, not you. For them it will be seen as enough to test my steadfastness in their time of need, not to expose my life to the mockery of wild animals. Indeed I was thinking it sufficient that I offered you an acceptable spectacle, when I raged with my arms and strength in the slaughter of your enemies. But it seemed more spectacular that I be demolished by the teeth of beasts!' With these and similar words, Wiprecht raved without control against the emperor, since he was energetic, passionate, unconquerable, spirited and proud in arms. Then Wiprecht departed from him, causing fear even in the emperor on account of his high spirits.

Since the emperor hoped to be able to draw Wiprecht back to him without any blandishments or promises of benefices, he judged it a better idea to appease him and soften his inflexibility of mind through other people, to whose words he might be better disposed. Therefore, the emperor exhorted the archbishop of Mainz, together with the rest of the aforesaid bishops and abbots, and other princes to go to him wisely. He entreated them earnestly that, in his stead, they each – inspired by the king's devotion to them and with a view to a twofold reward – bestow on Wiprecht some kind of benefice out of the incomes of their churches and offices, as they might see fit. Moreover, they should not doubt him to be entirely prepared to make up, as soon as it should be convenient, whatever amount they themselves should deem worthy. They therefore followed Wiprecht and spoke with persuasive words. Although he was reluctant for a long time, they finally bent the high-spirited man – with, however, this promise introduced: that they would all return home with him, if the emperor should do other than he had promised.

In the emperor's presence, they all carried out solemnly this handing over of benefices. The archbishop of Mainz conceded to Wiprecht a benefice of 1,300 talents, the archbishop of Cologne the whole district called Orla,[66] the bishops of Halberstadt and Münster fifty talents each, and the abbots of Fulda and Hersfeld 300 each. Finally, the emperor advanced to meet Wiprecht on his return and confessed that he had carelessly done wrong against a man so useful and most loyal to him and to the whole kingdom. Accordingly, he granted into his full possession the castle named Leisnig with its many appurtenances. Afterwards, at a gathering of the court in Allstedt, he granted him a benefice of 300 talents and Dornburg with its appurtenances. Later, he assigned him 300 talents at a court gathering held in Merseburg.[67]

Then, having received hostages from the duke of Verona, along with the silver he had demanded – namely five hundred shallow bowls, just as many silver and gold dishes, and 4,000 marks – the emperor finally obtained the desired peace. Wiprecht, together with the king of Bohemia's son, named Bořivoj, approached him and asked for permission to leave. The emperor sought Wiprecht's advice as to how to send off the Czech as befits imperial honour. Wiprecht said: 'In this, it will seem enough if you offer sufficient silver for his and his men's expenses, along with two bowls and as many dishes. Also, you should bestow two dishes on each of his *milites*, together with two sets of clothes, as is fitting the royal munificence. In addition, by letters you should make known to his father every act of strength they accomplished in your company.' Approving his advice, the emperor inquired once more: what recompense might Wiprecht himself request as gifts out of the royal offerings? Wiprecht indicated he was ready to request nothing now, but later when it might be convenient. Nevertheless, he indicated this desire: that, with the Czech king's son mediating and interceding wisely on his behalf (as he had confidence), he be commended to Bořivoj's father for remuneration. Thus, he might be recompensed for serving not the emperor but the Czech king, who was not unmindful of his own honour

---

66 This region takes its name from the river Orla, a tributary of the Saale in eastern Thuringia.

67 We are unable to assign dates to these courts.

and title, recently regained by Wiprecht's faithful and wise guidance.[68]
And so indeed, what Wiprecht had prudently recommended, the emperor
ordered done. Having dismissed them, he said farewell.

Thereafter, departing from the king with Wiprecht, the Czech king's
son saw his birthplace again. There, with a crowd of magnates gathered
together and *permission given to speak*,[69] they set forth the success of all
of their affairs. They also displayed the emperor's letters and the rewards
they had received from him.

Afterwards, Bořivoj grasped Wiprecht's hand and said, 'Father, the
lord emperor committed this man to your diligence for the attainment
of this request: that you might reward with a worthy recompense his
most devoted service, which he has thus far most vigorously shown to
the whole kingdom, with me as a witness.' The Czech king therefore
ordered that a shield of the most exquisite workmanship be brought
out, perfectly decorated with gold and silver engravings, and also a bow
with a quiver, which the king of Hungary had recently sent – and that
they be offered to Wiprecht with a great abundance of gold and silver.
But he wanted to take none of these things except the bow and quiver,
saying that he could acquire much gold and silver by the hard work of
his own strength. Judging therefore that Wiprecht wanted more and
better things, the king had another shield again brought out, one more
decorated and laden with better gifts, together with a chess board edged
in gold with pieces skilfully carved of ivory and crystal. But Wiprecht
did not want to take any of these things except the board and pieces.
A third time the king ordered a shield to be laden with similar things,
with an ivory horn placed on top; in addition, he offered twenty horses
outfitted with saddles ingeniously made. But from these Wiprecht took
nothing except the horn. Therefore the king's mind began to waver: what
was there of great enough value, that, having been offered, Wiprecht
would not refuse to accept?

The son, more privy than the father to Wiprecht's desire, drew
his father out privately and advised that he marry his daughter, now
grown-up, to him. Bořivoj asserted that this would be more to his
advantage for the defence of his territory than if he were to marry her

---

68 The implication here is that Wiprecht, by leading the Czech contingent promised
    by Vratislav when negotiating the royal title (see above, p. 40), has been serving
    Vratislav rather than Henry IV. Thus, his reward should come from Vratislav (who
    has already received his own reward from Henry in the form of the
    royal title).

69 Virgil, *Aeneid*, I.520, XI.248 and XI.378.

to the king of the Russians or Hungarians. The joyful king assented, and had her come forth. Named Judith, she was elegant in appearance and adorned with garments woven with gold and with various jewelled ornaments. Then, calling Wiprecht forward, he handed her over to his safe-keeping. Wiprecht accepted her with not a little thanks and, with the king nodding approval, commended all those ornaments to his chamberlains to be saved, thus providing himself future advantages. But Wiprecht refused to accept the part of that province [i.e., Bohemia] which the king had assigned to his daughter for her dowry; instead, he demanded and procured in exchange two districts outside it, namely Nisen and Bautzen.[70] Having accepted these, he built a castle by the name of Schwerzau, which would be a safe fortress for his wife.

Although prosperous things were thus following Wiprecht, he nevertheless could not endure prosperity and peace. Remembering the injuries once inflicted on him by the more noble men of this province,[71] he frequently carried off not a little plunder from them, falling upon them unexpectedly. Therefore it happened that once, crossing the boundaries of the town called Belgern, he laid waste to the nearby villages by plundering and was on his way back, with everyone having suffered. When this became known to Margrave Henry of Meissen,[72] he took his *milites* with him and pursued Wiprecht as he came away from Belgern. But Wiprecht steadfastly intercepted him. They came together in battle, and Margrave Henry's standard-bearer died, transfixed by a lance from Wiprecht's *miles* Hartwig.[73] With others falling on both sides and Wiprecht's adversaries ultimately forced to flee into the town, Wiprecht's *milites* carried off their plunder.

At another time, Wiprecht was thinking of taking revenge against certain men, whom he was preparing to attack secretly. Therefore, in the middle of the night, he came to a village called Lippendorf, where a

---

70 Bautzen (Budyšin) was historically the most important town in Upper Lusatia. The district of Nisen is most likely a region just to the west of Bautzen around Dohna (Donin). Bautzen and Nisen are often paired in extant charters. The name 'Nisen' may derive from the name of a people (Niseni, a comparable grammatical form to 'Balsami' above), while Bautzen/Budyšin was the name of a fortress.

71 Here, the author is no longer referring to Bohemia but, presumably, to the region around Pegau.

72 Henry I of Eilenburg (d. 1103), margrave of Meissen and Lusatia (the Saxon Ostmark). Henry IV did not appoint him margrave of Meissen until c. 1089, suggesting this story does not fit here chronologically.

73 It is not clear if this is the same person as the Hartwig referenced above (p. 37).

certain *miles*, one of his own familiars, lived. He hid himself there all day. On the following night he came secretly to Zeitz with this same man. Having discovered that Ekelin and Hageno, men most hostile to him, were present there, he returned to his castle of Schwerzau as quickly as possible.[74] He joined with his most select men, and falling upon Zeitz unexpectedly, seized it. He slew Ekelin with seventeen men. Hageno and the rest were forced to flee into the church of St James. Since he could not in any way bring about by threats that they come out – oh, the pain! – fire was cruelly thrown in, and the church was burned down. Having thus been forced to exit, they were greatly deprived of the light of their eyes because they had fled for the refuge of the church. At last, Wiprecht returned home, not without great destruction to the region.

In the year of the Lord 1079.[75] There was a battle between Henry [IV] and Rudolf in the place that is called Flarchheim,[76] where in the initial clash, the Saxons turned their backs. There Vratislav, duke and king of Bohemia, gained possession of Rudolf's royal lance; thereafter, with Emperor *Henry's permission, at every festivity it always preceded in procession whatever the insignia were from the duchy of that people.[77]* And Wiprecht, who was always prominent in warlike events, was present at this battle.[78]

In the year of the Lord 1080. King Vratislav of Bohemia, getting set to invade the Saxons, passed through the district of Nisen with Wiprecht as guide.[79] The Czech made a sudden incursion from Wurzen to Leipzig and laid waste to everything. He received advice from Wiprecht that he ought to wait for his coming at [Hohen]wussen, until Wiprecht had ravaged the places around Belgern. As these things were happening,

---

74 These are quite possibly the 'Hageno from Döbitzschen' and 'Vicelin from Profen' mentioned above (p. 37), rivals to Wiprecht since he first arrived in the region around Groitzsch.

75 The text moves backwards in time here. The events described in the preceding sections occurred during the 1080s.

76 The battle of Flarchheim (27 January 1080).

77 These two sentences have been copied verbatim from Frutolf of Michelsberg's chronicle, except for some alterations of titles (adding 'and King' for Vratislav; calling Henry 'emperor' in place of Frutolf's 'king') and omitting Frutolf's note that the battle took place 'in a very harsh winter' (*hieme nimis aspera*). Cf. *Frutolfs und Ekkehards Chroniken und die Anonyme Kaiserchronik*, 90 and Frutolf of Michelsberg, *Chronicle*, 117.

78 No other text names Wiprecht as present at this battle.

79 Vratislav was not yet king in 1080, although his coronation has already been mentioned in this text. Since 1075, Vratislav had been Henry IV's military ally and in return had been granted both Lusatia and Meissen. The marches remained a war zone between pro- and anti-royal forces until 1089 or 1090.

news of their invasion suddenly became known to everyone in the neighbourhood. Immediately giving the call to arms, many thousands quickly joined together. They approached the Czechs, who were placed in an uneasy position. Struggling against the enemy with all his men, the Czech nearly lost the vanguard. But when Wiprecht came up, they turned the Saxons to flight and killed very many of them. Thus was the returning man's skill with a sword made plain to the Czechs.

Meanwhile, the emperor returned from Italy and announced to the Czech his court at Regensburg.[80] There, he gathered an army. The Bavarians, along with the Czechs and the rest of the peoples from Germany, crossed through the territory of the town of Weida and arrived at a fortification by the name of Mölsen near the Elster River. There, the Saxons with King Rudolf, elected three years before, met the emperor.[81] The battle was engaged, and did not drag on long. The emperor's army began to flee and was cut down everywhere from Mölsen all the way to the village of Wiederau. While the Saxons were pursuing them zealously, King Rudolf was gravely wounded in the right arm and carried off to Merseburg. He died three days later, with great penance for so much rebellion and slaughter committed on his account. He was honourably buried in that same place.[82]

With the emperor's army scattered everywhere, each returned home, having abandoned the king. Vratislav and Wiprecht, who had been present at the same battle, led the emperor away with a few men through Bohemia.[83] They had not yet learned of King Rudolf's ruin.

Meanwhile, Betheric of Teuchern came upon Wiprecht's *milites* by chance.[84] Pursued by them as he fled, he died, struck down in the village

---

80 This is likely a reference to Henry IV's brief trip to Brixen (today's Bressanone in Italy) in late June 1080 to hold a council with various German and Italian bishops, preparatory to appointing Wibert of Ravenna pope in place of Gregory VII.

81 The Battle on the Elster (14 October 1080). Rudolf had been elected (anti-)king at Forchheim in March 1077.

82 i.e., Merseburg. Rudolf's death and burial are attested by many sources, and his bronze tomb effigy can still be seen in the cathedral.

83 Bruno of Merseburg, usually regarded by scholars as the most reliable source for the battle on the Elster, clearly indicates that Vratislav and the Czechs, together with men from Meissen, were not present that day. Henry had summoned them, but the fight was engaged before they arrived (Bruno of Merseburg, *Brunonis Saxonicum Bellum*, 386–9, ch. 121 and 392–3, ch. 123). No other source mentions Henry withdrawing through Bohemia after this battle, though he did so on other occasions of fighting in this region.

84 For Betheric, see above, p. 37.

called Queisau. After his violent death, Wiprecht reminded his *milites* Hartwig and Peter – who (as we mentioned before) had gone over to Betheric with the town of Groitzsch – that they should be mindful of their loyalty and open the town to him. They handed it over immediately, and he erected two well fortified towers in it.

At that time, Wiprecht received in benefice from Bishop Walram of Zeitz the district Bautzen, with 1,100 *mansi* adjacent to the same place.[85] Provided with these and many other estates and benefices (which it would be tedious to enumerate one by one), he gained extraordinary praise among the nobles of this province for his strength and integrity. But because praise accompanies strength and envy praise, many of the princes pursued him with manifest hatred, for all power is impatient with a partner.[86]

Hence, his rival, Margrave Ekbert of Brunswick, slowly consumed by envy,[87] strove to attack his lands with a large army.[88] He soon passed by the castle at Teuchern. Having heard this, Wiprecht ordered his men to grab their arms immediately and to attack that man, who was imagining nothing of the sort. The margrave, terrified by the unexpected attack, considered the safety of flight. But with his adversaries seriously pressing upon him in pursuit, the fight was engaged near the same castle. There, a certain *miles*, who was most dear to Ekbert, attacked Wiprecht with a lance. He thrust through Wiprecht's shield and knocked out two of his teeth. Wiprecht immediately pierced him with his sword and, with due retaliation, divided his forehead down the middle. Then he turned the margrave's whole multitude to flight.

In the year of the Lord 1081.

In the year of the Lord 1082.

In the year of the Lord 1083.

---

85 Bishop Walram of Zeitz-Naumburg (1091–1111). A *mansus* was a measurement of land.

86 See n. 25 above.

87 See n. 4 above.

88 Ekbert II (c. 1060–90), the son of Margrave Ekbert I of Meissen (d. 1068), inherited the march but then was dispossessed as a result of his participation in the Saxon rebellion against King Henry IV; he was twice reinstated and dispossessed over the course of the revolt. Both Wiprecht and Ekbert were militarily active in eastern Saxony from 1080 onwards, Wiprecht allied with the king and Ekbert alternating in his allegiances. As a result, Ekbert and Wiprecht were almost certainly enemies, off and on, in the decade before Ekbert's death in 1090. However, no other source describes outright warfare between them, such as this incident when Wiprecht lost two teeth.

In the year of the Lord 1084.
In the year of the Lord 1085.
In the year of the Lord 1086.
In the year of the Lord 1087.
In the year of the Lord 1088.
In the year of the Lord 1089.

In the year of the Lord 1090. Margrave Ekbert, having enlarged his army, was again thinking about attacking Wiprecht's territories. But before he drew near to them, he died dishonourably in a certain mill.[89]

Thereafter, Wiprecht received two sons from his most noble wife by the name of Judith, the daughter of King Vratislav of the Czechs: Wiprecht the younger and his brother Henry, as well as a daughter named Bertha.[90] And he went from day to day ever growing in stature with more fortunate successes, such that he seemed to be frightening not only to the princes of Saxony but even to Emperor Henry himself. The emperor began to harbour extreme jealousy toward him. Having forgotten justice – and not remembering that Wiprecht had been loyal to him and had been his partner up to this point in great and frequent dangers and labours – he strove to upset Wiprecht's position of great good fortune.

When everything had at last been set up around him according to his desire, Wiprecht, so as not to misuse the tranquillity of the time granted to him by God, now pondered how he might become fortunate before God. (On account of the enormity of his worldly good fortune men were languishing from a voracious envy.)[91] It was as if he heard the very author of his salvation threatening him, '*Transgressors, take it again to heart!*'[92] Afterwards Wiprecht, soon to be the founder of the monastery of Pegau, felt remorse in his heart – while God himself, who calls those whom He predestines, took pity. However late, Wiprecht at last turned inward toward himself, and before the eyes of his own mind

---

89 For a more detailed account of Ekbert's death in a mill, see *The life of Emperor Henry IV*, 112–14. For brief, slightly different, reports, see Bernold of St Blasien, *Chronicle*, 299 and Frutolf of Michelsberg, *Chronicle*, 128.

90 Wiprecht the younger appears frequently below in the text; he predeceased his father, probably in or after 1117. The second son, Henry, succeeded his father but died childless in 1135. The daughter, Bertha, married Dedo IV (d. 1124), the older brother of Conrad of Wettin; this Conrad would, after 1135, acquire much of Wiprecht of Groitzsch's patrimony.

91 Cf. Wisdom 6:25 (see n. 4 and n. 87 above).

92 Isaiah 46:8.

he recalled which and how many bad things he had done: namely, how often he had plundered other people's things; how many men he had afflicted with slaughter, fire and pillage; how many he had deprived not only of their resources, honours, treasures and towns but also of life itself. Oh, that I might leave out these things: how much [violence] he committed at Rome, at the threshold of the blessed apostles, and in the burning of the basilica of St James in Zeitz.[93]

Recalling all these things, Wiprecht groaned in his heart and in all earnestness beseeched Him, without whom human frailty has no strength at all, to guide his counsel. Oh, how effective always is the judgment pronounced from the mouths of the saints – or rather from the Holy Spirit – such that wherever iniquity is abundant, grace is more abundant. Undoubtedly summoning himself more inwardly, he was resuscitated from the deadly habit of vice. And with the divine voice penetrating the hardness of his heart of stone,[94] Wiprecht was reminded to go forth outwardly for confession and penance. He took himself in complete devotion of spirit to [Archbishop] Hartwig of Magdeburg[95] and [Bishop] Werner [of Merseburg].[96] He revealed to them the enormity of his guilt and his desire to render satisfaction. To such men, who knew how to heal the sicknesses of souls, he revealed himself as ready to render satisfaction in every way, according to their judgement and as far as he was able.

These men, to be sure, although they did not lack confidence that they would be able to correct him by their authority and opinion, nevertheless, for the sake of easing for him the form of his penance a little bit – which they judged best – persuaded him with flattery to go to the threshold of the blessed apostles, Rome, and to the feet of the lord pope. Wiprecht, not delaying at all, was disinclined to go there heavily laden. Therefore, taking little with him, he arrived at Rome, as he had been counselled. There, prostrate on the ground, he watered the threshold of the apostles, which he had previously defiled with blood, with the tears of true penance. Afterwards, the opportunity granted him, he was brought to the feet of the lord pope, to whom he confessed with the highest devotion, in sequence, the reason for his journey and the enormity and the foulness of his sins.[97]

---

93 See above, pp. 45 and 52.

94 Cf. Ezekiel 36:26 and Romans 2:5, among others.

95 Archbishop Hartwig of Magdeburg (1079–1102).

96 Bishop Werner of Merseburg (1059–93).

97 This might be a reference to either the reformist Pope Urban II (1088–99) or the imperial anti-pope Clement III (1084–1100).

Then, by the authority of his predecessors the pope, most splendid in his knowledge of the true and salvific medicine, most insightful in showing moderation in penance, and having first offered certain words for compelling more diligently a compunction to repentance, sent him to the patriarch of the Spanish, a man of apostolic authority[98] and admirable (even to the pope himself) on account of the merit of his life. That is to say, having consulted more privately, the pope counselled Wiprecht to mention to him the heavier labour of that trip or some need of an obstacle, with God arranging it. He also counselled Wiprecht to comply with all of the patriarch's commands and advice.

And so, Wiprecht hastened to the patriarch with ardent desire, and made fully known to him the things he had done thus far in his neighbourhood. The patriarch imposed penance on him – from ecclesiastical, not his own, judgement – measured in accordance with the magnitude of his crimes, and taking care *lest by chance he run in vain.*[99] Not as a harsh overseer of a fellow servant but as a neighbour with compassion,[100] with these salvific admonitions the patriarch instructed the spirit of the one in danger, who was hastening to race back to the harbour of salvation by his own rowing:

'Concerning those publicly penitent in our times, we indeed fear to pre-judge whether they be penitents or more like jokers – those who, after they are received in the church as reconciled, pretend to alter their former life. But because true justice lies not in beginning but in persevering, most beloved son, consider why you have travelled such a great distance. For the lord pope was able to give you – nay rather ought to give you more appropriately than I – remission of sins. But he wanted to test your patience with the labour of such a great journey, so that, having reaped the benefit of your perseverance, you may now receive from me a more relaxed measure of penance. Therefore, to your love I declare this advice most efficacious and salutary: redeem your sins through alms, which are strong enough to extinguish them

---

98 The implication here is that Wiprecht went on pilgrimage to Santiago de Compostela, the town in north-western Iberia considered the resting place of St James the Greater, one of the twelve Apostles. An increasingly popular pilgrimage destination in this period, it became an episcopal see only in 1094 and an archiepiscopal see in 1120. The author here seems either to possess a confused knowledge of all of this, to have conflated the situation at the time of his writing with the earlier period when Wiprecht travelled, or to be obfuscating the chronology deliberately.

99 Galatians 2:2.

100 Cf. Matthew 18:23–35.

completely, just like water on fire.[101] As for the rest, if the means are
abundant, construct at your own expense a temple to God, whose servant
a good will ought to be, for the veneration of the blessed James, whose
basilica you burned down. Also, bring together there as many servants
of God as you judge yourself able, according to the Lord's precept:
make the poor *your friends from the wealth of iniquity*.[102] Let these men
preserve the order of the Rule's observance, so that, when you have
departed from the present life, with constant prayers they will bring
it about that you are worthy to be received in the heavenly abode.'[103]

To this Wiprecht said: 'If your paternity judges it sufficient, I can
establish a monastic cell suitable for six brothers and can spend whatever
might meet their needs.' Prudently resisting, the patriarch said to him:
'*Those who sow sparingly, also reap sparingly*.[104] And he who will spend
in cheerfulness and abundance, will also receive abundantly.[105] Because
maintaining the Rule's observance in every way will not be possible
among so few, if you are in any way able, add the same number of others
to these [i.e., six plus six] – for together they will more easily be strong
in monastic order. Just as greater diseases need greater medicine, so
too do greater rewards follow heavier labours.' Since Wiprecht promised
himself ready to do everything he could, with God working with him
and granting life, the patriarch gave him relics, namely the knee of St
James.[106] Then he dismissed him, reconciled to the church, with the
remission of his sins and a blessing.

Thus were these things happily accomplished. As Wiprecht was
returning home, he detoured to his town of Leisnig, where his assembled
men received him with joy. He made known to them the causes and
results of his journey, in sequence, and took counsel with them as to
which place under his control seemed to be suitable for constructing a
monastery. And although different people offered different opinions
about what might be best, nevertheless the more prudent agreed that

---

101 Cf. Ecclesiasticus 3:33.

102 Luke 16:9.

103 Cf. John 14.

104 2 Corinthians 9:6.

105 Cf. 2 Corinthians 9:7–8.

106 The term is *poblitem* in Latin (*Annales Pegavienses*, 243), which likely comes from
poples, poplitis (knee). However, other scholars describe Wiprecht as receiving the
saint's thumb (*pollex, pollicis*). See, for example, Vogtherr, 'Wiprecht von Groitzsch
und das Jakobspatrozinium', 46.

he ought to look in the neighbourhood of his town of Groitzsch, in whatever place might be most suitable there.

Toward that end, as he was turning his mind to that same devout intention, Wiprecht passed by chance through a certain village named Eula, where there was a wooden church that had by then almost fallen apart from the old age of the wood. He withdrew into it for the sake of prayer, with his familiar named Giselher. For it was Wiprecht's custom that he never passed a church without saying a prayer. Rising, therefore, after saying his prayer – wondrous to say! – the chest of relics, which was placed upon the altar, seemed to be opened like a book by divine agency. With the brightness from it glittering in his face, it struck the chest of this very brave man with such great terror that he was scarcely able to remain in his place. Coming out, Wiprecht asked his aforesaid familiar if he had seen anything. After Giselher said that truly he had seen nothing yet had experienced immense terror, Wiprecht described what he had seen, and said he was of a mind to restore this very church. After he had ordered that to be done immediately out of his own expenses, he resumed his journey and reached Groitzsch.

There too, he was received with not a little exultation. Impatient of delay, Wiprecht made known to more prudent men the desire and wish he was incessantly turning over in his mind. It seemed to them that it ought to be done in a certain prominent place, adjacent to the same castle [i.e., Groitzsch], called Nible in antiquity, now Old Groitzsch. But, sensibly, this displeased certain more careful men with more profound advice; they prudently contended that if the castle itself should at some time be surrounded by a siege (as will be clear, this later happened) that place would be a refuge for the enemy and a source of desolation for those staying there.

Afterwards it pleased Wiprecht to designate for such a great work a place on this side of the river Elster, adjacent to the village of Pegau, where now a certain village called *Wolftitz* lies. For that place, quite pleasant and spacious, was then empty on this side of the nearby highway. But because the public highway created an opportunity – even a necessity – for everyone to be passing through frequently, and this would be a loss – even a catastrophe – for those ready to serve God there, that advice was also withdrawn as useless.

After Wiprecht had surveyed everything all around with diligent consideration, they looked toward the region west of the village of Pegau at a place chosen for this work – so we believe – by divine agency. It was most fitting but not every part of it lay in his control, for a certain Erpo possessed a castle bordering this place; since he did not possess an heir, he was bound most closely to Wiprecht by both consanguinity and friendship.[107] When Wiprecht had opened his mind to him, Erpo held that he was entirely in agreement with him. And so he donated that place, together with other benefices in Saxony, in order to renounce completely his ownership of it. Consequently, he ordered the place to be levelled, and the defences to be fully removed as well.

In the year of the Lord 1091. Divine clemency had led the way by inspiring Wiprecht, and that same clemency also followed after by working together with him. Therefore, because the charity kindled in him by divine agency was not able to be idle, he turned this over in his most wise mind all day and all night by frequent meditation: how might he properly begin the work of his most devout intention and more properly complete it? He judged it fitting to seek advice and comfort from his father-in-law, that is, from King Vratislav of Bohemia; therefore he did not neglect to go see him. Vratislav, joyfully favouring the praiseworthy petition of the man, since he was his son-in-law, put 700 talents into Wiprecht's hand. The king gladdened him not a little with words and promises that, in view of his help, he should act confidently and establish a work becoming to the honour of God and of St James with his encouragement and assistance.

Having returned, Wiprecht went to the lord Hartwig, archbishop of Magdeburg, entreating and inviting him to give the blessings of foundation and of cemeteries to the place under consideration.[108] He also invited [Bishops] Walram of Zeitz and Albuin of Merseburg[109] to come with him. Meeting together, they discharged the duties of the priestly office. After they had given the blessing, they advised Wiprecht that he should first carry on his own shoulders baskets of stones for the twelve corners of the foundation, the same number as in imitation of the deed of the most pious prince Constantine, who was the first and most powerful among the princes as a founder of Christ's churches.[110]

---

107 It is not clear who this Erpo was, or how he was related to Wiprecht. See below, p. 68, for more about Erpo and his castle.

108 Cemeteries and the sites of church foundations needed to be blessed before they could become sacred places.

109 For Walram, see n. 85 above. Bishop Albuin of Merseburg (1097–1112). Bishop Werner of Merseburg, mentioned above (p. 56), was still bishop in 1091, so either the bishop or the date is incorrect here. Since Vratislav died in 1092, the former is more likely – although the chronological obfuscation may be intentional, precisely to push the monastery's foundation earlier so as to assert a direct connection to Vratislav, and thus also his heirs.

110 Cf. *The donation of Constantine (Constitutum Constantini)*, 142, ch. 13.

Wiprecht complied readily. And he kindled so great an ardour in all his men for willing labour that, unlike the foundation of other churches laid by the labour of paid servants, the work surged eagerly from his armed band and from the perseverance of those yielding to them, such that within three years, without any break, it had risen up to the top of the towers. Meanwhile, next to the same work, he established a court for himself (in the place where a hospital is now located), in which he immediately had a chapel to God and the blessed confessor Nicholas constructed.[111]

In the year of the Lord 1092. Next, Wiprecht considered it advantageous to seek out some man of a pious way of life, who, joined with brothers, might *put the finishing touch on the same work*,[112] construct workshops,[113] and most especially introduce the divine office. Going to the monastery called [Münster]schwarzach,[114] well known to him since it was pre-eminent in piety, he obtained there the lord Bero and three other brothers, companions in such great labour. To Bero, Wiprecht commended the care of his monastery.

Once, Wiprecht gave Bero thirty marks for the use of the brothers and the expenses of the buildings. Bero lost them when going into the bathhouse, fastening the key to his belt. There was a certain man, a *conversus* from the laity,[115] corrupt in character and in cunning. His abbot had not at all noticed his deceitfulness, because he was of an exceedingly simple nature – and because good men sometimes disguise what they are, while in every endeavour bad men pretend to be what they are not. Thus Bero had taken him into his employ ahead of other men. This man, like Judas, having wickedly taken advantage[116] of benefits of this kind, finally, after a long time, stumbled (I think) upon the opportunity he had premeditated. With his abbot entering the bath, he stealthily stole the key and fled with the donated money.

---

111 Most likely the fourth-century Saint Nicholas of Myra, not Pope Nicholas I, who is mentioned in *The deeds of Count Ludwig of Arnstein*.

112 Seneca, *Ad Lucilium Epistolae morales* 71.28 and 101.8.

113 Cf. *RB 1980: the rule of St Benedict*, 186–7, ch. 4.

114 Münsterschwarzach was a Benedictine monastery on the Main River in Franconia. Bishop Adalbero of Würzburg (1045–90) and Abbot Ekbert (d. 1076/77) transformed it into one of the leading reformed monasteries of the late eleventh century.

115 *Conversus* is usually translated as 'lay brother', someone who lived apart from the monks or canons and typically performed menial chores for the religious community for the sake of his soul. However, *conversus* could also be used to refer to someone who had joined a religious house as an adult, not as a child oblate, and who was illiterate.

116 Cf. Luke 22:5–6.

Wiprecht learned this, having experienced the abbot's negligence not for the first time now. Although he considered it to have happened out of simplicity and not an evil desire, he nevertheless thought to remove the abbot from himself, because he realized that his place [i.e., Pegau] could not readily be advanced through such a man. The abbot promised to restore every loss that had occurred and returned to his monastery [Münsterschwarzach], having obtained a reprieve from Wiprecht, so that he might not incur the ill fame of such a great loss. Within a short time, he recovered from acquaintances and relatives the full amount of silver negligently lost. Then, having returned [to Pegau], for his whole life he laboured as much as he was able and yet increased the number of brothers not at all. He departed to the Lord without pastoral consecration, quite old, on the tenth Kalends of January [23 December], and was buried there.[117]

In the year of the Lord 1093. The lord Wiprecht had exhausted nearly everything that his father-in-law, namely King Vratislav of Bohemia, had given to him. So he sent to him again and was not disappointed by the king's usual encouragement. Vratislav sent him another 300 talents toward completing the work that had been started.

In the same year, *Vratislav, having fallen from his horse while hunting, died a sudden death*.[118] In the excellence of his honour, power and wealth he was surely a man incomparable to all his predecessors in his principate. He even struck fear in the emperor and all the German princes. Vratislav was nevertheless a most loyal joint-labourer for the kingdom, as he proved frequently in many times of need when King Henry [IV] was ruling. For that reason, the same emperor – not undeservedly – raised him up with the pre-eminence of the royal title. He was also the first among his people to be distinguished by a royal crown and the lance.[119] He

---

117 See below, p. 65, where Bero's death is reported again, with a different date.

118 *Frutolfs und Ekkehards Chroniken und die Anonyme Kaiserchronik*, 106 (Frutolf of Michelsberg, *Chronicle*, 129). Cosmas of Prague, *The chronicle of the Czechs*, 2.50, 179, dates his death to early January 1092 – and the scholarly consensus agrees with his date.

119 This must refer to Rudolf of Swabia's lance (see above, p. 52), which Vratislav was allowed to carry after its capture at the battle of Flarchheim. Note that this passage seems to contradict the story told above (p. 38), where Wiprecht states that Vratislav's ancestor 'Buogo' was the first leader of the Czechs to attain the royal title.

left behind five sons, one of whom was called Bořivoj;[120] after his father died, he obtained the duchy for some time.[121] Another son was Ulrich, who later, when Lothar was ruling, obtained the same principate.[122]

In the year of the Lord 1094.

In the year of the Lord 1095. *The finishing touch was put*[123] upon the church of the monastery of Pegau. And by the industry of the lord Bero, who governed that place commended to him and was not lazy in administering it, many workshops were established for the use of the brothers.[124]

In the year of the Lord 1096. On the seventh Kalends of August [26 July], the church of the monastery of Pegau was dedicated by the venerable lord Hartwig, Archbishop of Magdeburg, working together with Bishops Albuin of Merseburg, Walram of Zeitz and Hezilo of Havelberg, in the presence of the lord Wiprecht, the founder of the same place, and with very many other nobles and his sons, Wiprecht and Henry, also present.[125] On the same day, the lady Countess Judith, daughter of the Czech king Vratislav, came forth crowned and royally adorned in clothes woven with gold.

That very day, upon the altar, she dedicated to God and St James these two remarkable items: a crown inlaid with gold and gems, and a robe woven with gold, resembling a dalmatic[126] and of the most precious

---

120 Vratislav fathered six sons, two of whom predeceased him – one as a child (presumably the one omitted from the count here). All four of those surviving him ruled as duke of Bohemia over the course of the next three decades: Břetislav II, Bořivoj II, Vladislav I and Soběslav I (named in some texts, as here, Ulrich). Bořivoj was not King Vratislav's immediate successor, as implied here (see Cosmas of Prague, *The chronicle of the Czechs*, 3.7, 189 and 3.10, 192); however, this is the same Bořivoj mentioned above (p. 40).

121 This vague statement may be deliberate obfuscation or result from simple uncertainty: Bořivoj assumed the throne more than once, but never managed to rule as duke for any length of time; he was repeatedly challenged and/or ousted by his cousins and brothers.

122 Another name for Vratislav's youngest son, Soběslav, duke of Bohemia from 1125 to 1140.

123 Seneca, *Ad Lucilium Epistolae morales* 71.28 and 101.8 (cf. above, n. 112).

124 See the very different description of Bero above, under the year 1092.

125 Albuin would not become bishop until 1097 (see n. 109 above). Little is known about Bishop Hezilo of Havelberg, who died some time after the year 1108.

126 A calf-length garment with relatively wide sleeves, ornamented with stripes down the front and around the cuff, chiefly worn by deacons. See Miller, *Clothing the Clergy*, 249.

workmanship, which she was wearing under a cloak also woven with gold. For those wanting to know about these things – where they ended up – let him lament! For, as we have learned, the lord Abbot Windolf[127] later used the crown advantageously as payment for possessions to be bought in Thuringia. But, as for the robe, lord Wiprecht the younger, about to travel to Italy in the service of the emperor in his father's place, later offered it for – and promised to pay back – as much silver as it might be worth.[128] Bishop Burchard of Münster (nicknamed 'the Red'),[129] having inspected the robe, gave forty marks for it. But, when Wiprecht returned from Italy, many obstacles hindered him, and he was not able to pay back the silver before his death.

This is a summary of the possessions of the church of Pegau, which the lord Margrave Wiprecht built in honour of the Holy Trinity and St Mary and St James the apostle.[130] He endowed it with the town adjacent to it, together with all its appurtenances: woods, meadows, and pastures; rights of way (in and out); waters and watercourses; millstones and mills; vacant plots, tilled and untilled fields; fishing and hunting rights; and all uses that can be stated or named, except one of the roads, the outermost, situated toward the north. Later, to increase its endowment, he gave the same church two villages, one of which is called Hilpritz, the other Pörsten, with the adjacent vineyards and meadows and a mill, as well as nine *mansi* in *Stonice* and in Lausick ten *solidi*, with which lamps should be bought for illuminating the chapel of St Mary.[131] Then, as the piety and number of brothers grew over the course of time, the lord Wiprecht gave more for the brothers' support, namely these villages: *Muchelice, Bořice, Karlsdorf,*[132] *Heinrichsdorf* and Lippendorf,

127 See below, p. 66.

128 This is probably a reference to Henry V's Italian expedition of 1111, though below (pp. 78–80) the text suggests that Henry V was not on good terms with the two Wiprechts in this period.

129 Bishop Burchard of Münster (1098–1118).

130 This list, which includes many common legal phrases found in charters, suggests that the author of this passage had access to at least some of the monastery's early charters, although none but the original papal privilege for Pegau survives today (see below, p. 71).

131 The location of *Stonice* is not known with certainty. A *solidus*, also known in Germany as a 'schilling', was usually equivalent to twelve silver pennies. The passage here thus seems to indicate that the monastery of Pegau received income, rather than property, at Lausick.

132 Karlsdorf is mentioned below, p. 91, as a grant made by Wiprecht on his deathbed, suggesting that this passage was written after his death and was intended to summarize the monastery's property holdings at some point during the second or third quarter of the twelfth century.

with meadows and pastures and all their other appurtenances; and in *Borkovice* four *mansi*; and the church in Lausick with the tithes of 16 villages;[133] and the church in *Dietmarsdorf,* plus two *mansi* and one mill in the same village; and the church in *Cloveldechesdorf,* and nine *mansi* in *Suchsdorf.*[134] What things were handed over to our church after these, by his children and by very many other people loyal to him, we will mention in the appropriate place;[135] now let us return to those things from which we digressed a little.

The celebration of the aforesaid dedication solemnly extended over five days, and the lady Countess Judith, to everyone's admiration, came forth adorned with garlands of changing design, equally inlaid, one for each of the five days. Therefore, after everything was suitably arranged according to his will, the lord Wiprecht bid farewell to everyone and dismissed the whole assembled crowd. Afterwards, he gave for the adornment of the pulpit crystal and ivory chess pieces with carvings in relief.[136]

In the year of the Lord 1097.

In the year of the Lord 1098.

In the year of the Lord 1099. At Aachen, on the Lord's Epiphany [6 January], Emperor Henry made his son Henry V king.[137]

In the year of the Lord 1100. The lord Abbot Bero, thus far looking out for this place both as much as he was able and as well as he knew, was finally ready to receive the rewards for his labours and migrated to the Lord. He was buried in the brothers' old chapter hall near the entrance of the church, on the seventh Kalends of January [26 December].[138]

In the year of the Lord 1101. At that time, strict observance of the Rule, which laudably had begun spreading everywhere then after the custom of Hirsau,[139] was flourishing at Corvey, a royal abbey, above all

---

133 For the significance of tithes in this period, see Eldevik, *Episcopal power.*

134 The names of these villages have been formed by appending conventional German or Slavic placename suffixes ('-dorf' or '-ice', respectively) to German or Slavic personal names. Those in italics cannot be securely identified today; the modernized spellings here are approximations. Hilpritz ('Hilpertice' in the manuscript, reflecting the Slavic pronunciation of the personal name Gilbert) is now called Rippach.

135 No such list of grants appears anywhere in the *Annales Pegavienses.*

136 Presumably these are the same ones described above, p. 50.

137 Cf. Frutolf of Michelsberg, *Chronicle,* 137.

138 Cf. above, under the year 1092.

139 The monastery of Hirsau in Swabia was an important centre of Benedictine reform in the late eleventh and early twelfth centuries; its reforming ideas were greatly influenced by those of Cluny (see the general introduction).

other Saxon monasteries.[140] There, the lord Abbot Markward, a man worthy of veneration and remembrance, presided at that time.[141] Arriving there, the lord Wiprecht laid bare to him, in sequence, all the things afflicting his mind: namely that the condition and piety of his monastery had thus far advanced less than he had hoped toward an improvement of the Rule's observance. But the sole reason for this was the fact that, for such a great work to be begun, he did not have suitable partners in the plan. Therefore, whatever seemed best to the abbot's prudence, Wiprecht promised himself ready to do. He promised he would be fully deserving of this, by the abundance of his compliance, if Markward would appoint from the community of that holy congregation [i.e., Corvey] whomever he judged likely to be advantageous to Pegau – with several companions in this labour alongside him. Thereupon he promised himself ready to furnish from his own estates everything needed for their use, if this alone might satisfy his request.

The abbot, steadfast in piety and justice, received gladly Wiprecht's request and desire in Christ; he asked for the advice and will of the whole community about this matter. With everyone agreeing with him on it – and in order not to disappoint such a great man in so pious a vow – that venerable monk lord Windolf was judged with their unanimous consent to be suitable and likely to be advantageous for this work. And not without merit. For, on account of his continence of life and attention to piety, he was at that time head of a certain cell belonging to the same monastery (whose heads are called priors), where he had energetically presided over the brothers entrusted to him. Previously, it is reported, he had been in charge of the students and had laudably become renowned for his knowledge of letters [i.e., at Corvey].[142] He had also held a canonry in the priory called Heiligenstadt. But having set it aside for Christ, conquered by the love of piety, he was received at Corvey.[143] Therefore, since he laid the foundation for perfection from the beginning, no one doubted that he would become perfect later,

---

140 The Saxon monastery of Corvey, a Carolingian foundation, played a pivotal role in disseminating Hirsau reform ideas within Saxony during the later eleventh century.

141 Abbot Markward of Corvey (1081–1107).

142 i.e., his formal education.

143 Monastic authors in this period commonly exhibited a low regard for canons, since they did not live according to as strict a rule as monks. The implication here is that Windolf showed greater dedication to God by renouncing his position as canon and becoming a monk at Corvey.

advancing himself day to day by developing virtues.[144] Concerning the rest, however, for those wanting to know, it will be set forth more clearly with light and by certain tests.

Therefore, the lord Windolf was promoted as abbot, and other brothers joined with him for the easing of this great labour. One of them, Ludiger, who afterwards became abbot in Reinsdorf,[145] was appointed his prior. And he was endowed with many necessities, among them these books: an antiphonal and a gradual, a small missal book, the Rule and a Psalter. They have remained at our house until today. In addition, the lord Abbot Markward gave him relics of St Vitus the Martyr[146] and of other saints. Bidding farewell to everyone, he dismissed them, having faithfully entrusted Windolf to the safe keeping of the lord Wiprecht.

Since not a small disagreement had arisen between royal power (*regnum*) and the power of the priesthood (*sacerdotium*) at that time, such that none of the priests of that province deigned to communicate with Emperor Henry [IV],[147] the lord Wiprecht brought his abbot with him to Archbishop Ruothard of Mainz, who was then at Erfurt, and arranged for Windolf to be elevated by the pastoral benediction through him.[148] At the same time on the same day an abbot of that town by the name of Burchard was consecrated with him.[149]

Afterwards, having returned home with Abbot Windolf, the lord Wiprecht handed his monastery over to Windolf's safe keeping, so that, in that place, he might care for his own soul to Wiprecht's advantage in all things. Windolf received the place – however undeveloped, unformed and uncultivated it had been up to this time – under his care. He

---

144 Cf. *RB 1980: the rule of St Benedict*, 294–7, ch. 73.

145 See below, under the year 1110, for more on this monastery.

146 i.e., from Corvey.

147 This is a reference to the disagreement of the late eleventh century that modern scholarship terms the Investiture Controversy (see the general introduction). Put simply: Pope Gregory VII sought to limit royal control over episcopal elections and investiture while King Henry IV insisted that he had the right as king to choose bishops and invest them with the symbols of their office. In the course of this dispute, Henry IV was twice excommunicated.

148 Archbishop Ruothard of Mainz (1089–1109) rebelled against Henry IV in 1098, was exiled from his see, and subsequently joined the faction that had long opposed Henry's rule. Although Wiprecht chiefly supported Henry IV, for some reason he turned to this embattled archbishop to secure his abbot's consecration – a decision the author justifies by reminding his readers that the emperor was an excommunicate at the time.

149 See *Annales Sancti Petri Erphesfurdenses*, 17, where it is reported that Burchard became abbot of St Peter's in Erfurt on 8 February 1103.

was nevertheless very sure that God especially would be his partner. Like some very skilled carver of a seal, assessing the timidity of his predecessor on the basis of the very poor start to all the workshops, he consigned the previous buildings to oblivion and began to construct better ones. By the industry of his own labour and also supported through everything by the generosity of the lord Wiprecht, he brought them to perfection. Indeed, having inspected the place, Windolf had unformed and marshy places levelled and the filth from briars and other squalor eradicated. He enlarged and increased everything. And in the church commended to him – again, like on a seal – he wisely carved out an image of perfect elegance that bears witness to the accomplishment of its maker still today.

Among other things, Windolf increased the number of brothers to forty and to a number greater than that. By their daily labour, he levelled the castle of the lord Erpo (about whom we spoke above), which was heaped together by an impregnable pile of earth with entrenchments and ramparts.[150] He made a garden there, stuffed with a diverse abundance of fruits and herbs, which frequently gladdened that same city of God. Afterwards, along the river Wyhra on the eastern side, he began to cultivate the place still called *Abtsdorf* after him, that is, to completely tear out trees and shrubs all around, and, with the thickness of the forests cleared, to expand the lands ready for the plough. With a church built there and with a manor abundantly endowed for the inhabitants' use, he established that it was to be for our brothers in perpetuity. By his own labour he also established a village by the name of *Wolftitz* next to the village of Pegau, and increased its annual render to the value of a talent.[151] For the use of the brothers, he also rendered a certain place toward the western side of that village profitable by an annual payment of eight *solidi*.

The lord Wiprecht, inspecting and attentively approving Windolf's industry and his attentiveness in the place commended to him, was a most generous partner with him in all things. He charged all his men with what most had to be done. They finished it not only when he was a witness but even devotedly afterwards,[152] as much out of love for their lord as for the remedy of their own souls, conferring on that monastery

---

150 See above, p. 60.

151 For this village, see above, p. 59.

152 i.e., both while Wiprecht was still living and after his death.

– even beyond ordinary benefits – very many estates (which we will mention in the appropriate place).[153]

In the year of the Lord 1104.[154] After this, the lord Wiprecht had certain uncultivated land in the diocese of Merseburg ploughed. Then, going to the regions of Franconia – where the lady Sigena, his mother, had been married in Lengenfeld (as we remember having said before)[155] – he transferred from there very many peasants of that province. He ordered them to cultivate the aforesaid district, having completely uprooted the forest, and to possess it thereafter by hereditary right. And (if we might insert something ridiculous) any one of them, accompanied by his small household, could even name after his own name the village or the property planted by his own labour.

Therefore, when a great many villages had been established between the rivers Mulde and Wyhra, the lord Wiprecht was not yet weary of his most devout intention. But in tireless labour, striving after a work of piety, he founded another monastery on the aforesaid uncultivated land in the village, namely, of Lausick.[156] Desiring that a cell suitable for at least six brothers be created there, he arranged for this place to be the parish church of all the neighbouring villages, and he wanted it to be subject to the monastery of Pegau. Because he was not able to accomplish this – nor should he have been – without the consent or permission of the lord Albuin and the entire clergy of Merseburg, he himself went with a humble petition to address their will concerning this. These men, great in respect to piety and devotion, rightly granted the things he asked for and desired. They decided that the things they had conceded ought to be made unalterable by the authority of the whole church; they agreed that the bishop should grant a privilege concerning the tithes of all the villages pertaining to that parish church and also of others lying in the burgward of Groitzsch, below the Wyhra and Schnauder rivers. We transcribe a copy of it here, as an example:[157]

---

153 Cf. above, n. 135; again, there is no such list of grants anywhere in the *Annales Pegavienses.*

154 The text does not include entries for 1102 or 1103. The earliest reference in an extant charter to Wiprecht's eldest son, Wiprecht, dates from this period; he and his father are named together in the witness list of a charter of Bishop Walram of Zeitz-Naumburg from the year 1103 (*CDSR* I A 2, 5, nr. 3).

155 See above, p. 35.

156 For this village, see above, under the year 1096.

157 Cf. *CDSR* I A 2, 7–8, nr. 7.

In the name of the holy and indivisible Trinity, Albuin, by the grace of God bishop of Merseburg. Let it be known to all the faithful both future and present, how, because of the lord Wiprecht and Abbot Windolf's intervention and for the remedy of my soul, we handed over to the monastery of Pegau, established in honour of St James, and to its spiritual head, Windolf, the tithes of the villages, the names of which are written below, and of others, if they are yet to be established around these places: Časlavsdorf, Ottendorf, Čadorf, Münchroth, Lausick, Suoerdorf, Sulansdorf, Bělansdorf, Milansdorf, Drogisdorf, Čazindorf, Vladsdorf, Vizecká, Eberhardsdorf, Moisdorf, Sečevice, Kosovo.[158] *These are situated in the burgward of Groitzsch, in the county of Margrave Udo, between the rivers Wyhra and Schnauder.*[159] *Done in the year 1105, in the twelfth indiction,*[160] *on the ninth Kalends of October* [23 September], *in the ninth year of his ordination* [as bishop], *with the canons of that church consenting: vidame Hubert,*[161] *dean Dietold, Walter the master of students, and the laymen Ludiger, Henry and Giselbert and very many other clerics and laymen. I, Albuin, signed with my own hand. The land is filled with the mercy of the Lord.*[162] *However, if anyone, with the devil's urging, should be an impious violator of this act, let him know that he will be damned forever by the chain of anathema.*

In the year of the Lord 1106.[163] The lord count Wiprecht saw to the favourable conditions of his monastery not only in the present but also into the future. On the advice of the lord abbot Windolf and the rest of

---

158 Most of these place names have been formed by appending the German suffix '-dorf' to either a Slavic (Milan, Časlav) or a German (Otto, Eberhard) personal name. Again, the modernized spellings here are approximations. None but Lausick can be identified securely today.

159 This is presumably a reference to Udo III of Stade (d. 1106), son of the Udo II mentioned above (above p. 36).

160 The indiction was a way of reckoning time, based on a cycle of fifteen years, that originated at the time of the Roman empire.

161 A vidame (*vicedominus*) was a bishop's deputy.

162 Psalm 32.5.

163 The year 1105 is omitted. Other texts show Wiprecht deeply implicated in the political instability around this time. *The 1106 continuation of Frutolf's chronicle*, 182, describes him assisting Henry IV in escaping from his rebellious son – in late summer 1105 – by conducting him from Bohemia to the Rhineland. Henry IV's own widely circulated letter to King Philip I of France, written from imprisonment in early 1106, names Wiprecht as the envoy sent by Henry V the previous December to demand the imperial regalia from his father (*Imperial lives and letters*, 193). And Ekkehard of Aura, *Chronicle*, 224, claims that 'Count Wiprecht', apparently endeavouring to cross the Alps as a pilgrim to Italy in 1106, was captured in Trent by a rogue follower of Henry IV and then released on condition of reconciliation with him.

those most loyal to him, he decreed that he was transferring that place over to the right or power of the apostolic see in perpetuity, so that it would not come to be harassed by the lordship of any secular person in the future.[164] Hence, he sent in his place a *miles* by the name Luvo (a familiar of his, diligent in dealing with business and lawsuits) to Rome, to the threshold of the apostles. Luvo was to bind that monastery to the Roman liberty by faithful representation and to bring it about that the pope give a privilege concerning this same transfer.[165] Therefore, the lord pope Paschal, the second of this name, administering the vicarship of blessed Peter, was made aware of the reasons for Luvo's journey.[166] Supported by apostolic authority, he sanctioned the monastery of Pegau by this confirmation of the privilege and with the impression of his seal:[167]

Bishop Paschal [II], servant of the servants of God, to the faithful throughout Saxony, greetings and apostolic blessing. A desire that is known to pertain to pious intention and the salvation of souls, with God as its author, must be fulfilled without any delay. Accordingly Wiprecht, illustrious count of the Saxon people, built for his and his men's salvation a monastery in the diocese of Merseburg, in a place on his own property called Pegau. With the admirable miles *Luvo sent in his place, he offered this monastery upon the altar of the blessed Peter and transferred it in perpetuity into the right of the apostolic see. The lord Wiprecht nevertheless made an exception of the advocacy, which he was prepared to hold himself.[168] After him either the first born of his posterity, if indeed he should want to preside over the church justly and beneficially, should be advocate; or if, however, his posterity should fail – may God avert it! – the abbot of that place, with the sounder advice of his brothers, should choose an advocate – whomever he will want – advantageous to him and to the church. Therefore, following up his laudable desire, we sanction by the authority of the present decree the following: both the aforesaid place and everything pertaining to it shall always remain secure and undiminished under*

164 It became common practice in the German kingdom during the late eleventh and early twelfth centuries for nobles, as one aspect of the monastic reform agendas popular in this period, to hand over their new monastic foundations into papal protection – instead of into royal protection, which had been the earlier practice.

165 Papal privileges of this kind are common during this period, with most of the new monastic foundations of this period seeking such documents from Rome. Cf. *The life of Bishop Otto of Bamberg*, I.22 and I.29.

166 Pope Paschal II (1099–1118).

167 This papal privilege survives in the original, which is the basis for the edition in *CDSR* I A 2, 8–9, nr. 9.

168 Church advocates were local nobles responsible for defending a religious house's properties and for judging capital offences on the religious house's estates.

the protection of the apostolic see, to the profit of God's servants residing there in every kind of use. Nevertheless, we also sanction that an annual payment of one gold piece shall be paid to the Lateran palace.[169] *No man is at all permitted rashly to disturb that place, or to take away or diminish its possessions, or to appropriate them for his own uses, even for seemingly pious reasons. Truly, we have decreed that burial in that place shall be entirely free, such that no one may stand in the way of those who have resolved to be buried there as an act of devotion and a final wish – unless by chance they might be excommunicates. The brothers of that place ought to receive chrism, holy oil, the consecrations of altars and basilicas, and the ordinations of monks who are to be promoted to holy orders, from the bishop in whose diocese they are – if he should have the grace and communion of the apostolic see, and if he should wish to furnish these things freely and without impropriety. Otherwise, they should receive the sacraments of consecration from whatever catholic bishop they might choose. Furthermore, no one may be put in charge as abbot there through any secret stratagem or violence, except the man the brothers by common counsel – or a part of the brothers of sounder counsel – elect, according to the Rule of St Benedict and the fear of God.*[170] *But if anyone – and let this not be! – should want to go against this decree of ours meant to be enduring in perpetuity, let him be struck with anathema, and let him suffer the ruin of his honour and his office, unless he corrects his presumption with suitable penance. For those observing these things, on the other hand, may peace and mercy be preserved eternally by God. Amen. BY THE WORD OF THE LORD THE HEAVENS WERE MADE.*[171]

In the same year, Emperor Henry III [IV] died.[172]

In the year of the Lord 1107.

In the year of the Lord 1108.

In the year of the Lord 1109. In this year, Henry, the fourth [fifth] king of this name, arranged to celebrate Christmas at Mainz. The German princes solemnly came together there from all directions, supported by a great deal of pomp. Wiprecht too was present with his sons, Wiprecht and Henry. But for them – oh the pain! – that same feast was turned into mourning. For the lady countess Judith, worthy of everyone's veneration and remembrance, died – with God piously arranging it (as we hope and wish) on account of her most generous

---

169 i.e., to the pope.

170 *RB 1980: the rule of St Benedict*, 280–5, ch. 64.

171 Psalm 32:6. This sentence is written all in capitals in the manuscript.

172 Henry IV died early in the year 1106 in the midst of an uprising against him led by his son, Henry V.

good will towards our monastery. Ready to sing on the nativity of her Saviour, she joined with the saints in the angelic song, *'Glory in the highest to the lamb, who takes away the sins of the world.'*[173] And ready to delight in the bosom of Abraham[174] in the resting place for the earthly amongst the heavenly, she went the way of all flesh on her patrimony called Bautzen on the sixteenth Kalends of January [17 December].

Messengers were therefore sent quickly in both directions to report her death: not only to the lord Wiprecht and their sons, but also to the princes of Bohemia, the lady Judith's brothers. Meanwhile, everyone came together in groups for her funeral. Indeed, having received such sad news through the messengers, the lord Wiprecht, with a tearful plaint about the passing of his wife, obtained permission from the emperor to return home immediately. He sent a legate ahead as soon as possible to have the body brought in the meantime to the monastery at Pegau, where Abbot Windolf received it with honour and his brothers received it solemnly with grief and chanting. The lord Wiprecht himself very swiftly followed with his men.

Finally, on Wiprecht's arrival there and with the princes of Bohemia meeting up with him simultaneously, there arose great lamentations. A crowd of people gathered, who had flocked together from all directions within four days. On account of this, the body brought to Pegau remained continuously placed on top of a bier and unburied. Besides the bishop of Meissen, who had come with everything needed for the funeral rites, the lord Wiprecht invited [Bishops] Albuin of Merseburg and Walram of Zeitz, who came surrounded by ranks of clerics. They devoutly performed the funeral office with due veneration.

In the end, how do such great and festive funeral rites deserve to be distinguished or delimited? What description might satisfy the reader? A short one, to be sure. For what could be said more briefly or heard more truly from us than that dirt is consigned to dirt, ashes to ashes?[175] But without doubt they are settled in the sole hope of resurrection and rebirth; falling blessedly asleep in the Lord, they rest in peace.[176] May God, the redeemer of our souls, who lives and reigns with the Father and Holy Spirit (etc.), grant this peace and the grace of rebirth to our lady Judith.

---

173 'Glory in the highest' refers to the *Gloria in excelsis,* part of the liturgy of the Mass, while the 'lamb, who takes away the sins of the world' is a reference to another part of the liturgy, the *Agnus Dei,* from immediately before communion.

174 Cf. Luke 16:22.

175 Cf. Genesis 3:19 and Ecclesiastes 12:7.

176 Cf. Psalm 4:9–10 and Revelation 13:14.

But let it be known that the body does not lie in the place where the memorial made for her is visible; instead it is at the foot of the altar of the Holy Cross, a spot which still remains marked by some indication. At that time, this altar was positioned in a higher place.

With these things thus accomplished, the lord Wiprecht exercised his usual generosity toward our place and donated these things specifically listed for the remedy of his wife's soul: namely her most precious cloak, extraordinarily and quite skilfully woven with gold (from which the best chasuble[177] was made – not however of the same size, insofar as it was cut into various pieces, both advantageously and disadvantageously; also, it is well-known that its very extensive gold-embroidery was transferred to another ecclesiastical cloak). To this he also added: a chest, very large and decorated to the utmost degree both with gold and with gems and enamel; three very large crosses also ornamented with enamel, gems and gold, and with their bases silver; and a silver pitcher fit for holy water. In addition to these things: two candelabra embellished with work that is cast and Greek;[178] the finest covering for the main altar, which they say was from his household; and the finest cloth, that on the highest feast days is placed upon the pulpit, on which the gospel is customarily read aloud. Out of all these things, some of them are not now among us; for some were spent in time of famine, and it happened that others were broken up for the purpose of buying estates.

Besides these things, while she was still living, the lady Judith had given to this church a green chasuble with gold embroidery. But also, she endowed the basilica of St Nicholas with the material for the preparation of both the altar and the priest and with two royal *mansi* in the village of *Borkovice*[179] for the use, that is, of the priest who should perpetually celebrate the solemnities of the Mass there.

Who indeed may set forth in words how much – not only on the thirtieth day[180] but also beyond it – the most generous lord Wiprecht

---

177 A poncho-style liturgical garment worn by the priest saying Mass. Although the eleventh-century form was cape-like and used copious fabric, during the twelfth century the form narrowed so that the priest's arms were freer. Cf. Miller, *Clothing the Clergy*, 248.

178 Ackley, 'Re-approaching the Western medieval church treasury inventory', 25–6 has guided our translation here.

179 Mentioned above, p. 65.

180 Cf. *Ottonian Germany*, 281, where Thietmar of Merseburg writes: 'The third, seventh, and thirtieth days following the departure of any believer should be dedicated to his remembrance, because these days embody the mystery of our faith in the Trinity and the sevenfold gifts of the Holy Spirit.'

mercifully expended in giving with largesse to the sick, the poor, orphans and widows and in liberally relieving their hunger, nakedness, poverty, and all of their needs? Who, in the end, has the means to say or to know with what a crowd and with what generosity he performed the thirty-day anniversary of his most beloved wife's death? Since this short report of ours is able to capture nothing worthy of such a great festivity, it seems proper to leave these things to the prudence and judgement of the reader.

In the year of the Lord 1110. After this, the lord Wiprecht, having finally received consolation concerning his wife's death, considered it necessary – although reluctantly and with difficulty – to make preparations for another wife, a mother of sorts for his household. Thus he decided to marry the widow of lord Kuno, the most noble prince of Beichlingen, by the name of Kunigunde.[181] Because she was still turning over in her mind the subject of widowhood, at first she hesitated to assent to his request. But afterwards, having considered sounder counsel with her men, since she was not then able to withstand the many powerful invaders of her estates – of which her husband had left her an abundance – she consented to the requested union of marriage, even if not out of desire but necessity. For she was gravely harassed by the insolence of the same men, by whose deceitfulness her most noble husband (who suspected nothing evil from them since they were his own men) had been secretly killed, contrary to justice and divine law; one of them was called Elger of Ilfeld, the other Christian of Rothenburg.[182]

Therefore, when he obtained her consent, the lord Wiprecht was quite cheered. Not only did he arrange his own happy union, but indeed he persuaded her to betrothe to his own eldest son, namely Wiprecht, her daughter by the name Kunigunde, the most elegant and renowned compared with her other four daughters. After he had achieved this, together as one they – that is the father with the son and both mother and daughter – performed the wedding ceremonies generously (beyond what might be able to be said now). And they betrothed the rest of the four sisters to the most noble princes of Saxony and Thuringia. Finally,

---

181 Kuno of Beichlingen (d. 1103) was the third son of Count Otto of Northeim and his wife Richenza. Kunigunde (d. 1140) was the daughter of Otto, count of Weimar-Orlamünde and margrave of Meissen (d. 1067). This marriage thus strengthened Wiprecht's connections to some of the leading families in Saxony.

182 No other source for Kuno's murder names these individuals as responsible. *The 1106 continuation of Frutolf's chronicle*, 174, instead blames the 'conspiracy of a certain wretched man', an anonymous individual of, it emphasizes, the 'lowest' status.

the marriage pact was strengthened by this reciprocity and by an oath from the aforesaid matron that if this countess should submit to nature first, the lord Wiprecht and his heirs would obtain her patrimony.

Among the rest of her estates she held an abbey within the borders of Saxony and Thuringia called Oldisleben, which, above everything else, she commended especially to the care and lordship of the lord Wiprecht, her husband.[183] For its resources had been greatly squandered and its piety destroyed under the direction of Lupert, the abbot of that monastery, whose impiety had already been made known to the lord Wiprecht. After he was deservedly deposed, that place was assigned to the industry of the lord abbot Windolf, so that its condition might be restored by some means, with him providing priors and useful brothers there, and with Wiprecht working together with him.

After Windolf had advantageously seen to this place for a little while to the best of his ability, he finally grew weary of the double labour, because *a mind focused on many things derives less from any one of them*.[184] Worrying about the failure of the monastery of Pegau as a consequence of his looking after Oldisleben, it seemed more fitting that he put someone else in charge there and lighten his own labour in the process. Toward this end he got the lord Hillin at Corvey, whose industry he had put to the test already long ago, because Hillin had distinguished himself and had administered the priorship at Pegau quite vigorously. Hillin was placed at the monastery's head; after he had presided there for many years, he died happily on the journey to Jerusalem, when King Conrad [III] was leading the army of the Christians, in the retinue of the lord Count Bernhard of Plötzkau on the second Ides of March [14 March].[185]

In addition to these things, an increase of power – nay rather of good fortune – came to the lord Wiprecht during this same time, because a certain Vizo of Vitzenburg, a noble and very rich man joined to him by consanguinity, reached his end and left him the heir of all his estates.[186] From some of his estates he had established a community of nuns in

---

183 Oldisleben had probably been founded by Kunigunde and her previous husband, Kuno of Beichlingen.

184 A Latin motto (*pluribus intentus, minor est ad singula sensus*) of unknown source.

185 This reference to the Second Crusade indicates that this passage was written sometime after 1148/1149. For Count Bernhard's role in the crusade, see Phillips, *The Second Crusade*, 179–82.

186 As with Erpo, mentioned above, pp. 59–60; it is not clear how this Vizo was related to Wiprecht. No other source from this period mentions him.

that same castle.[187] After Vizo died, the lord Wiprecht allowed his venerable mother, the lady Sigena, then widowed for the second time, to rest there in holy conversation until the end of her life; he spent as much as was proper for her needs. After some time, crossing over to the Lord on the sixth Kalends of March [24 February], she was buried in the church there with two abbesses, who had presided over that place's community.

At the same time, a certain very rich matron, granddaughter of the above-mentioned Count Frederick of Lengenfeld, gave herself to the same place with her own estates worth fifteen talents.[188] Squandering this wealth in the freehandedness of nobility, with goods for herself and with the number of her companions, she gravely offended the lord Wiprecht, whose spirit was always restrained with respect to the pious way of life. He did not long hide his punishment of this offence. Its location seemed to bring about no small opportunity for impiety, and so he thought to change not only the very order – or rather, disorder – but even the location of the place. Therefore, under threat, he ordered the aforesaid group of virgins, since they were fools,[189] to desert the place, so that they might not disadvantageously occupy thereafter a place that those serving God might be able to inhabit advantageously.

Wiprecht took advice from the lord Bishop Otto of Bamberg,[190] whose reputation for piety and devotion had by then spread very widely: he should found a monastery along the Unstrut River, in the vicinity of that same castle, and having brought monks together there, he should confirm for them the estates of the aforesaid place. Wiprecht did not delay at all in complying; in a place called Reinsdorf, he began again to be a founder of the pious way of life. He summoned his abbot Windolf, so that some man, industrious and advantageous for the work, might be put in charge of that place. The abbot, eager to satisfy him quickly in all things, thought to put in charge of that monastery a venerable brother,

---

187 The convent at Vitzenburg had actually been founded in the latter half of the tenth century.

188 For Frederick, see above, p. 35. Since Frederick was the second husband of Sigena, Wiprecht's mother, the matron mentioned here was possibly one of Wiprecht's relatives. The author may be deliberately leaving her nameless in order to avoid linking Wiprecht too closely with a family scandal.

189 Cf. Matthew 25:1–13 for the parable of the wise and foolish virgins.

190 Cf. *The life of Bishop Otto of Bamberg*, I.13, for a much more succinct account of how the community at Vitzenburg was moved to Reinsdorf.

the lord Ludiger, whom we mentioned above.[191] Ludiger had been given
to him as prior but had been received back again at Corvey, where he was
administering the office of dean when Windolf arranged to be given him
as abbot. And so Ludiger was recalled to Pegau and elected according to
the Rule. Meanwhile, the lord Wiprecht sent a messenger swiftly ahead
and ordered the aforesaid sisters to give up the place as soon as possible;
he demanded that they depart without any hesitation and that they not
presume to wait for his arrival on any account, since he himself would
be following after with the abbots and brothers.

In the year of the Lord 1110.[192] Therefore, after the younger Henry
[V] had gained hold of the kingdom,[193] he deprived the son of King
Vratislav of Bohemia, by the name of Bořivoj, of his kingdom and
substituted for him a certain Svatopluk by name.[194] This greatly pained
Wiprecht.[195] He earnestly begged the king with the highest devotion
that Bořivoj might be restored. Nevertheless, he was unable to obtain
this, and he frequently reproached the king on account of it. The king
advised Svatopluk that he should behead all the leading men who were
called Vršovici, and he obeyed.[196]

In the year 1111.[197] Next Henry V proclaimed to his men an expedition
against Poland, and commanded Wiprecht to set out at the same time.[198]

---

191 Cf. above, under the year 1101.

192 There is a break in the manuscript here. The first entry for the year 1110 ends
on the top half of fol. 210r, the remainder of which is blank. This second entry
for the year 1110 begins on the top of fol. 210v. The two entries for the year 1110
are another indication that this text is a compilation of multiple sources (see the
introduction). The hand however remains the same.

193 See above, n. 172, for the fact that Henry V had already succeeded his father in 1106.

194 Svatopluk, duke of Bohemia (1107–09), was Bořivoj's cousin. Note that, by comparison
to Cosmas of Prague, this text offers a confused account of events. Henry V did
invade Bohemia in 1110, but in support of Vladislav, Bořivoj's younger brother, who
challenged Bořivoj's claim to the Czech throne after the assassination of Svatopluk.
Svatopluk had previously ousted Bořivoj in 1107, ultimately, if not initially, with
Henry's support. The massacre of the Vršovici, correctly attributed here to Svatopluk,
occurred in 1108.

195 This is the same Bořivoj mentioned earlier in the text, leading the Czech contingent
– under Wiprecht's tutelage – on Henry IV's Italian campaign.

196 Cf. Cosmas of Prague, *The chronicle of the Czechs*, 3.24, 211–13.

197 Note that for the remainder of the text, each entry opens with just 'Anno' rather
than 'Anno Domini'.

198 Cosmas of Prague, *The chronicle of the Czechs*, 3.27, 214, dates the Polish campaign
to 1109, and states that the Czechs joined with Henry's forces in September of
that year. He claims that Svatopluk's assassin was sent by one of the Vršovici, who
had escaped their slaughter the previous year – and dates the duke's death to 21
September. Cf. *The anonymous imperial chronicle*, 210–11.

Taking two thousand men, he advanced. Since Svatopluk considered the king hostile [to Wiprecht] on account of Bořivoj, he secretly had much discussion with the king concerning Wiprecht – which was not concealed from Wiprecht's industry for long.

In fact, Svatopluk quite often returned from counsels of this sort in the middle of the night, passing in front of Wiprecht's tents on the way to his own. Finally, Wiprecht arranged with a certain *miles* of his that he might secretly slay the unsuspecting Svatopluk as he was passing by, just as he had yesterday and the day before. The same man diligently investigated his passing and, having launched a sharp spear into him, transfixed the duke between the shoulders.[199] At his falling, the *miles* fled to Wiprecht's camp.

Thereafter, a clamour arose among the Czechs. When the duke's death became known to them, they fled headlong without delay[200] and left the king behind in a very anxious situation. Called forth by the king, Wiprecht presented himself. The king earnestly begged Wiprecht to lead him and his men away from Poland. This he gladly promised to do, if Henry would restore Bořivoj to his paternal principate. At length, unable to oppose his request, Henry agreed (since led by necessity) and commanded that Wiprecht return that man to his paternal seat. And so the king departed Poland in haste, with Wiprecht leading the way.

But the young Wiprecht, Wiprecht's son, on his father's order, returned Bořivoj to Prague, seat of the principate.[201]

When the king arrived in the lands of Germany, at Naumburg,[202] he learned that the younger Wiprecht had returned Bořivoj and was still tarrying in Bohemia. He preferred Vladislav, namely the brother of

---

199 Cosmas of Prague, *The chronicle of the Czechs*, 3.27, 215, similarly describes Svatopluk speared between the shoulder blades while returning from Henry's 'court'.

200 Cf. Cosmas of Prague, *The chronicle of the Czechs*, 3.27, 215, where they fled to Prague, because enthronement there would decide the succession.

201 Cosmas of Prague, *The chronicle of the Czechs*, 3.28–30, 216–19, identifies one of Wiprecht's sons as 'Václav'; this is most likely an alternative, Czech name for the younger Wiprecht. Cosmas tells this story differently, and at length. According to him, Bořivoj consulted with the elder Wiprecht after learning that Vladislav had been enthroned (two days after Svatopluk's death). Bořivoj then returned to Vyšehrad (with only a brief appearance in Prague), where he was encircled by the forces of Svatopluk's younger brother Otto. Vladislav, aborting a trip to Regensburg in response to an imperial summons, found himself barred from Prague; at that moment, the younger Wiprecht ('Václav') appeared with an army in support of Bořivoj, only to be defeated by Vladislav.

202 Pertz, the editor of the Latin edition, suggests Nuremberg for *Nuenburc* here (*Annales Pegavienses*, 251, n. 49); however, Naumburg seems more plausible given the narrative and accords as well with medieval spelling conventions.

Svatopluk,[203] whom he had deceitfully raised up to the principate from below[204] in place of his brother, without Wiprecht knowing. With Vladislav goading him and working together with him, Henry entered Bohemia and pursued the younger Wiprecht and Bořivoj, without their knowing of his deceit. When they learned of his coming and his deceit, they fled to protection. The king besieged Bořivoj in Vyšehrad and Wiprecht in Prague [Castle]. After they had resisted most vigorously for seven days, Henry finally prevailed and led them away with him as captives.[205] He put them under guard in Hammerstein.

In the Year 1112. The elder Wiprecht, when he learned what had happened, was deeply pained. He was able to redeem his son by no other agreement, until he handed over to the king the town of Leisnig and the districts of Nisen and Bautzen,[206] together with the town of Morungen.[207] The king immediately granted all this in benefice to Count Hoier of Mansfeld, a man most familiar to him.[208] The younger Wiprecht, not long after his release, arrived with the king in Thuringia. There, Henry enfeoffed him with a certain castle called Eckartsberga.

In the Year 1113. Consequently, the king persecuted the elder Wiprecht with a hatred now manifest.[209] He decided to attack Groitzsch, with Vladislav bringing him help. The younger Wiprecht too, hoping to be enfeoffed with the town of Naumburg, was a help to the king against

---

203 Vladislav I, duke of Bohemia (1110–25), was actually Bořivoj's younger brother and Svatopluk's cousin.

204 i.e., Vladislav assumed the throne outside the accepted order of succession, according to which Bořivoj had a prior claim. The implication here seems to be that Henry agreed to this at Svatopluk's request. However, according to Cosmas of Prague, the Czechs swore an oath at Svatopluk's enthronement that Vladislav would succeed him and Henry only became involved at Vladislav's request, upon the promise of 500 marks (Cosmas of Prague, *The chronicle of the Czechs*, 3.32, 221).

205 Again Cosmas's account differs (Cosmas of Prague, *The chronicle of the Czechs*, 3.32, 221): Henry and his army entered Bohemia on 1 January 1110, summoned Bořivoj and the younger Wiprecht to a meeting under safe conduct, and then arrested them without a hearing.

206 Henry IV had granted Leisnig to the elder Wiprecht for his service on the Rome expedition (see above, p. 49). Nisen and Bautzen were his widow Judith's dowry lands (see above, p. 51).

207 Cf. p. 34 above, where Morungen is identified as part of the dowry of Wiprecht's mother.

208 Cf. below for Hoier, who was a key supporter of Henry V in eastern Saxony.

209 Cf. *The anonymous imperial chronicle*, 216, which names Wiprecht among the instigators of rebellion against Henry in this year.

his father. The elder Wiprecht, however, gathered together certain of his most select *milites* in the town's fortress, with military equipment and tools.

Vladislav, when he had arrived there from the king's army, strove to capture the town with his men by a sudden attack, but he lost more than 500 of his men.[210] The king, giving up on its capture, departed from there after eight days and enfeoffed a certain familiar of his with the town of Naumburg. And so Wiprecht [the younger] deserted him and returned to his father.

In the Year 1114. Therefore, taking precautions against the king's coming again, Wiprecht [the elder] pledged friendship with Count-palatine Siegfried of Orlamünde and with Count Ludwig of Thuringia.[211] They came together to talk at Warnstedt to agree upon some kind of pact. Hoier, having learned of their meeting against the king, arrived unexpectedly with thirty men. Because they were too weak in arms and in the number of their *milites* to make a stand, Ludwig escaped by fleeing, Count-palatine Siegfried was killed, and Wiprecht, injured by many wounds and captured, was carried away and delivered into custody in Leisnig. Then, brought before the king at the court held in Würzburg, in the presence of the princes, he was condemned by all to death.

Wiprecht was therefore handed over for beheading to a certain *miles* of Plisna,[212] by the name Conrad. He delayed in carrying out the orders and was putting off Wiprecht's death in the field, waiting for some other, better messenger from the king. All the princes, meanwhile, suggested to the younger Wiprecht that, in order to revoke the death sentence – that is, for the redemption of his father – he, being loyal, should offer the king Groitzsch with all his father's estates. When he had done that, the king indeed gave Wiprecht his life but ordered him kept in his most fortified town of Trifels for about three years.

Having learned this, the younger Wiprecht and his brother Henry joined with the Saxons against the king. On account of this, together with Count Ludwig [of Thuringia], they were judged guilty of treason. And so, while their father was placed in captivity for three years, they

---

210 Cosmas of Prague, *The chronicle of the Czechs*, says nothing about Vladislav's participation in attacks on Wiprecht.

211 Count Siegfried of Orlamünde and Ballenstedt, count-palatine of the Rhine (d. 1113) and Count Ludwig ('the Leaper') of Thuringia (d. 1123). Ekkehard of Aura, *Chronicle*, 244 and *Cronica S. Petri Erfordensis Moderna*, 161 list these events under the year 1113, and scholars have generally followed their dating.

212 Now Altenburg.

protected themselves and their men in the hiding places of the forests, deprived of the comforts of men, like wild animals.

In the Year 1115. Meanwhile, Emperor Henry, incapable of imposing moderation on his own insolence, violently harassed all the princes of Saxony with a previously unheard-of tax imposed on everyone. Thus, after he had captured Bishop Reinhard of Halberstadt, the count-palatine of Sommerschenburg, Frederick of Arnsberg, and Rudolf of the Nordmark, he deprived each of his dignities and replaced them with others favourable to him.[213]

Like-minded men, roused by this injury, united together with Duke Lothar of Saxony, the younger Wiprecht and his brother Henry, and others equally injured by the emperor. They held many small gatherings at the same time. Finally, crowded together next to Creuzburg, they confirmed by an oath the pact they had undertaken. Setting out from there, they built the castle called Walbeck to injure the king; from it, they harassed Count Hoier by every means.

The younger Wiprecht, concealing himself in a hiding place of the forest next to Gundorf, relieved his own need by frequently attacking his adversaries. Then, in the month of November, the falling leaves illuminated the forests' shadows. Judging that the forests' hiding places would not be at all safe for him any longer, he sent a representative to Adelgot, his cousin, then archbishop [of Magdeburg].[214] Wiprecht requested that Adelgot allow him to spend the winter in some fortress under his authority together with his wife Kunigunde and a few *milites*, for under the open sky winter would not permit him to be hidden. The bishop, feeling sympathy for his need, sent a noble man by the name of Adalbert and arranged for Wiprecht, together with his wife, a certain Suidger, another Brun, and five of his ministerials, to be put up in a town beyond the Elbe called Loburg. The prefect of this town, by the name of Přibron, was still for the most part a pagan, because beyond the Elbe in those times it was rare for a Christian to be found.[215]

213 Bishop Reinhard of Halberstadt (1107–23); Count-palatine Frederick I of Sommerschenburg (d. 1120); Count Frederick of Arnsberg (d. 1124); and Count Rudolf of Stade, margrave of the Nordmark (d. 1124). Helmold of Bosau, *The chronicle of the Slavs*, 135–6 reports that, fearing a Saxon rebellion coalescing around Archbishop Adalbert of Mainz, Henry V 'overran all Saxony and wrought very great havoc in the country, delivering its princes either to death, or at least into captivity'. But he then lists Bishop Reinhard and Count Frederick among those who 'survived' and led forces to meet Henry V at Welfesholz.

214 Adelgot and the younger Wiprecht were first cousins.

215 Cf. *The life of Bishop Otto of Bamberg*.

As soon as this fact became known to the emperor, he summoned
the archbishop to the court announced at Goslar. The archbishop did
not know that he would be treated deceitfully, contrary to his own
interests. [The younger] Wiprecht sent a representative from among
his own men with the archbishop to court, so that if anything should
be done there concerning him, he might find out through his agent.
And when it was then late in the evening on the next day after that,
the emperor was ready to sit with a crowd of princes and to deal with
the state of the *res publica*. A certain familiar of the archbishop was
secretly forewarned by his own nephew, who was in the king's service,
that the archbishop would be surrounded by the king's deceptions, and
not only would he be deposed the next day but he would even be
captured with all his men. Having learned these things, that man brought
them to the attention of his lord. Without any delay, in the darkness
of that very night, with his enemies unaware and horses swiftly mounted,
the archbishop fled to Magdeburg with his men before midnight. Come
morning, the king learned of it and bore gravely the contempt of royal
majesty. Therefore, he lodged an accusation about this before the princes,
by whose favour the king's audacity was fed, and the absent archbishop
was deposed. On the spot, it was also decreed that punishment be
carried out against the Saxons, as men in contempt of the *res publica*.
An expedition was announced to all his men for forty days hence,
namely for the fourth Ides of February [February 10]. Meanwhile they
united the king's army at Wallhausen, while the Saxons on the other
hand struggled against him to the best of their abilities.

Arriving at the appointed time and at a place called Welfesholz,[216]
the battle was put off until the next day on account of the harshness
of the winter and the inconvenience of the snows there. Night passed.
At the time of the first rising of the dawn, during the solemnities of
the Mass, Bishop Reinhard [of Halberstadt] made a speech to the
people, warning them to beg for divine clemency and sufficiently assuring
them that God would never be absent from those invoking his mercy
in truth. After the solemnities of the Mass were completed, they
steadfastly awaited the king's arrival and manfully exhorted themselves
to the defence of liberty and the fatherland. Arriving, the emperor
arranged his battle lines. Hoier was placed in the first group with his

---

216 The Battle of Welfesholz (11 February 1115) was a decisive victory for the Saxons
   led by Duke Lothar against Emperor Henry V. Among other accounts, cf. Ekkehard
   of Aura, *Chronicle*, 246 and Helmold of Bosau, *The chronicle of the Slavs*, 136.

men. Then, ahead of everyone, he moved a little away from his men
with a certain Lutolf and, adding vainglory to audacity, leaped alone
from his horse and ran headlong against the Saxons, wielding his
unsheathed sword in his hand. The younger Wiprecht, accompanied
by two most excellent men, the brothers Conrad and Herman, approached
Hoier without delay and with a strong effort hurled a spear into his
chest. Lutolf immediately extracted the spear, and Hoier, roused, attacked
Wiprecht with his sword; but Wiprecht's shield protected him, and the
blow was brought to naught. Immediately, Wiprecht knocked Hoier
down, bouncing his sword off the centre of his head. As Hoier struggled
to rise, he was left exposed at the edge of his coat of mail, and Wiprecht
pierced him through with his sword.

Consequently, a war cry was offered up, and the wedges of both
sides' armies joined together in battle. The Saxons acted manfully for
themselves and their fatherland. They approached their enemies – who
were struggling without hope or fear, like sheep – with such fury that
twenty or thirty died from one of the Saxons. The battle was fought
all day; intervening night broke it off. And so, vanquished, the king
was put to flight by the Saxons, who held out all night in that same
place in dread of ambush. When the victors learned the next day that
the king had fled to Bavaria, they returned home.

In the Year 1116. A monastery, called Neuwerk, was founded at
Halle by the venerable Archbishop Adelgot of Magdeburg. *Count Ludwig*
[of Thuringia] *was released from chains.*[217] Count Erwin was made a
monk.[218] In the city of Mainz, when the citizens assembled together
with Arnold, the count of the same city, the king was compelled to
release [Arch]bishop Adalbert of Mainz from chains.

In the Year 1117. *On the third Nones of January* [3 January], *before
sunset, there was a great earthquake. The moon, changed into blood,*[219] *seemed
to vanish. In Swabia a certain terrible thing happened: the earth, bubbling up
as high as houses, suddenly fell away into an abyss. The air seemed to be mixed
equally with fire and blood.*[220]

The younger Wiprecht earnestly asked Dedo of Krosigk, who
sympathized with his misery, to receive him with his men into some

---

217 *Cronica S. Petri Erfordensis moderna*, 161.

218 Count Erwin I of Tonna-Gleichen, a Thuringian lord from the region of Erfurt.
He became a monk at Reinhardsbrunn.

219 Cf. Revelation 6:12.

220 *Cronica S. Petri Erfordensis moderna*, 161–2.

fortress of his. But Dedo declared himself wary of the insolence of Wiprecht's *milites*, so Wiprecht urged that at least a churchyard be granted to him.[221]

Dedo agreed, and after everyone in the vicinity gathered an abundance of trees and stones for him, Wiprecht built a secure refuge for himself and his men within fourteen days. And after he had violently attacked everything all around, he divided it all among his *milites* in benefice. Then, almost nine weeks having passed, he occupied the town of *Devin* through ambushes, and he plundered such a great abundance of gold and silver, clothes, horses and other things that each of his *milites* relieved his poverty in that place. Accordingly, having gained control of this town, he subjugated twenty-four castles around it in a short time. Then, with Archbishop Adelgot of Magdeburg bringing help and Margravine Gertrude (that is, the mother of Queen Richinza)[222] assisting, he besieged and obtained Groitzsch with 2,000 *milites*. Archbishop Adelgot, together with the bishop of Halberstadt and Count-palatine Frederick, with Wiprecht too and Ludwig [of Thuringia], surrounded Naumburg by siege and laid waste to a large part of the adjacent province of Thuringia.

And because the army was running to and fro all around to plunder fodder, Henry, nicknamed 'Big Head,' inflicted many misfortunes on them through ambushes.[223] For this reason, Wiprecht and Ludwig with other of the more noble men decided to take care of plundering fodder themselves,[224] in order to be able to lay an ambush for that man. They encountered him, and after following the fleeing man into the castle of Arnsburg, they captured him and led him to the archbishop and the others princes. Having heard this, the townsmen handed over Naumburg.

Also, when the emperor learned these things, he was finally compelled then to release from captivity the elder Wiprecht and Ludwig, as well as Burchard of Meissen, in return for the release of Henry

---

221 Churchyards and cemeteries were places of sanctuary and short-term asylum.

222 Queen Richinza (d. 1141), wife of Emperor Lothar III; her mother, Gertrude (d. 1117), was married three times, on the final occasion to Margrave Henry I of Eilenburg (see above, n. 72).

223 Henry appears with this nickname (*Heinricus cognomine cum capite*) among the witnesses in a charter of Emperor Henry V from 1114, in which Count Erwin and Hoier are also named; see *Die Urkunden Heinrichs V*: www.mgh.de/ddhv/dhv_135.htm (accessed 2 August 2016).

224 In other words, this kind of pillaging for supplies was usually left to lesser men.

'Big Head'.[225] Dismissed, therefore, [the elder] Wiprecht returned to Groitzsch. But he was kept at a distance from it by the townsmen until the emperor, having sent a legate, ordered that it be restored to him.[226]

From there, [the elder] Wiprecht fell upon Leisnig with an army. But the garrison resisted him; after he had spent much labour and much time, he finally obtained it and expelled the townsmen. At the same time, he received in benefice from Archbishop Adelgot of Magdeburg a prefecture endowed with 1,000 shields and 500 talents.[227]

Therefore, with everything of his restored, he proceeded to the court announced for Worms and rendered thanks to the emperor for the recovery of his possessions. And, having promised 2,000 talents, he begged that the emperor might distinguish him with the Lusatian march. The emperor reckoned it would be safe for him to admit a man of such great strength to the company of his familiars by means of such a benefice; so he distinguished Wiprecht with the dignity he desired. And thereafter, among the rest of the princes, the emperor considered him equal both in honour and in familiarity. But before he granted Wiprecht permission to return home, the emperor presented him with an ecclesiastical cloak, dalmatic and tunic, all quite seemly;[228] the bishop of Münster, Burchard 'the Red', had offered these vestments to the emperor.[229] Thus, with prosperity following him, Wiprecht returned to his own lands, distinguished by royal largesse.

In the Year 1118.[230] *Pope Paschal II died;* he was the first to give to the monastery of Pegau a privilege, which was procured by Wiprecht,

---

225 Burchard, burgrave of Meissen. The Ludwig mentioned here is presumably Count Ludwig of Thuringia. However, the entry above reported his release in 1116 (a date which accords with the later account offered in *Annalista Saxo*, 754). Most likely the discrepancy results from the amalgamation of two different source texts in this section.

226 The discrepancy here is more difficult to explain. Just above, the text plainly states that the younger Wiprecht retook Groitzsch by force; it is therefore not clear why imperial intervention would have been necessary to compel the townsmen to admit the elder Wiprecht. The text has most likely omitted mention of events that occurred between these two incidents.

227 See above, p. 34, for the family connection between Wiprecht and Adelgot. Prefecture (*praefectura*) is another term for the advocacy over the archbishopric.

228 These are all types of liturgical vestments; see Miller, *Clothing the Clergy.*

229 Cf. above, under the year 1096, where Bishop Burchard purchased the cloak that Wiprecht the younger had been given by the monks of Pegau.

230 For the italicized sections of this and the following entries, see *Cronica S. Petri Erfordensis moderna*, 162–4.

the founder of that monastery and afterwards margrave in Lusatia.[231] *In Paschal's place, Gelasius (who was formerly John) was appointed.[232] Soon expelled by heretics, he reached Gaul [i.e., France] by fleeing with his men. A great council was assembled at Cologne under Cardinal Cuno [Conrad], bishop of the city of Palestrina.[233] And there was another council under the same man in Fritzlar. The Saxons, with the citizens of the town of Mainz, violently attacked the town of Oppenheim and destroyed it; with flames consuming it from all sides, they killed almost 2,000 of each sex. The castle Kyffhausen was also ruined, destroyed completely by the great strength and fortitude of the Saxons, though not without the death of very many and wounds to countless. Emperor Henry V returned from Italy.* Poppo of Henneberg died.[234] There occurred a flood of the rivers.

In the Year 1119. *Pope Gelasius II died, and in his place Calixtus, [arch]bishop of Vienne, was appointed pope by seven cardinals and by the remaining clergy, as well as by those Romans expelled with Pope Gelasius [II] who were living in exile among the Gauls, and also by all the bishops of Gaul.[235] There was an assembly of the king and the princes of the whole kingdom at the village of Eckstein upon the banks of the river Main.[236] A synod was celebrated by 450 bishops and abbots under Pope Calixtus in the town of Reims.* In the same year, Archbishop Adelgot of Magdeburg, acceptable to both God and men, fell asleep in the Lord. Ruotger succeeded him.[237]

In the Year 1120. *All the princes of the German kingdom proclaimed that a conference was to be held at Fulda concerning the kingdom's dissension. Having sent messengers there, the king, at Worms with the flatterers* in his party, *put off dealing with the matter through every trick possible, by imploring and promising. Because a few of the Saxons returned to the king and all the*

---

231 See above, pp. 71–72.

232 Pope Gelasius II (1118–19), formerly John of Gaeta.

233 Cf. *The 1125 continuation of Frutolf's chronicle*, 265–6.

234 Count Poppo II of Henneberg, a prominent lord in the regions of Thuringia and Franconia.

235 Pope Calixtus II (1119–24).

236 *Annales Pegavienses*, 254, n. 65 suggests this is the village of Hörstein on the Main, in part because the Erfurt chronicle from which this text is copied spells it 'Erstein'. Cf. *The 1125 continuation of Frutolf's chronicle*, 267, where the specific site of the assembly is not named.

237 Archbishop Ruotger [Rugger] of Magdeburg (1119–24), a relative of Wiprecht (see above, p. 35). Cf. *Gesta Archiepiscoporum Magdeburgensium*, 411, where Wiprecht is credited with helping to arrange his election as archbishop.

rest of the princes returned to their own lands, he frustrated their plan for a meeting. Duke Welf died.[238] *Frederick, count-palatine of Saxony, died.*[239] Beatrix, the widow of Poppo of Henneberg, died.[240]

In the Year 1121. *Bishop Erlung of Würzburg died.*[241] *But soon, dissension arose among both the clergy and the commoners. The king's party favoured a certain Gebhard, but the other, no less supported by the help of Duke Frederick of Swabia and also of his brother Duke Conrad, appointed Ruotger. A short time later he abandoned the bishopric, having been expelled by the bishops of Mainz, Worms and Speyer.*[242]

The sun, obscured by air full of smoke and stinking, and as if turned into blood, seemed to lack the light of its usual brightness from the ninth hour of the day until the third day.

In the Year 1122. *At Worms two cardinals, sent by Pope Calixtus, absolved of excommunication the king and all the supporters of his party. First, however, the king himself denied under oath every heretical depravity for which he had been excommunicated and* promised faith and obedience *to the Catholic Church.*[243]

In the Year 1123. *Bishop Reinhard of Halberstadt died, and in his place Otto was appointed.*[244] *Bishop Dietrich of Zeitz was killed unexpectedly, and in his place Richwin was appointed.*[245] *Count Ludwig,* founder of the monastery of Reinhardsbrunn, *died, having been made a monk* there.[246]

Margrave Henry the younger died,[247] *in his place Emperor Henry appointed two margraves, a certain very rich Wiprecht and Count Herman of Winzenburg. But Adalbert and Conrad, counts from Saxony, supported by the help of Duke*

---

238 Duke Welf V of Bavaria.

239 Frederick of Sommerschenburg, count-palatine of Saxony.

240 Poppo's death is recorded under the year 1118 above. Beatrix's family origins are not known definitively.

241 Cf. *The 1125 continuation of Frutolf's chronicle*, 273, where Erlung's death and the subsequent dispute are listed under 1122.

242 Cf. *Cronica S. Petri Erfordensis moderna*, 163, the source for this entry, where the additional word *ordinatus* changes significantly the meaning of this final sentence – attributing Ruotger's ordination to these bishops rather than his expulsion.

243 This is a reference to the famous Concordat of Worms. See the general introduction.

244 Bishop Otto of Halberstadt (1123–35).

245 Cf. *The 1125 continuation of Frutolf's chronicle*, 279 for the story of Dietrich's death. Bishop Richwin of Zeitz-Naumburg (1123–25).

246 Count Ludwig ('the Leaper') of Thuringia.

247 Henry II of Eilenburg, margrave of Meissen and Lusatia (the Saxon Ostmark), died childless.

Lothar and of other Saxons, expelled those men [Wiprecht and Herman]
and then assailed their lands and likewise their dignities.[248]

At almost the same time, [Arch]*bishop Adalbert of Mainz demanded tithes
of produce from the provincials who inhabit the march of Duderstadt, and
they strongly resisted. It happened that some of them were killed by* milites *of
the bishop, others were maimed, and several were even led away as captives.
For that reason, the Thuringians, agitated and fearing something similar for
themselves, came together from all parts of their territory on Tretenburg hill.
Soon, they prepared to break into the city of Erfurt – where the bishop was by
chance then staying – with twenty* milites. *And they would have accomplished
what they had started by their labour, if the same bishop, since he was a man
well-endowed with natural genius, had not turned them back by prudent counsel.*

At the same time, near Worms, spirits in the likeness of an army,
horsemen and armed, appeared and were wandering about; they were
confessing themselves to be the spirits of the many *milites* recently
killed.[249]

In the Year 1124. In the preceding passages, we recounted to the best
of our ability and knowledge the most noble lineage of the lord margrave
Wiprecht, founder of the monastery of Pegau. Then, we recounted as
well his hard work from boyhood in strengthening mind and body. We
also recounted how, enriched above others with estates and benefices
acquired in both peace and war, he eventually grew powerful in this
province, which is called Sorbia,[250] and how he obtained the princely
dignity and also the principality in Lusatia, as well as the main prefecture
in Magdeburg.[251] Amongst all of this, in both his foundation of and
joint labour at Pegau and other monasteries, he fervently endeavoured
to render satisfaction to God and the saints for the enormity of his sins.
He also put divine worship before all earthly riches. Having nevertheless
omitted many things for the sake of brevity, now it remains to be said
how he died a blessed death.

---

248 The extant sources do not agree on what happened to Henry II of Eilenburg's
marches after his death. Emperor Henry V and Duke Lothar of Saxony each granted
the two marches to their own supporters. Wiprecht of Groitzsch received one,
possibly both, from Henry V (other sources do not mention Herman of Winzenburg),
while Conrad of Wettin and Adalbert (Albert) the Bear each received one from
Lothar. Cf. *Annalista Saxo*, 759–60 and *Annales Patherbrunnenses*, 144.

249 Cf. *The 1125 continuation of Frutolf's chronicle*, 278.

250 Cf. Cosmas of Prague, *The chronicle of the Czechs*, where Sorbia is used to designate
the march of Meissen (60, n. 142).

251 For this 'prefecture', see above, n. 227.

Once during the winter, Wiprecht was spending the night in the village of Halle, where he was attending to the lawsuits of the advocacy.[252] In the still of the night, when everyone was lost in a deep sleep from safety and happiness after the day was done, the fire from the nearby hearth set alight the straw for the *milites'* beds, which was scattered about negligently here and there in the evening. After the fire had grown stronger for awhile, only the prince, awakened from sleep, was roused. Unable to bear any delay – yet silently, as he was semi-nude – he got up and set about extinguishing the straw by stomping on it with the bare soles of his feet. He accomplished this with everyone else unaware and, half-burned, returned to his blanket. On account of this fire, little by little he reached a state of such weakness that he never recovered from it.

Come morning, the situation became clear from the obvious signs and moved everyone to both compassion and wonder. Ordering that he be returned from there to his home at Groitzsch, he first turned aside toward his refuge, Pegau, as had always been his custom before. There, he poured out at length a prayer from the depths of his heart; then, with his men bringing him out in their arms, he withdrew immediately for town, so that the presence of his weakness might not disturb the brothers too much. There, as his sickness grew worse all winter, finally disgusted by the unfitness of the exterior man, he turned his whole self over to God, who alone cures the infirmity of the interior man, in order to redeem his life from eternal ruin.[253]

He therefore sent for the son of his sister, Archbishop Ruotger of Magdeburg,[254] for other neighbouring bishops (Arnold of Merseburg, Richwin of Zeitz, Gotbold of Meissen),[255] and for his venerable abbot Windolf. He sought from them aid and counsel for the remedy of his soul. Seeing him to be in desperate circumstances, after many speeches of compassion and consolation, they began to advise him to adopt the habit of the monastic life. How willingly and devotedly Wiprecht paid

---

252 This is probably a reference to the advocacy over the monastery of Neuwerk, which Archbishop Adelgot of Magdeburg had founded in 1116. Since this was an archiepiscopal foundation, the archbishop's advocate (i.e., Wiprecht) would probably have been Neuwerk's advocate as well.

253 Cf. 2 Corinthians 4:16.

254 For this genealogical connection, see above, p. 35, and the family tree.

255 Bishop Arnold of Merseburg (1120–26); Bishop Richwin of Zeitz-Naumburg (1123–25); and Bishop Gotbold of Meissen (1119–40).

attention to such counsel can better be concluded from the following: immediately, in the presence of those same bishops, with the surrender of his sword he renounced both military and all secular affairs, thoroughly hating them. On the following day, carried to Pegau, he was received with the greatest sorrow of the brothers, and having received the habit, with great contrition of spirit he made the vow of the Rule's intention before the main altar in the brothers' presence. Then he was led away in the arms of the many. Thereafter, so it is said, he strove to practice obedience with such great attentiveness that he would consent to take nothing of either food or drink, nor to be seen or visited by any of his men, not even his son, without being given permission, very much devoting himself to silence and obedience.

And so, with God calling, after a few days he was released. As bishops and laymen performed the funeral rites with a large crowd – individual bishops saying mass for him on individual days – he was honourably commended to the earth and buried between his wife and son in the middle of his church.[256] It is well known that on the same day he handed over on behalf of his soul the estate called *Karlsdorf*.[257] Wiprecht passed away on the eleventh Kalends of June [22 May].

---

256 Wiprecht's eldest son, Wiprecht *iunior*, last appears in the text under the year 1116/17, suggesting he died in or soon after these years. However, the text makes no mention of his death.

257 See above, under the year 1096, for the first reference to Wiprecht's grant of *Karlsdorf*.

THE LIFE OF BISHOP OTTO OF BAMBERG (D. 1139), BY A MONK OF PRÜFENING

INTRODUCTION

Few if any German prelates of the twelfth century had as extraordinary a career as Bishop Otto I of Bamberg. His influence stretched from the shores of the Baltic to the papal see in Rome. Prior to his becoming bishop in 1102, he had already earned a reputation for his service at court, first among the Poles and later with Emperor Henry IV. Then, as bishop of one of the most important dioceses in the German kingdom, he founded and endowed numerous monastic communities while also pursuing territorial strategies that strengthened significantly his bishopric's control of the region in and around Bamberg. These successful activities, by themselves, would have made Otto stand out from the crowd of German bishops during his day. But he cemented his legacy by undertaking two missions in the 1120s to Christianize the Pomeranians, a pagan Slavic people living on the Baltic coast in what is today northern Poland. According to his *vita*, he frequently risked serious injury and even death as he struggled against the local pagan priests for the hearts and minds of the people of Pomerania. While he was not completely successful, he laid the groundwork for the gradual adoption of Christianity in the region during subsequent decades. In 1189, only a half-century after his death, he was canonized for his efforts as a missionary bishop, and his tomb in the monastery of Michelsberg in Bamberg remains a pilgrimage site to this day.

The text translated here is the earliest *vita* for Otto and is divided into three books. The first concerns Otto's early life, his time at the courts of the Polish duke and German emperor, and his work as a monastic founder and reformer. The second and third books offer a remarkable account of his missionary activities in the towns of Pomerania. In these sections of the *vita*, readers will find one of the most detailed surviving descriptions of how medieval Christians sought to convert pagans and convince them of the errors of their ways. In such a text, hagiographical *topoi* are inevitable; miracles have a prominent role to play in this conversion narrative. But alongside these miracles are many stories of Otto's interactions with fellow missionaries, pagans and early converts; all of these stories paint a vivid picture of life along the religious frontier of north-eastern Europe during the twelfth century.

Context

Otto was probably born in the 1060s. As his *vita* reports, he was from Swabia, in the south-west of the German kingdom, and was of noble birth. Although little is known about his family, some scholars have suggested that his mother was related to the Staufen, a lineage that would produce a line of German kings and emperors during the twelfth and thirteenth centuries.[1] By the late 1080s, the young Otto had become an important figure at the court of Duke Władysław I Herman of Poland (1079–1102), where he used his influence to convince the duke to marry Judith, the sister of the German Emperor Henry IV (1056–1106). He then served as Judith's chaplain for a time in Poland before returning to the German kingdom to join Henry IV's court. Under Henry, he served in a variety of positions, including for a time overseer of the construction of the cathedral in Speyer.[2] Otto's worldly career thus reveals a skilled courtier, one who was adept at winning favour and reaping rewards from his patrons.[3] His appointment as bishop of Bamberg in eastern Franconia in 1102 was the culmination of his efforts to rise through the ranks at court through loyal service.

Although Bamberg is a small, rather sleepy town today, it was the seat of one of the most important bishoprics in the German kingdom during the early twelfth century. The diocese had been established only a century earlier, in 1007, by Emperor Henry II. This childless ruler, the last from the Ottonian dynasty, had lavished his new foundation with extensive gifts of relics, manuscripts, rights and properties – not just

---

1 *Die Prüfeninger Vita*, 49. King Conrad III (1138–52), the first ruler from the Staufen lineage, was king when Otto died.

2 Ebo and Herbord of Michelsberg, the authors of two other early *vitae* of Otto (see below, p. 95), both mention his work on the Speyer cathedral: *Heiligenleben zur deutsch-slawischen Geschichte*, 192–3 and 480–3.

3 Jaeger, *The origins of courtliness*, 49–53.

in eastern Franconia but also across Bavaria and the south-east of the German kingdom. For example, the bishops of Bamberg possessed the town of Villach in southern Austria for three-quarters of a millennium from 1007 until 1759, when Empress Maria Theresa finally purchased it and integrated the town into the Habsburg territories.[4] Throughout the eleventh century, the bishops of Bamberg continued to expand their influence while remaining closely linked to the German rulers; Emperor Henry III even arranged the elevation of Bishop Suidger of Bamberg to the papal see as Pope Clement II (1046–47). During this period, the cathedral school also became one of the leading centres of education in the German-speaking lands. Thus, when Otto was appointed bishop of Bamberg, he acquired one of the foremost ecclesiastical positions in the kingdom.[5]

Throughout his time as bishop, Otto remained a prominent figure in imperial politics; charters and various chronicles attest to the leading role he played at key moments in the 1110s, 1120s and 1130s.[6] However, the text translated here has very little to say about this aspect of his career. Instead, after discussing his early years and his work founding and endowing monasteries and churches as bishop, it turns to his efforts to bring Christianity to Pomerania in 1124–25 and 1128.[7] As the *vita* makes clear, his connections to the Polish court were a crucial factor in his missionary activities. Duke Bolesław III 'the Wrymouth' of Poland (1102–38) had recently conquered Pomerania, and he supported Otto's missionary work as part of his broader strategy of further subduing the region.[8] The Slavic peoples of Pomerania had encountered Christians before; their own duke in this period, Warcisław I, was himself a convert.[9] But Warcisław's control over the elites in the towns of Pomerania, especially in the wealthy trading hubs of Wolin and Szczecin, was limited. As a result, paganism was well-entrenched in the region, and Bishop Otto and his fellow missionaries struggled to gain a foothold.

---

4 For Bamberg's territories outside Franconia, see Klebel, 'Bamberger Besitz in Österreich und Bayern'.

5 For a more detailed discussion of the early history of the bishopric of Bamberg, see Schneidmüller, 'Die einzigartig geliebte Stadt'.

6 See, for example, *Chronicles of the Investiture Contest*, 172, 224, 245 and 272 and *MGH DD L. III*, 2–3, nr. 2; 102–3, nr. 66; and 109–11, nr. 71.

7 For an excellent overview of the history of this region of the Baltic coast during the early twelfth century, see Christiansen, *The northern crusades*, 6–47.

8 Bartlett, 'The conversion of a pagan society', 194–5.

9 See below, II.3.

It was only after his death, in the year 1140, that the first bishop for Pomerania was finally consecrated.[10]

Text and authorship

Although the text of this *vita* nowhere explicitly states that it was written at the monastery of Prüfening just outside Regensburg in Bavaria, scholars are in agreement that the text stems from this religious community. Prüfening was one of the monasteries established by Bishop Otto, and the lengthy foundation story reported about this house early in the *vita* leaves little doubt that the text's author was a monk there.[11] The date of the text's composition, on the other hand, is more difficult to determine than its place of origin. There exist three early *vitae* of Bishop Otto, all written between approximately 1140 and 1160: the one by a monk of Prüfening translated here, a second by Ebo of Michelsberg, and a third by Herbord of Michelsberg. During the nineteenth and early twentieth centuries, scholars argued that Ebo and Herbord's were the oldest, with the Prüfening monk copying from their works when writing his own.[12] This older argument is the principal reason why the only other English translation of any of these three texts, which was published in 1920, includes excerpts from Ebo and Herbord's works but not the monk of Prüfening's.[13] The weight of scholarly consensus has shifted in recent years, however, and the text translated here is now viewed as the oldest of the three. Jürgen Petersohn, in his 1999 edition for the *Monumenta Germaniae Historica*, posits a date range of between 1140 and 1146 on the basis of his close analysis of the text.[14]

For the first book of the *vita*, the monk of Prüfening relied heavily on a text known as the *Relatio de piis operibus Ottonis episcopi Bambergensis (Report on the pious works of Bishop Otto of Bamberg)*.[15] Written in Bamberg,

---

10 For a more detailed discussion of Pomerania in this period, see Bartlett, 'The conversion of a pagan society' and Petersohn, *Der südliche Ostseeraum*.

11 See below, I.10. Weinrich, the translator of the *vita* in *Heiligenleben zur deutsch-slawischen Geschichte*, assigns the name Wolfger of Prüfening to the author of the text translated here, but there is no general agreement on which monk at Prüfening wrote the work.

12 Wattenbach, for example, in his *Deutschlands Geschichtsquellen*, vol. 1, 371, states that it was written after the other two *vitae*.

13 *The life of Otto, apostle of Pomerania*.

14 *Die Prüfeninger Vita*. See also Petersohn, 'Otto von Bamberg'.

15 *Relatio de piis operibus*, 1151–66. Petersohn indicates in his edition of the *vita* (*Die Prüfeninger Vita*) which passages were taken from this earlier work.

this was a record of Otto's monastic foundations, his other support for
religious communities, and his work strengthening the territorial and
lordly prerogatives of his bishopric.[16] However, the first book of the
vita includes more than just a copy of this text; the chapter on the
foundation of Prüfening, for example, does not appear in the *Relatio*.[17]
For the second and third books of the *vita*, which give an account of
Otto's missionary work in Pomerania, scholars have identified only one
contemporary written source utilized by the author, namely a report
on the first mission in 1124–25 that has also been preserved in a chronicle
from the same period.[18] Although the Prüfening monk gives no indication
that he participated in either of the missions to Pomerania, his *vita* was
written soon enough after Otto's death that it is probable the author
gathered most of his material from the oral accounts of those who did.[19]
The monk also relied heavily on Sulpicius Severus's fourth-century *vita*
of St Martin of Tours, a text rich with stories of Martin's efforts to
convert pagans in late antique Gaul, as a model for much of his
narrative.

The life translated here is the shortest of the three mid-twelfth-century
vitae of Bishop Otto. Ebo of Michelsberg, who wrote the next oldest
vita some time between 1151 and 1159, used the Prüfening monk's text
as a source and mimicked its structure; his text is also divided into
three books, with the first one concerning Otto's early life and work
in and around Bamberg, and the other two his missions to Pomerania.
However, Ebo's text frequently gives more details than the Prüfening
monk's, an indication that its author had other, independent sources.[20]
The third author, Herbord of Michelsberg, writing in 1159, adopted
the form of a three-person conversation, giving his *vita* a strikingly
different character than the earlier two. He included information about
Otto that does not appear in either Ebo's or the Prüfening monk's texts,
but he also had a tendency to digress in the midst of his narrative; his
work contains a well-known description of the women's convent at
Admont, for example, that has little if anything to do with Bishop
Otto.[21] All three versions of Otto's life can be read together fruitfully,

---

16 *Die Prüfeninger Vita*, 6.

17 See below, I.10.

18 Cf. below, II.21, and *The 1125 continuation of Frutolf's chronicle*, 283–4.

19 *Die Prüfeninger Vita*, 7–8.

20 Petersohn, 'Otto von Bamberg', 9.

21 *Heiligenleben zur deutsch-slawischen Geschichte*, 322–31.

but the text translated here is an independent work that can also be appreciated on its own.

Manuscripts and editions

The life of Bishop Otto of Bamberg by a monk of Prüfening survives in three manuscripts from the late twelfth and early thirteenth centuries.[22] All three of these codices include portions of the *Magnum Legendarium Austriacum (MLA)*, an extensive collection of saints' lives compiled and copied at several Austrian monasteries around the year 1200.[23] Given the bishopric of Bamberg's extensive property holdings in Austria, and the Regensburg monastery of Prüfening's location on the Danube River upstream from Austria, it is not surprising that the text attracted interest in Austria and found its way into this great compendium of hagiographical works. These manuscripts, as well as later ones, formed the basis for Petersohn's 1999 scholarly edition of the text.[24] In 2005, a facing-page Latin edition with German translation appeared in a volume that also includes the other two early *vitae* by Ebo and Herbord of Michelsberg.[25]

Notes on this translation

In preparing this translation, I am deeply indebted to Petersohn's 1999 Latin edition as well as Weinrich's 2005 German translation. However, the biblical, classical and post-classical source citations identified by Petersohn have not all been noted here. Rather than indicating every individual word and short phrase that the Prüfening monk seems to have borrowed from other texts, I have chosen to include a more modest number of source citations; most of these either call attention to the impressive range of the author's textual knowledge or show how much he relied on particular sources at key moments in his text. For the many passages he has excerpted from the writings of Sulpicius Severus,

---

22 *Die Prüfeninger Vita*, 21–5.

23 For a recent overview of this collection, see Ó Riain, 'The *Magnum Legendarium Austriacum*'. This same collection also preserves the only extant copy of *The life of an unnamed magistra of Admont* translated in this volume.

24 *Die Prüfeninger Vita*.

25 *Heiligenleben zur deutsch-slawischen Geschichte*. The Latin edition of the Prüfening *vita* is based on Petersohn's. Note that this volume includes only excerpts of Ebo's text, not the complete work.

the translations are mine, while the footnotes direct the reader to alternate
published English translations. I have used the modern, Polish spellings
for all Pomeranian place names. The chapter numbers, which do not
appear in medieval copies of the *vita*, follow Petersohn's edition.

Although the anonymous monk of Prüfening who wrote this text relied
heavily on other sources in some places, much of this *Life* nevertheless
reads like a well-crafted narrative. It describes Otto's youth, and especially
his missionary activities, in a lively – and, at times, humorous – style.
Book II, in particular, offers a vivid account of Otto's efforts to convert
the pagan Pomeranians to Christianity while travelling from town to
town along the Baltic coast. I have tried to capture the energy and
excitement of the monk's story as best as possible in this translation.

TRANSLATION

Prologue to the life of Bishop Otto of Bamberg

After Moses was victorious against Amalec, the Lord ordered him to
commit to writing both the ruin of his enemies and the victory of the
Israelite people.[1] For so we read it written in Exodus: And *the Lord
said to Moses: 'Write this for a memorial in a book, and deliver it to the ears
of Josue: for I will destroy the memory of Amalec from under heaven.'*[2] But
why recall these things of such ancient origin? Namely so that[3] you pay
attention: if the punishment of the condemned will be described for
this purpose, to show that their wicked acts must be avoided, how much
more ought the deeds of excellent fathers be written down, so that
those who wish to do so may find the strength to imitate their virtues?
For if the ruin of their memory, whose memory must be destroyed from
under heaven, may be commanded, how much more must the life of
any saint be committed to writing? That verse in the Psalm agrees
with this: *The just shall be in everlasting remembrance.*[4]

For this reason, it is fitting that our mutual father, Bishop Otto, be
placed in the memory of men. Removed from human affairs, he crossed
over to the joy of the angels. When he was still rooted in this body, he
was made worthy by the continual achievement of good works, such

1 Cf. Exodus 17:8ff.

2 Exodus 17:14.

3 Jerome, *Epistulae*, 10.2.1; 52.4.1; and 58.4.1.

4 Psalm 111:7.

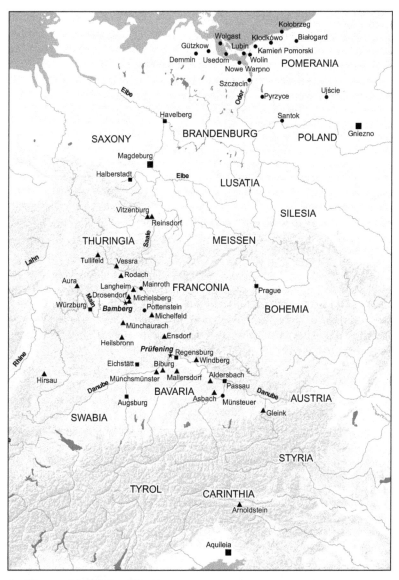

4　The world of Otto of Bamberg

that his memory should be in the heart and mouth of the faithful in an
eternal blessing. Therefore, we have undertaken to write down some
things concerning his deeds, with the Lord helping, both to edify the
readers and to honour the deeds. So that no one may judge what we
write to be unbelievable, we relate only those things we ourselves know
for certain, or well known and pious people verified for us. Thus do we
await from God the reward for our labour, so long as we follow the
pure and simple truth of history.[5]

The life of the same. Book I

[1.] In our memory, there was a certain venerable bishop, worthy to
God, named Otto, who was descended from a pious and noble lineage
of Swabians.[6] Truly, I would say that many men would have rejoiced
at his birth, if they could have known beforehand the course of his life.
Let me describe this life in a few words: he was a father of the poor[7]
and a *consoler of mourners*,[8] and he seemed to be – as far as it looks to
human consideration – a pillar of the church, the honour of his time,
and a mirror of holy faith. Who does not know how great a source of
joy it would be for the then-unknowing world, when this child of such
great innate character was born into the world? Then, born blessedly
and raised prosperously, he was instructed extremely well in sacred
texts, doubtlessly in the proper manner; he who was going to become
a doctor of the church learned then what he would later teach. After
he reached maturity, he conducted himself in such a way that he excited
many people's affection for him. These people were given to understand
clearly that he would be a man of great merit, he who already as a boy
was devoted to God.

[2.] Already, he had come forth in manly strength of spirit;[9] preparing
himself for greater devotion to the virtues, he was eager to say and do
only those things befitting a man. Good to everyone, better to his own

5 The latter half of this prologue draws heavily on the works of Sulpicius Severus,
  especially his *Vita Sancti Martini* (*The life of Saint Martin of Tours*).
6 For his family background, see the introduction to this text.
7 Otto is also called *pater pauperum Christi* ('father of Christ's poor') in the necrology
  of the monastery of Michelsberg in Bamberg. See *Die Prüfeninger Vita*, 49, n. 16.
8 Job 29:25.
9 Cf. Boethius, *The consolation of philosophy*, I.2.

men, even better to himself, he already devoted himself to others' success, and he received from them suitable rewards for his labour.

Then, it happened that he left his fatherland behind and sought out the lands of the Poles. He stayed there for some time and came to know not only the customs of that people but also their language so perfectly that, if you had heard him speaking this barbarous language, you would not have thought the man was German. Truly, divine providence granted this grace to him: that he could understand and speak the language of this barbarian people, he who would later guide this same barbarian people to the faith.[10] But we will speak about this more fully in another place; we return now to the narrative's proper order.

And so, the prudent and faithful man, wanting to disburse to his fellow servants the wealth he had received,[11] gave his attention to teaching their boys [i.e., the Poles']. By this means he procured his livelihood in a foreign land. Indeed, he used these wages like a good labourer, while he also took care to restrain the boys he instructed from childish foolishness.

[3.] In these ways, he moved all the wise men to have affection for him, such that the bishops of that land [i.e., of the Poles], having heard about the adolescent's reputation, genuinely loved him. They were amazed not only at *the polish of his speech, the grasp of his memory, the quickness of his intellect, and the earnestness* of his learning,[12] but also at the elegance of his manners. On account of this, it happened that he began to assist these bishops and serve with them at home and abroad, and thus he obtained among them a position of familiarity that was not the lowest.[13] When he had stayed a very long time in their service, he likewise found grace with the prince of the people, namely Duke Bolesław.[14] Because he served everyone piously and faithfully, his labour was offset by the benefits he received from them.

10 The author is possibly confused here. The Poles had already been Christianized before Otto's arrival in the region. Moreover, the author reports that the bishop used an interpreter when preaching to the Pomeranians (see below, III.8).

11 Cf. Matthew 25:14ff. for the parable of the man who gave money to his servants.

12 Jerome, *Epistulae*, 39.1.2.

13 The term *familiaritas* is common throughout this text in various grammatical forms. It is translated here simply as 'familiarity', because it does not seem to imply any kind of fixed or formal relationship of either kinship, household, or vassalic status. It suggests loyalty, intimacy and physical proximity but only generically.

14 Bolesław III 'the Wrymouth' was duke of Poland from 1102 to 1138; however, Otto's initial arrival in Poland occurred earlier than 1102, during the rule of Bolesław III's father, Duke Władysław I Herman (1079–1102).

Although he seemed to be rich in all goods and to abound in fortunate successes in this foreign land, nevertheless he did not neglect
to return to his homeland and to visit his own men. Since the God of
his salvation was always at hand, he was allowed to have a favourable
journey both going and returning. Even though he took care of his own
men and especially the members of his household, nevertheless he did
not withdraw himself from the familiarity and service of bishops and
princes. Indeed, he served them in very many ways, but especially in
carrying out their public and private embassies here and there. From
this, it happened that he frequented the palace of King Henry, who was
the fourth of this name to hold the Roman empire.[15] He found so much
favour in the eyes of the king[16] and of his magnates that they bound
him very tightly to their own service and friendship.

[4.] At this time, the king's sister, named Judith, was staying in attendance on her brother. *Although happy in other respects, he* often *experienced*
the ill luck *of misfortune* on account of her,[17] and because he had been
unable to maintain her respectably, he arranged to join her in a respectable
marriage.[18] The most faithful Otto concerned himself with this business
for the sake of the king's honour and that of the kingdom. He did not
stop suggesting to the duke of the Poles that he should seek that beautiful
and noble woman in marriage, since she was the daughter of a king and
the brother of another king.[19] He asserted it would be a great benefit
to his [i.e., the duke's] and to his men's honour – and would protect
the peace – on account of the relationship it would create with the king.

And so, the duke agreed with the sound advice of this prudent man,
whose hard work he had previously come to know. He sent respectable
messengers directly to the king, not without gifts, and he sought and
received his sister from him as his wife.[20] In her service, our Otto,
directed by the king, entered Poland again and assisted and ministered

---

15 King Henry IV of the German kingdom (1056–1106). He also plays a prominent
     role in *The deeds of Margrave Wiprecht of Groitzsch.*

16 Cf. Genesis 18:3 and 33:10.

17 Einhard, *Vita Karoli*, ch. 19, where Charlemagne's relationship with his daughters
     is discussed (Einhard, *The life of Charlemagne, 33*).

18 The chronicler Bernold of St Blasien reports that she had been unfaithful to her
     first husband, King Solomon of Hungary, and was maintained in Regensburg by
     her brother. See Bernold of St Blasien, *Chronicle, 273–4.*

19 i.e., like Henry IV, she was a child of Emperor Henry III (1039–56).

20 Judith probably married Duke Władysław I Herman of Poland in the year 1088.
     See *Die Prüfeninger Vita, 53,* n. 45.

to her faithfully. He performed the office of arch-chaplain to a singular degree, and that most noble woman loved and cherished him. She sometimes directed precious gifts to her brother, the king, through him. After he had served her for many years and had been honoured by her with many gifts, he received permission to return and went back to the royal hall.[21] Having attached himself to the king's service, he later could not be separated from him.

From this, it happened that Otto went from being an esteemed man to being the most highly esteemed, not only to the king but also to all the magnates. They recommended his character in every possible way and judged it most worthy of any honour whatsoever. And so the king appointed this industrious man principal chancellor of his palace and undertook to invest him with the benefices attached to the same office. If I wished to explain how excellent he was in this office and how many people he benefited, the day would fail me before the words.

[5.] At that time, our Otto had other fellow ministers at the royal court, who were full of wisdom and the spirit of knowledge and distinguished by the integrity of their characters. Of them, we saw several afterwards become bishops. For whenever it was announced to the ears of the king that the bishop of any church had died, he immediately said that his Otto had to be substituted for him. Our Otto, recommending his other chaplains, protested that this one or that one was more suitable for such an office, explaining that this one excelled him in virtue and that that one had exerted himself more for the king's honour. And so it happened that after Otto had refused appointment to two episcopacies, namely Halberstadt and Augsburg, they were given to others – divine providence doubtless reserving him for another church.[22]

[6.] At this time, Bishop Rupert was the head of the church of Bamberg.[23] When he died, the pastoral ring and staff were brought to the king, until he should provide a suitable priest for the same church – on the advice of his magnates and with the consent also of the clergy and the people. It happened that, because the choice was delayed for almost six

---

21 He probably returned to Henry IV's court in the year 1097. See *Die Prüfeninger Vita*, 53, n. 47.

22 *Heiligenleben zur Deutsch-Slawischen Geschichte*, 126, suggests that the archbishopric of Bremen is meant here, rather than Halberstadt; the chancellor Humbert received Bremen in 1101. Bishop Siegfried II of Augsburg died in 1096 and was succeeded by Herman (1096/97–1133).

23 Bishop Rupert of Bamberg (1075–1102).

full months, the church stood vacant. Then, the feast day of the Lord's birth arrived.[24] King Henry [IV] called together all the well-respected members of the clergy, ready to discuss with them the state of the church of Bamberg and the choice of a bishop. But they requested a stay in the proceedings, and it was granted, because they were impeded by zealous factions and were unable to agree on any person. They placed the selection of a bishop in the king's judgement.[25]

Immediately, that man ordered the ring to be brought to him, and through this ring he solemnly invested the chancellor Otto with the *regalia* and appointed him bishop of the church of Bamberg.[26] The king also took care to entrust him carefully to two bishops, namely those of Würzburg and Augsburg, to lead him honourably to his see.[27]

The whole city [i.e., Bamberg] then roused itself to joy at the entrance of the blessed man. It decorated not only the churches but also the streets with cloths spread and hung everywhere, so that it might receive the bishop chosen for it with appropriate pomp. He would later distinguish it above almost all neighbouring cities with amazing decorations both inside and out. But he entered the city humbly, clothed in vestments of mourning, his feet bare. Thus did the clergy and people receive him *in a voice of joy and praise.*[28] He deserved to be raised to the episcopal dignity.

[7.][29] And so, after Bishop Otto had first been given the prelacy of the holy church of Bamberg by divine gift, he committed all his enthusiastic devotion to it; he shone forth in his character with the splendour of his

24 It was common for there to be large assemblies at the royal court during the Christmas season, making this a popular time for the king to discuss important matters with the magnates.

25 During the period of the Investiture Controversy, Pope Gregory VII (1073–85) and his successors sought to limit royal control over episcopal elections and investiture, while King Henry IV insisted that he had the right as king to choose bishops and invest them with the symbols of their office. See the general introduction for more on this point.

26 The *regalia* were those elements of episcopal authority that derived from the king (including lands and other forms of income), rather than those elements that concerned the spiritual aspects of the episcopal office. For more on this point, see the general introduction and Weinfurter, *The Salian century*, 169–73.

27 Bishop Emehard of Würzburg (1089–1105) and Bishop Herman of Augsburg (see n. 22 above).

28 Psalm 41:5.

29 With the exception of Chapter 10, all of the chapters from this one to Chapter 30 of Book I are drawn, at least partially, from an earlier work, the *Relatio de piis operibus Ottonis episcopi Bambergensis.* For more on this source, see the introduction to this text.

virtues, and he glorified God, who was glorifying him, through his works. For he pursued in everything the honour of Christ, the salvation of the people, and contempt of himself; he knew not to seek in all these things his own profits, but those of the Lord.

In the meantime, he went to the apostolic see. He was consecrated bishop in the city of Anagni by Pope Paschal [II] on the solemn day of Pentecost, with the Holy Spirit cooperating, and he received the bishop's mitre.[30] It was also at this time that the same Roman pontiff distinguished him with the use of the cross and pallium; to be clear, the apostolic see intended these symbols – as it had already in the past – for all who succeeded him canonically in this church in perpetuity.[31]

[8.] Thereafter, strengthened more and more in the grace of Christ, he strove to be *a fruitful olive tree in the house* of the Lord,[32] a tree which knew no drought and had no experience whatsoever of being barren. For he was eager to disburse to the peoples the wealth of the word;[33] in exchange for this, he knew that he would one day be placed over all the goods of the Lord. For this reason, he was excited about the pastoral office entrusted to him, and he watched over ecclesiastical business day and night, giving attention to how he might – for the honour of the Lord – either augment the properties of his holy church by acquisition or recover properties that had been lost. From this, it happened that he cast his hand toward everything that had been taken away from the same church up to that time, whether through violence or fraud or any iniquity. And, in as much as God's mercy deigned to favour him, he laboured to bring everything back and succeeded in restoring it.

[9.] Then, because the whole of pious Otto's ambition burned to spread praise of the divine name, he constructed some monasteries from their foundations; he even finished at great expense a few that had been previously started – but poorly – which were either bestowed on the church of Bamberg by princes or by other faithful of Christ, or which he acquired for a suitable price. Indeed, we put all of this together in

---

30 Pope Paschal II (1099–1118) consecrated Otto in Anagni on 13 May 1106.

31 This is a reference to the bishops of Bamberg's right to receive the symbols of their spiritual authority directly from the papacy rather than one of the German archbishops; this right had been confirmed in two papal privileges for the bishops of Bamberg from 2 January 1053 and 15 April 1111: *Die Prüfeninger Vita*, 57, n. 70 and *Relatio de piis operibus Ottonis episcopi Bambergensis*, 1157, n. 2.

32 Psalm 51:10.

33 See above, n. 11.

writing, so that we may offer it to those wanting to taste the honeycomb amassed by our most prudent bee. And so, he was inflamed by such a great desire for the religious life that there was almost no monastic order considered acceptable in his days and territories, from which he did not continually receive pious men. He entrusted to these men the leadership of the monasteries he constructed. The first fruit of his desire was a monastery called Aura, which was constructed in the diocese of Würzburg in honour of St Lawrence.[34]

[10.] His second foundation was the monastery he constructed and consecrated in the Bavarian duchy, in the Regensburg diocese, in the Danubian *pagus*,[35] he resolved that the new monastery be named for St George.[36] The occasion for its construction was this – so it is told. One time, a general assembly of bishops and princes was held at Regensburg, and this bishop, having been invited, came.[37] He ignored the city, however, and withdrew into a certain field situated toward the city's western end, since solitude was always a friend to him. He directed a tent to be set up for him in this place. While he was resting there, he was shown a wondrous vision at night. And behold, he saw an enormous ladder that extended all the way to heaven, just as it had appeared formerly to the patriarch Jacob in his sleep, *on which angels were shown* to him – truly, without a doubt, to the bishop – *descending and ascending*.[38] While he focused his contemplation on high and tried to follow the ascending angels with his sharp eyesight, he awoke. Roused from sleep, he was overcome by great awe, such that he was given to understand plainly that there was something of the divine in this same place.

In the meantime, after he had returned to himself, the bishop recalled that dream or example of St Jacob from the Old Testament, and he began to rejoice in the vision. And so, *he set up a stone for a pillar*, and *pouring the oil* of blessing *on top of it*,[39] he consecrated the altar he had

---

34 Otto founded the Benedictine monastery of Aura in 1108. Its first abbot was Ekkehard of Aura, who is better known as a chronicler of the late Salian period. See *Chronicles of the Investiture Controversy*, 44–8 and 66–9.

35 A *pagus* was an administrative district.

36 This is the monastery of Prüfening, founded in 1109, where this text was written.

37 This is probably a reference to King Henry V's court session at Regensburg in the summer of 1108. See *Die Prüfeninger Vita*, 59, n. 87.

38 Cf. Genesis 28:12–22 for the story of Jacob's ladder; see also *RB 1980: the rule of St Benedict*, 192–3, ch. 7.

39 Genesis 28:18.

constructed. Here it happened that, in the place where two nut trees were planted long ago and still stand today, it often sounded like bells were ringing. Their sound was heard plainly by the inhabitants, so that the Lord might announce with manifest proofs that this same dwelling place ought to be delivered up for divine services. And so, time passed, and the blessed man acquired that place partly by purchase and partly by legitimate exchange. He improved it on behalf of the abbey with great expense and labour. Soon, he sent an abbot and brothers there, whom he had obtained from Hirsau, introducing for the first time to the regions of Bavaria the discipline of this monastic order.[40]

It happened that very many of the townspeople, visiting this place out of curiosity, praised the tonsure and habit of these servants of God, together with the modesty of their manners. They marvelled especially at their reception of guests, their care of the poor, then too their washing of feet – which they did continually, according to divine mandate and example, both to each other and also to arriving pilgrims – and other holy obligations of this sort. That man, filled with God, loved this place always with the most sincere love. He cultivated it, he enriched it, and he loved always the progress of the brothers living there.[41] It suffices to say these things about his second foundation.

[11.] These are the other monasteries, which he constructed and in which he introduced monks and the monastic way of life: Münchaurach, under the protection of the blessed Peter, in the diocese of Würzburg;[42] Michelfeld, in honour of the blessed John the Evangelist,[43] and Langheim, in honour of the blessed virgin Mary,[44] both in his own diocese [i.e., of Bamberg]; Ensdorf, in honour of the blessed James;[45] one in the castle Mallersdorf in honour of the blessed apostle John;[46] another,

---

40 The Benedictine monastery of Hirsau was an important centre for monastic reform in the decades around the year 1100; see the general introduction and also *The deeds of Margrave Wiprecht of Groitzsch*. The claim that Prüfening was the first Bavarian monastery reformed from Hirsau is not entirely accurate.

41 See below, p. 113, where comparable language is used for the monastery of Michelsberg.

42 Benedictine monastery, founded c. 1124–27.

43 Benedictine monastery, founded in 1119.

44 Cistercian monastery, founded in 1132. The author of *The life of Mechthild of Diessen*, Engelhard, was a monk at Langheim.

45 Benedictine monastery, founded in 1121.

46 Benedictine monastery, founded in 1109 and acquired by Bamberg c. 1129–31.

named Münchsmünster, in honour of the blessed Peter;[47] Biburg[48] and
Windberg,[49] which is a house of regular canons under the protection of
the blessed Mary, each one in the bishopric of Regensburg; Reinsdorf,
in the bishopric of Halberstadt, in honour of St John the Baptist;[50]
Heilsbronn, in the bishopric of Eichstätt, under the protection of the
blessed Virgin Mary;[51] Aldersbach, another house of regular canons, in
honour of blessed Peter;[52] Asbach, in honour of St Matthew;[53] Gleink, in
honour of St Andrew the Apostle, in the diocese of Passau;[54] and another,
in the castle of Arnoldstein, which is in the bishopric of Aquileia, in
honour of St George.[55] And so, he added by his zeal to the six abbatial
sceptres that he found [i.e., when he became bishop], fourteen others,
with God supporting him.[56] In addition, he dedicated five cells for divine
worship: St Getreu in Bamberg, St George in Rodach, one in Drosendorf,
one in Tullifeld, and another one in Vessra under the protection of the
blessed Virgin Mary.[57]

[12.] Some of these monasteries, as we said, he founded on his own
property; some, which were begun by other faithful men, he finished; and
others, handed over to the church of Bamberg through the munificence
of kings and princes, he advanced toward the privilege of a better
condition, with the Lord helping. These last ones we will divide out
separately, so that we may show which ones he received from whom.

[13.] He subjected the abbey of Vitzenburg,[58] which changed its location
and name and is now called Reinsdorf, to the holy church of Bamberg,

47 Benedictine monastery, founded c. 1131–33.

48 Benedictine monastery, founded c. 1125–33.

49 Augustinian house of canons, founded c. 1125.

50 Benedictine monastery, probably founded in 1112.

51 Cistercian monastery, founded in 1132.

52 Augustinian house of canons, founded c. 1123–32.

53 Benedictine monastery, founded c. 1090 and acquired by Bamberg before 1125.

54 Benedictine monastery, founded 1123.

55 Benedictine monastery, founded 1106.

56 There are indeed fourteen monastic houses named in this chapter, but that does
    not include Aura or Prüfening from the preceding chapters. The six monasteries
    that already belonged to Bamberg prior to his becoming bishop are not named
    here but include (to mention only one) the Benedictine house of Michelsberg in
    Bamberg, founded in 1015.

57 St Getreu was founded in 1123/24; Rodach before 1135; Drosendorf before 1139;
    Tullifeld (near Neidhartshausen) c. 1127–39; and Vessra c. 1131–35.

58 For the monastic community at Vitzenburg, see also *The deeds of Margrave Wiprecht
    of Groitzsch*, pp. 76–77.

along with the properties pertaining to it from the munificence of Henry IV [V], having received privileges of royal authority.[59] He also doubled the same monastery's properties, for, since previously it had nothing except sixty-two *mansi*, he increased that number by just as many *mansi*.[60]

[14.] Emperor Lothar [III] gave the abbey located in the castle Mallersdorf to the church of Bamberg; the bishop expanded it with buildings, possessions and very many other properties.[61]

[15.] He acquired the abbey called Münchsmünster, with the church of blessed Sixtus and its other appurtenances, from Duke Henry of Bavaria and Margrave Diepold for an enormous amount of both gold and silver.[62] The most Christian emperor Lothar [III] assigned it to the ownership of the holy church of Bamberg by a royal privilege, and this was confirmed by a papal privilege of Pope Innocent II as well.[63]

[16.] He received the abbey called Gleink near the Enns River from Margrave Leopold and added twenty *mansi* and 50 marks to it.[64] He constructed a monks' cell in Arnoldstein after he had destroyed the fortification there. That castle, which had been alienated from the Bamberg church for forty-five years, he recovered with great labour, together with ninety-five *mansi*, and he gave another sixty *mansi* to the same place.[65]

[17.] The church of Bamberg had lost the estate at Asbach a long time ago. He reclaimed it through shrewd management, and establishing a monks' cell there, he enriched that place with a large gift of estates.

---

59 Emperor Henry V issued a privilege on 25 March 1121, in which he granted the monastery to the Bamberg church; see *Die Urkunden Heinrichs V.*: www.mgh.de/ddhv/dhv_229.htm (accessed 2 August 2016).

60 A *mansus* was a measurement of land.

61 There is no extant charter of Emperor Lothar III (1125–37) concerning the grant of Mallersdorf to the Bamberg church.

62 Duke Henry X the Proud of Bavaria (1126–38) and Margrave Diepold III of Vohburg (d. 1146).

63 *MGH DD L. III*, 85–7, nr. 54 [23 October 1123] and 102–3, nr. 66 [6 June 1134]. Pope Innocent II (1130–43) issued a privilege concerning Münchsmünster and other Bamberg monasteries on 23 January 1139: *Germania Pontificia* III.3, 269–70, nr. 62.

64 Margrave Leopold of Styria (1122–29). A *marca* (mark) was a unit of weight, usually the equivalent of approximately 8 ounces. Presumably, silver is meant here.

65 The idea of converting an ageing fortification into a monastery can also be seen in some of the other texts translated in this volume. See especially *The deeds of Count Ludwig of Arnstein*.

[18.] He received the cell at Rodach, which had been donated to the Bamberg church along with sixty *mansi* by Countess-palatine Agnes and her sister.[66] He also bought the properties surrounding the same church for 275 marks, along with the ministerials,[67] fields, woods, meadows, pastures and mills – and every other use and right, by which Duke Cuno was known to have held the same estate.[68]

[19.] Count Godebold had begun to build the cell at Vessra.[69] Afterwards, he donated it to the Bamberg church. Otto received it and granted very many properties to it for the use of those living there.

[20.] He distributed to all his monasteries everywhere the estates he had acquired in suitable places by very great labour and at enormous expense. Thus did he prepare daily offerings to the omnipotent God from his possessions in ever watchful concern. Who could count how much he bestowed on the same churches in furnishings – namely in altarcloths, stoles and chasubles, gold and silver chalices, crosses, reliquaries, pitchers, bottles, hangings, tapestries, books of each Testament, and various codices? Clearly, so great was the abundance of these objects that the number seemed to just about exceed estimation, and it was amazing that so much had been able to be conferred on so many places by one man.

[21.] Moreover, he perceived that the structure of his monasteries would stand more firmly, if the pillar of papal authority supported it. Nor could this structure be destroyed easily, if it were surrounded by blessed Peter's protection. Therefore, he placed it under the guardianship of Rome's defences and received a document of this sort from the apostolic see:[70]

Bishop Calixtus, servant of the servants of God, to the venerable brother Bishop Otto of Bamberg, greetings and apostolic blessing. We ought not only to favour the good endeavours of our brothers but also to incite their spirits toward them. Therefore, most dear and venerable brother Bishop Otto of Bamberg, we are favourably disposed toward your requests. We receive into the protection

---

66 Agnes was married to the count-palatine of Saxony, Frederick of Putelendorf (d. 1125). She and her sister, Adelheid, were granddaughters of Judith of Schweinfurt, a prominent heiress from the region west of Bamberg.

67 For ministerials, see the general introduction.

68 Conrad (Cuno) of Zütphen, duke of Bavaria (1049–53), was the first husband of Judith of Schweinfurt. Thus, the properties mentioned in this chapter all seem to have been part of the extensive Schweinfurter inheritance.

69 Count Godebold II of Henneberg, burgrave of Würzburg (1096–1144).

70 This privilege of Pope Calixtus II (1119–24) dates from 3 April 1123: *Germania Pontificia* III.3, 265–6, nr. 50.

of blessed Peter and his Roman church these monasteries, which must be defended against the wickedness of perverse men: St John the Baptist in Reinsdorf, St John the Evangelist in Michelfeld, St James in Ensdorf, St Lawrence the martyr in Vessra, and St George the martyr in Prüfening. You constructed them at your own expense, you gave them to the Bamberg church, and you asked that they be strengthened by the protection of the apostolic see. Therefore, we establish that all the possessions, estates and properties, which your fraternity granted to the same monasteries out of consideration of divine love, and those which the other faithful have given as a lawful offering, and those which might happen to be acquired or offered justly and legally in the future, remain secure and undiminished for these monasteries, with the Lord as surety. Also, let them receive the ordinations of their abbots or monks from the catholic diocesan bishops. Also, we decree that the care and administration of these monasteries' properties should remain in yours and your successors' authority and power. Also, let no man have the opportunity to disturb the same monasteries, or take away their possessions, or keep the possessions they take away, or diminish and exhaust them imprudently. But let all their things be preserved intact, for the sustenance and management of those to whom they were granted, and let them be useful and beneficial in all ways. Therefore, if any secular or ecclesiastical person, knowing this document with our decree, should try to challenge it rashly, let him be warned a second and third time; if the person should not make amends with suitable satisfaction, let him lose the dignity of his office and his honour, and let him learn that he is, by divine judgement, guilty on account of the perpetrated injustice. And let him become unworthy of the most sacred body and blood of God and of our lord redeemer Jesus Christ, and let him be subject to strict retribution in the Final Judgement. On the other hand, may those protecting these same monasteries' rights have the peace of our lord Jesus Christ, so that they may secure the fruits of their good deeds here and may discover the rewards of eternal peace before the strict Judge. Written by the hand of Gervase, scribe and notary of the holy palace.

[22.] It is pleasing to consider now with what zeal and with what diligence he wanted the order of the holy, monastic way of life to be observed in his monasteries. For this reason, after he had requested from the Roman see a papal privilege of confirmation, he received a document of this sort:[71]

Bishop Innocent, servant of the servants of God, to the venerable brother Bishop Otto of Bamberg and to all his successors canonically placed in his

71 This privilege of Pope Innocent II (1130–43) dates from 28 October 1131: *Germania Pontificia* III.3, 268, nr. 57.

position, greetings and apostolic blessing. As often as that is sought from us, which is known to accord with honesty and the religious way of life, it is proper that we grant it with a cheerful spirit and that we impart a suitable decision, so that faithful devotion may obtain swift effect. Venerable brother Bishop Otto, we therefore agree to your petition's requests, mercifully, from the accustomed gentleness of the apostolic see. We establish, first and foremost, that the condition of the monastic way of life, which was instituted in the churches entrusted to you through your diligence and with the Lord cooperating, be preserved firmly and continuously in these times. Also, we establish that no one may be placed in the same churches through the heresy of simony, but let honourable people be appointed there, who are recommended especially by the dignity of their character and their standing. Also, we decree that the rule of the holy, monastic way of life should remain in the monasteries, which either were constructed long ago in your diocese, or which you established yourself in view of devotion, or which you were able to unite to your church in other just ways, or finally which were constructed within your diocese by another of the faithful inspired by divine grace. Let no one be permitted to change the form of the same monastic regulation in any way, unless by chance he should want to advance it toward the privilege of a better condition, with the Lord assisting. And let this not be entrusted to the sole judgement of anyone; rather, we establish that it ought to be done with the advice and consent of all the monasteries pertaining to the Bamberg church, or to the sounder part.[72] If anyone should try to challenge this decree rashly, let him be warned a second and third time; if he does not set his deed right with suitable satisfaction, let him become unworthy of the most sacred body and blood of God and of our lord redeemer Jesus Christ, and let him be subject to strict retribution in the Final Judgement. Let those protecting the rights of the same places acquire our grace and the grace of the omnipotent God and the blessed apostles Peter and Paul.

[23.] I judge that this must not be omitted: he rebuilt the monastery of St Michael [i.e., Michelsberg in Bamberg] from its foundations with the entrance hall and all of the buildings of the cloister and also the basilica of St Mary with the sacristy and the chapel of blessed Bartholomew; he built the chapel above the gate too, and also the lodging house and the circuit of the wall with all the workshops.[73]

---

72 This language of the 'sounder part' is taken from the discussion of abbatial elections in the Benedictine Rule: *RB 1980: the rule of St Benedict*, 280–5, ch. 64.

73 For this monastery, see above, n. 56. Otto's construction projects occurred in the period 1117–21, after an earthquake in 1117 had damaged the monastery.

[24.] The same blessed man ordered a well to be made in the middle of the cloister [i.e., Michelsberg], and he also made a watercourse, at great expense, that led fresh water from a neighbouring mountain into the cloister through lead pipes. He granted to the same place very many furnishings, among them two silver bowls for receiving offerings, and a very precious chasuble with a gold-embroidered border. He also gave a cross fashioned nobly with gold and gems, with the salvific wood[74] hidden in it along with relics of the saints, which he named the Saviour's Cross; he offered it most devotedly to the blessed Archangel [i.e., Michael] with the threat of his ban, declaring that it was never to be removed from that monastery for any emergency.[75] For that man, worthy to God, loved this place always and cherished it; he restored this monastery, enriched it, sought its glory, granted property to it, elevated it,[76] and decreed he was to be buried in it.[77] Indeed, the same man gave to the monastery for the use of the brothers eight estates purchased for almost 500 pounds, establishing that a light be tended day and night continuously at his tomb, and that on the anniversary of his death an extra allowance be offered to the brothers, both canons and monks, and additional alms for the poor.

[25.] Having run through these things, it seems worth the effort for me to describe the buildings that this blessed man constructed in diverse places, besides those mentioned above. In the cathedral,[78] he laid the floor, decorated the columns with gypsum work, elevated the choir of St George, ordered painting to be done, covered the same church with a copper roof, and finally made new all the buildings of the cloister for each kind of workshop. Concerning these things, I deem it superfluous to relate more, especially because viewing the appearance of the church and cloister shows these things better. This church stands out so much in workmanship and decoration from almost all the churches of the kingdom that, not without merit, with us silent, it invites any curious viewer to praise its builder.[79] For all of this, he gave – among other

---

74 i.e., a piece of the true cross.

75 Cf. *The deeds of Margrave Wiprecht of Groitzsch*, in which some of the objects granted to the monastery of Pegau are sold or pawned.

76 See p. 107 above, where comparable language is used for Prüfening.

77 For his burial at Michelsberg, see p. 149.

78 i.e., the cathedral church in Bamberg.

79 Unfortunately, there was a fire in the cathedral in 1185. The cathedral that stands in Bamberg today was built in the thirteenth century.

things – an estate at Mainroth, which brings revenues of twenty talents annually and which he had bought for thirty pounds of silver and a talent of gold.[80] He established that ten talents from these should belong to them [i.e., the cathedral canons] as an extra allowance, and the other part should belong to the hospital house of St George.[81]

[26.] Furthermore, he gave to St Stephen's as an offering for the brothers an estate, which brings eleven ounces each year;[82] seven of these ounces provide an extra allowance for them in remembrance of the anniversary of his death, while the other four ounces belong to them for their annual market right. Also, among his other good works of piety there, he built a cloister with workshops and constructed a tower.

He gave very many properties to the brothers of St James and finished the towers of the church.[83]

At St Gangolf, he built the towers and gave several properties to the brothers.[84]

He also constructed the chapel of St Egidius with its hospital building, granting to the same place estates that bring twenty talents annually.[85]

Also, beyond the river, he built the chapel of St Gertrude with its hospital building.[86] He assigned very many estates to it and decreed that thereafter six pennies be given each day for receiving pilgrims. He provided very many other properties – to enumerate them would take too long – to these and other places. And these are in Bamberg! For, *uncertain is the number*[87] of churches, houses and towers he constructed in other regions: in towns and in their environs, in castles, villages, valleys and mountains.

---

80 A talent (*talentum*) was a unit of weight; in Germany in this period it was equivalent to a pound. The 'twenty talents' in revenue here is almost certainly silver, since the silver penny (*denarius*) was the only coin in circulation during this time. Gold, of significantly higher value than silver, is usually stipulated explicitly, as it is here with 'a talent of gold'.

81 i.e., the hospital affiliated with the cathedral. See *Die Prüfeninger Vita*, 72–3, n. 183.

82 St Stephen's in Bamberg, a collegiate church founded c. 1007–9.

83 St James's in Bamberg, a collegiate church founded c. 1065.

84 St Gangolf's in Bamberg, a collegiate church founded c. 1057–59.

85 The St. Egidius hospital in Bamberg was founded by Otto in or before the year 1112.

86 The Regnitz River divides Bamberg. The hospital of St Gertrude was established in what is now the Theuerstadt section of Bamberg in 1102/03.

87 Job 15:20.

[27.] In addition, he acquired innumerable properties by beneficial foresight for his own holy church.[88] Among these, he subjected to episcopal authority and power six fortifications, which had not been held prior to him [i.e., by the church of Bamberg]. Of these, he acquired the castle called Pottenstein,[89] situated nearly in the middle of his bishopric, for 530 pounds of silver and seventeen talents of gold, providing in this way not a little increase in peace for both himself and his successors. It is certain that, with the properties of the church placed in a circle all around, there is the firm protection of defence, *there is a tower of strength against the face of the* ravaging *enemies.*[90]

[28.] In the diocese of Passau, the church of Bamberg has held up until now all the tithes from its own possessions; a bishop of the same place, by the name Reginmar, attempted to take these tithes away from it.[91] But the pious Otto perceived that the loss to his church on account of this would not be small, and he wanted to be mindful of that church's advantage in all ways. So he gave the parish of Münsteuer and one vineyard through the hand of King Henry [V] to the Passau church.[92] In addition, he gave a talent of gold to the bishop, and in this way, he confirmed for the Bamberg church every right to the tithes, having received this right from the hand of Ulrich, advocate of Passau.[93]

Otto also acquired the tithes from newly cultivated lands in the Regensburg bishopric in a reasonable exchange. Then, two Roman pontiffs (Honorius and Innocent)[94] and three Regensburg bishops succeeding one another in order (namely Hartwig, Conrad and Henry)[95] confirmed by privilege the firmest guarantees for his own holy church in perpetuity; and he assigned the tithes to the monastery of blessed

---

88 The diocesan church of Bamberg is meant here.

89 See *Die Prüfeninger Vita*, 74, n. 202 and *Heiligenleben zur deutsch-slawischen Geschichte*, 140, n. 55 for more on the location of this castle.

90 Psalm 60:4.

91 Bishop Reginmar of Passau (1121–38). For the significance of tithes in this period, see Eldevik, *Episcopal power*.

92 There is no extant charter of Emperor Henry V concerning this grant.

93 See *Die Regesten der Bischöfe von Passau 731–1206*, 166, nr. 545. The advocate of Passau at this time was Ulrich of Wilhering-Waxenberg.

94 A privilege of Pope Honorius II (1124–30) from 21 January 1125–30, and a privilege of Pope Innocent II (1130–43) from 22 October 1136 are meant here. See *Germania Pontificia* I, 296–7, nr. 2 and 297, nr. 4.

95 Bishop Hartwig I of Regensburg (1105–26); Bishop Conrad I of Regensburg (1126–32); and Bishop Henry I of Regensburg (1132–55).

George [i.e., Prüfening], which he constructed in Bavaria, and granted them to the servants of Christ living there for their food and clothing.

[29.] So that it would be impossible for any of the bishops succeeding him to add anything to his arrangements or to rescind what he had well ordered, the apostolic see favourably received his petition about these matters and presented to him a document of confirmation of this sort:[96]

Bishop Calixtus, servant of the servants of God, to the venerable brother Bishop Otto of Bamberg, greetings and apostolic blessing. The teachings of the holy fathers and the canonical decrees demonstrate that the estates and possessions of churches, which are called – not without merit – the pledges of the faithful, the redemption prices of sinners and the patrimonies of the poor, ought not to be sold or alienated. For they are devoted to the service of the divine majesty and the benefit of the heavenly mysteries, and it is not appropriate for them to be received into another's right or changed in form to another kind of service. Truly, let us speak with the words of the blessed Pope Symmachus: 'We do not permit the possessions that anyone gave or bequeathed by free will to a church for its own use to be alienated by any claim whatsoever, or by selling them piecemeal, or by any sort of pretext.'[97] *Therefore, we agree to your just requests and ordain by our present document's confirmation that the* mansi, *which were given for the service of your episcopal table, remain, in future times, in the same condition in which they are recognized to be well administered by you. We decree that none of your successors or any other person is permitted to sell them or hand them over in benefice to laymen or exchange them for other benefits. But, just as you arranged, one penny from each of the aforesaid* mansi *shall be assigned every year to the Bamberg church for the soul of Emperor Henry* [II], *its founder, in order to furnish lights.*[98] *Also, let no one have the ability in the future to alter the abbeys and houses of regular canons, strengthened through your hard work in the order of the monastic way of life, nor the other houses you established properly. Moreover, if anyone presumes to challenge this our confirmation by a rash undertaking, he will be subject to the chain of excommunication.*

[30.] The blessed bishop, although he was complete in God and preferred to devote all his things to heavenly treasures, nevertheless, since he

---

96 This privilege of Pope Calixtus II (1119–24) dates from 13 April 1124: *Germania Pontificia* III.3, 266–7, nr. 51.

97 From a letter of Pope Symmachus in the Pseudo-Isidorean Decretals: *Decretales Pseudo-Isidorianae*, 657.

98 Emperor Henry II (1002–24).

was capable and prudent, rendered to God the things that are God's and did not deny to the world what was the world's.[99] For he served the kings of the world honourably and faithfully, above all other bishops, at home and abroad. He earned the familiarity of the princes too. He preserved unviolated for his church's ministerials their special rights.[100] Finally, he protected his household and everything attached to it with the strongest guard of piety and with the wing of maternal affection.

[31.] But I think that this should not be omitted: after the whole church of Bamberg flourished again, restored to a state of pristine splendour by the kindness of its pastor, it also began to flourish through his hard work in the study of all learning. For he took care to put very excellent masters in charge in his church, and people saw their honest life and splendid talents. And because the church's pastor was dedicated to works of mercy and the ecclesiastical school abounded in the study of all learning, as was said, it happened that a very great multitude of noble and rich clerics, but especially of the poor and pilgrims, coming from diverse and remote parts of the world, flocked there. They did so, because sustenance and instruction were made available to them there, provided by the kindness of that father.

[32.] That blessed man was always joined to strangers and the destitute by the deepest love for compassion, such that he frequently took up the company of pilgrims and of those accustomed to visit the sepulchre of the Lord and the threshold of the apostles and other places of the saints for the sake of prayer.[101] The devout man offered that they participate daily in his prayers, and in return he took care to recommend himself to their prayers very intently. Moreover, if at any time he was asked something in God's name by any of the needy, he stopped [what he was doing] immediately in reverence of the Lord's name, and he did not presume to proceed further before he heard the request of the person who had approached him to ask a favour.

But because we have mentioned briefly these things concerning his first works, and since we have begun to speak about pilgrims, let us

---

99 Cf. Matthew 22:21; Mark 12:17; and Luke 20:25.

100 A charter of Bishop Gunther of Bamberg from c. 1060 had guaranteed the rights of the church's ministerials while detailing their duties and obligations. See Arnold, *German knighthood*, 27.

101 The 'sepulchre of the Lord' is a reference to pilgrimages to Jerusalem; the 'threshold of the apostles' is a reference to pilgrimages to Rome. For the latter, see *The deeds of Margrave Wiprecht of Groitzsch*, p. 56.

make an end to these things and come to the start of his pilgrimage
and preaching.

Prologue of the second book

As I mentioned before in the last part of this work, it is not my plan
to set forth in writing everything I have learned about the venerable
man Bishop Otto, but only those things that are most well known –
although I would have omitted very many of these out of zeal for
brevity. For I have judged it sufficient to record only excellent things,
because one must look out for the readers, lest a heaped up abundance
of actions elicit from them any disgust.[102] For this reason, I have not
crowded everything into one part, but I have separated it into three
parts, the first of which has already been set forth. I have designated
these beforehand with their chapters and prefaces, so that the reading
may be less disagreeable, when it is resumed with a new beginning.

Book II

[1.] Meanwhile, pious Otto's heart grew hot with so great a desire for
pilgrimage and preaching that he decided to go to the regions of the
pagan Pomeranians, so that he might recall them from their error and
lead them toward the way of truth and to knowledge of Christ, the son
of God. After he had received permission to preach from Pope Calixtus
II of blessed memory and had selected suitable ministers from each and
every holy order as companions for his journey, he set out on his way
in the year of the incarnation of the Lord 1124, in the second indiction,[103]
in the month of June after the end of Pentecost.[104] Escorted honourably
by his men, he came to Bohemia. He was received there by the venerable
bishop of the city [i.e., Prague] and by all the clergy and people with

---

102 As is the case with the opening Prologue of this work, this one relies heavily on
   the Prologue to Sulpicius Severus's *Vita Sancti Martini.* See n. 5 above.

103 The indiction was a way of reckoning time, based on a cycle of fifteen years, that
   originated at the time of the Roman empire.

104 Pope Calixtus II (1119–24). Pentecost fell on 25 May in the year 1124, but the
   exact date of Otto's departure is unknown; see *Die Prüfeninger Vita*, 81, n. 12. See
   also *The 1125 continuation of Frutolf's chronicle*, 283, where the pope's approval of
   Otto's mission is also mentioned.

great honour and exultation.[105] There, as in all the churches he entered as far as the city of Gniezno, the response for the apostles was chanted on meeting the apostolic priest: '*The fellow-citizens of the apostles and the servants of God have come today, bringing peace and illuminating the fatherland, to give peace to the heathen and to free the people of the Lord.*'[106] This was done in such a way that you would have noticed he shared praise in common with the blessed apostles, with whom he shared his office in common too.

[2.] He rose then and said farewell to his friends and faithful followers, who had accompanied him as an escort. He departed from the land of the Czechs and directed his journey toward Poland. At length, when the journey was finished, Duke Bolesław of Poland received him honourably, for the duke rejoiced at that time in the arrival of such a great guest, no differently than if he had received the Saviour himself as a guest. Indeed, he did not just receive him devotedly; he also, as long as he was able, retained him kindly and treated him courteously. Then, when the bishop departed, the duke escorted him with so much courteous service that through every stage of his journey, up to the farthest limits of the duchy, the duke attended to him and his men generously. Thus, the duke had him conducted by industrious men, with the appropriate veneration, to Count Paul of Santok,[107] who was to conduct him just as honourably to Duke Warcisław of Pomerania.[108] Paul, after he had received the bishop, escorted him in great haste with almost sixty *milites* to that duke.[109] The duke, when he heard news of his arrival, joyfully came to meet the approaching bishop with no fewer than 300 armed men near the river Warta.

[3.] Now Warcisław had already abandoned the worship of idols and had received the basics of the true faith some time ago. For this reason, it happened that the barbarian people, whom he held under his authority,

105 Bishop Meinhard of Prague (1122–34).

106 This was a common response during the Mass to celebrate the entrance of a bishop; see *Die Prüfeninger Vita*, 82, n. 17. Notker the Stammerer also reports that Charlemagne's father Pippin entered Rome to the same welcome: Notker the Stammerer, *The deeds of Charlemagne*, II.15, 106.

107 Santok was an important border fortification for the Poles along the frontier with Pomerania. Nothing else is known about Count Paul.

108 Duke Warcisław I of Pomerania, who appears in sources from the 1120s and early 1130s.

109 For the term *milites*, see the general introduction.

detested him on account of their hatred for Christ's name. Thus, he rejoiced exceedingly at the bishop's arrival, since that man was about to guide the same nation, freed from the darkness of unbelief, to faith. Immediately, he bound two *milites*, who had also come to believe earlier, to the bishop's service; he made it their duty to escort the holy priest of the Lord through unknown places and protect him from the unbelievers' attacks. However, the bishop, on account of the fact that it was evident that these two had been in contact with pagans, first announced their penance; only then did he want to have contact with them and converse with them and share a common table.[110] However, he made the penance announced for them mild, so that the men, up until then rough in faith, neither became weaker, oppressed by the burden of a harsh judgement, nor, on the other hand, did they believe that they were not at fault, as if the bishop had received them without any penance and had dismissed them unpunished.

[4.] He had already entered the outermost territory of the Pomeranians, where the city of Pyrzyce presented itself as the first front.[111] Scarcely had the bishop uttered the first word of prayer when – behold! – some men, who had made their homes not far off from the town, came together eagerly – stirred by divine inspiration – to gain the grace of holy baptism. This was done by the exalted plan of the Divinity, so that when he [i.e., Otto] perceived that the pagans had been guided by divine grace and were ready for the word, hoping a better end would arise from a good beginning, he would in no way cease the urgent preaching he had begun, overcome by the labour or broken by desperation. Therefore, he baptized everyone whom he found there, and only then did he enter the city of Pyrzyce. When he finished preaching, he baptized almost 500 people of both sexes.

After he gave them regulations for preserving the faith, he came in a similar way to another city, called Kamień Pomorski, with the Lord supporting him. Truly, while he preached there for three full months, he converted to the Lord 3,585 of both sexes. Each may see in this

---

110 It was a sin for Christians to consort with pagans; see below, p. 134.

111 Throughout Books II and III of the text, I have chosen to translate *civitas* as 'city'. Wolin and Szczecin were unquestionably large, important centres in this period, worthy of that title. But the author routinely uses *civitas* to describe almost every place Otto visited during his missions. This may well be a subtle form of exaggeration, in order to imply that the towns where Otto was preaching were much larger than they really were.

what he wants to see. Some may wonder at the faith received by the pagans, others at the hard work of this singular teacher. I, to be clear, because I do not doubt that all these things return glory to God, consider nothing in all of them so wondrous as this: that the more this great man preached a call for justice, the more he converted, because omnipotent God inspired his faithful follower with certain (so I would say) rewards, until he might grant him numerous fruits in return for his numerous labours.

[5.] Thereafter, the third city was Wolin. It derived its name from Julius Caesar, who had built it a long time ago, and it was situated near the Oder River not far from the sea.[112] When the inhabitants of Wolin heard that many of the inhabitants of Kamień Pomorski had received the doctrine of faith, they did not accept this with even mindedness.[113] They [i.e., the inhabitants of Wolin] came together, dismayed, and began not only to deride the converts but also to disparage the holy bishop and his companions. Indeed, they called the bishop a magician and impostor, and the inhabitants of Kamień Pomorski foolish destroyers of the fatherland, who had renounced the laws of their fathers and had attempted to follow the error of a foreign people.

Therefore, the holy prelate decided to go to this city, and he asked for and received from Duke Warcisław an escort there. In every town he entered, he withdrew into the duke's residence, since the people would not rage against someone who had taken refuge under the protection of their prince. For these pagans preserved that ancient custom that as long as someone lived freely in the prince's house, he should endure no trouble from anyone – unless, after the prince had been consulted first, he should be shown to be guilty of a grave crime. Otherwise, there was hardly a safe place remaining anywhere for the bishop to stay. Indeed, he could not present himself for public appearances without grave danger to him and his men. For every time he appeared in public to preach, you would have seen the barbarians with swords and clubs, *just as chance had armed them.*[114] They erupted in competition: some hurled dust, others

---

112 In Latin, Wolin is Iulin (Julin), giving it a name similar to that of Julius Caesar. Hence, this foundation myth, despite the fact that Julius Caesar was never anywhere near the region of Pomerania.

113 The text uses the terms *Iulinenses* and *Chaminenses* to refer to the inhabitants of these cities; I have chosen to translate these as 'the inhabitants of Wolin' and 'the inhabitants of Kamień Pomorski' to avoid unnecessarily complicated terminology.

114 Sallust, *The War with Catiline*, 56.3.

repeatedly threw stones. They gnashed their teeth and shouted loudly, such that they all seemed to have conspired equally in the death of this one man, having overlooked no method of injuring him.

[6.] Seeing this, the bishop thought to approach them in another way, so that he might conquer with gifts those whom he had not been able to conquer with reason. For up until that time, the inhabitants of Wolin had venerably worshipped – and *I do not know whether I should laugh or cry* about this[115] – Julius Caesar's lance, which they had preserved.[116] This lance was so worn away by rust that the iron parts would not be of any use in the future. Nevertheless, the bishop, in order that he might free them from such great error, wanted to buy it for 50 talents of silver. He did not consider this expenditure from his own things to be a great burden in any way, provided that the pagans, having sold this fake, bought their salvation. Indeed, the bishop thought to do this as a faithful and prudent negotiator, for whom business was conducted on the basis of the salvation of souls. But the pagans, impious and unbelieving as they were, refused vehemently, saying that the lance was of a very divine nature, that nothing transitory or perishable could be compared to it, and hence that for no price would it ever be torn away from them. It was evident that the lance was their protection, a defence for their fatherland and their symbol of victory.

Meanwhile, when the bishop, venerable and worthy to God, was addressing the people in splendid language – behold! – someone from the crowd, raging and full of frenzy,[117] rushed at the holy priest and struck him so strongly with a green piece of wood he was holding by chance in his hand that he [i.e., Otto] was cast to the ground and seemed lifeless as he lay there. One of his companions, whom the spirit of God had touched very deeply, saw the priest lying there from a distance; he shouted, 'Thanks be to God', because he believed that the bishop had been killed innocently by the guilty and had achieved the glory of a martyr. He was not mistaken in his opinion, because, even though the bishop escaped the hands of his persecutor, nevertheless he did not deserve to lose the martyr's palm, which he desired. Meanwhile, that man [i.e., Otto] was helped up by others' hands, and he spread out

---

115 Jerome, *Epistulae*, 51.5.1.

116 See above, n. 112.

117 Cf. Luke 12:13 and Sulpicius Severus, *Dialogus Tertius*, 15.2 (*The Third Dialogue*, 246).

his own hands to the heavens, rejoicing and giving thanks to God that he had merited receiving at least one blow in his [i.e., God's] name.

[7.] What more is there to say? The barbaric people did not fear to rage constantly against the holy priest of the Lord – to such a degree that, after they had inflicted him with the grave injustice of their words and blows, they finally drove him from their territory. He left the town, and he arranged to remain with his companions on the other bank of the aforesaid river for about a week, until he learned how this business would end. For he hoped that the pagans, after they had considered reason, could be changed more easily to mildness if perhaps he withdrew from them a little ways, since they hated his presence so much. But his hard work made no progress on this. You would have seen the barbarians, their spirits inflamed, rage more and more wildly that they would never believe, except on the advice of the inhabitants of Szczecin. The distinguished preacher should preferably go and convert them, since they were considered the leaders of the whole people [i.e., the Pomeranians]. Then, after those people had converted, nothing would remain for them but to follow, as quickly as possible, the path of truth the bishop had promised to show them. They were not saying this in order to follow the inhabitants of Szczecin toward life, but because they thought they were sending the bishop toward death. They believed, without a doubt, that those people, who surpassed the others in their multitude and power, would be more willing to lay hands on the bishop.

At length, after the bishop had consulted with his men, he determined to put himself at risk. He anticipated, on account of Jesus' benevolence, that those whom he could not conquer with human intellect, the more glorious son of God would triumph over afterwards. Thus, he left the inhabitants of Wolin behind and, ascending the Oder by ship, arrived at the city of Szczecin. It stretched from the foot of a mountain to its heights and was fortified by three different sorts of natural and man-made defences.[118] It was considered the capital of the whole province.

[8.] In this city, for nine straight weeks, he stood firm and did not stop preaching the word of life. However, the hardened pagans refused to hear or receive the doctrine of faith. He went out into public every Sunday in order to preach, clothed in his priestly vestments, not only

---

118 Archaeological evidence confirms that Szczecin was a large town, with perhaps 5,000 inhabitants in this period, and possessed a well-fortified castle hill. See Leciejewicz, 'Die Entstehung der Stadt Szczecin', 225–6.

to imbue his sermon with more authority but also to soothe the pagans' savage hearts with his white appearance. But the barbaric people, still persisting in their unbelief, turned to sticks and stones, as was their custom, such that they frequently attacked the holy priest with clubs and rocks. The armed people drove him away with these things, which he had tried to restrain them from worshipping.

One day, he was holding the pastoral staff in his hand and preaching the word of the Lord. Because there was much opposition, a certain man threw a rock and wounded the bishop's hand gravely, such that he also struck the staff with the rock's blow. Nevertheless the bishop, lest by chance this be seen and bragged about afterwards, had the mark on the damaged staff polished and removed. Then, the bishop really did not know what to do, where to turn. Should he insist on preaching? But the crowd of pagans had been unable to see the bishop or hear Christ. Should he stop preaching? But the obligation to preach, his neighbour's need, and Christ's charity all pressed him to be an example. And so, completely *converted to the Lord*,[119] he prayed for his [i.e., the Lord's] help both day and night, spending all his time (which was not spent caring for his body) in psalmody and prayer together with his clerics, who numbered eighteen. Not long after, the Lord arranged to put an end to these great labours. Accordingly, he lent a ready ear to his faithful servant, who was praying for the salvation of the pagans, and deigned to collect them immediately for his holy church through his ministry.

[9.] For these people, the first opportunity for conversion and salvation was this: Domasław, one of the foremost men of the city, formerly a Christian, had received two sons from his still pagan wife.[120] However, overcome by his illicit love for her, he deserted his faith and abandoned these infants to the darkness of unbelief. Later, after they had finished their pubescent years, although they were attractive in appearance, perceptive in nature, and prudent in eloquence – oh the pain! – they were ignorant of their creator, the creator of all things, the son of God. These boys began to frequent the bishop's private chamber by God's will and to confer often with him in conversation. The bishop talked

---

119 2 Corinthians 3:16.

120 In Ebo of Michelsberg's *vita* of Bishop Otto, this Domasław is described as being of noble descent and as being a trusted adviser of Duke Warcisław I of Pomerania. See *Heiligenleben zur deutsch-slawischen Geschichte*, 230.

briefly and suitably to them – to the extent their age permitted – about the illumination of faith, the future judgement, the immortality of the soul, the hope of resurrection, and the glory of the blessed. Finally, lamenting their ignorance and the error of unbelief instilled as it were by birth, he said, 'Alas, little children, do you not listen to anything from us, who have come for the sake of your salvation? Why do you refuse to recognize him, who made you of such excellent form? Come, dearest ones, to the true and catholic faith; recognize the creator of you and all things, so that in the eyes of him, by whom you were created, you might be able to discover grace and mercy.'

He added some other words to these, and he restored them with the word of life, with food and drink. And he joyfully offered them some small presents now and then, of the sort that this age was doubtlessly accustomed to seek. Because of this, the boys' spirit was gradually guided toward the faith. At last, they broke out in this voice, with the Holy Spirit supporting them: 'Father, these things are new, which you provide; they were never announced to our ears. We heard that our father was once a Christian. There is no one who does not know that our mother is such a staunch pagan that he was corrupted by her example and her illicit love and fell from the faith. To be sure, we would meet with their displeasure, if we did anything else. Nevertheless, we declare that we will *put everything to the ultimate test*[121] for the faith, which you preach, provided that you, having sworn, assert in the name of your God, whose priest you are, that we, having turned from the laws of our fathers,[122] will be blessed with Christ.'

The bishop was amazed by the children's unexpected faith, and he promised them eternal life and salvation, if indeed they persisted in this intention. What more is there to say? The boys were baptized on the feast of the blessed martyrs Crispin and Crispian [25 October], not without serious risk to their lives, because their father had been absent for a long time and their mother, likewise, knew absolutely nothing about it. For they did not dare to disclose their feelings to her in any way, because they no doubt feared that they would suffer either death or harsh bodily tortures. But omnipotent God – *who, although he may be great in great things, nevertheless performs wonders more gloriously in the smallest things*[123] – not only freed the boys from their parents'

121 Sallust, *The War with Catiline*, 26.5.

122 Cf. 2 Machabees 7:24.

123 *Corpus Orationum*, III, nos. 1778–9.

hands but also converted their parents and their fatherland to recognition of his name by their example.

[10.] Scarcely had those things transpired when – behold! – the prelate's messengers, whom he had sent a little while before to the duke of the Poles to complain about his rejection and the injury inflicted on him, returned. Others from the duke's side arrived with them, carrying both harsh mandates for the pagans and pleasing ones for the bishop. For they said that their lord was moved with the appropriate indignation when he learned that they were harassing the bishop with all sorts of injuries, and he warned them that by no means should the bishop have any trouble thereafter. Otherwise, he would arrive with an army as quickly as possible and exact the greatest revenge upon them in the custom of victors. But if they consented to listen to the bishop and to receive the word of God, they would suffer no harm from him or any of his men. On the contrary, they would have perpetual peace, just like other Christians, provided that they did not refuse in any way to preserve their faith toward him and to go with him against his enemies, as often as his private necessity or the utility of the *res publica* demanded it.[124]

So, having been given this choice, the pagans called together innumerable people from the countryside and villages and inquired diligently which of the two they should choose. There were many speeches in favour of one or the other. At last, they promised that they would do everything commanded, provided that they would be safe henceforth from the slaughter, fires and other hostilities of the sort they had often endured before from the same duke.

[11.] After this promise had been made, the bishop rejoiced at Christ's glory. But he refused to hand them the sacraments of the faith until they destroyed the temples of their gods and finally cleansed their city of all the filth of idolatry. Now, in this city were two houses, which their ancestors called *continas*, because enclosed inside them were images of the gods.[125] These houses were built with enormous care and skill and were not separated from one another by very much space. In them,

---

124 I have chosen to leave untranslated *res publica*, literally 'public affairs,' rather than rendering it as 'State' or something comparable.

125 In the language of the western Slavs, a *kotina* was a small house containing religious images and other religious accessories. See Moszyński, *Die vorchristliche Religion*, 118–20.

the foolish populace of pagans worshiped the god Triglav.[126] In addition, the townspeople were accustomed to feed a horse of outstanding appearance, who was called the god Triglav's horse. For his saddle was decorated with gold and silver, as might befit a god, and was watched over in one of the *continas* by a priest of the idols. Evidently, the divine horse was fitted out with this saddle and appeared at the appointed time and place, when that pagan people, deluded by diverse errors, came together to seek auguries.

Indeed, there was a custom of this sort concerning auguries: after a great many spears had been placed in a scattered fashion, they made Triglav's horse pass through them. If it so happened that the horse touched none of them while walking around, it seemed a strong augury that they should proceed and mount their horses in order to pillage. But if it happened to touch any of them while walking, they judged the possibility of riding to be divinely forbidden to them. In that case, they immediately gathered together to cast lots, so that they might learn, by considering these, whether they would be better off pillaging by boat or on foot. They were accustomed to pay a tithe from all the plunder they took, and they always frequented the aforesaid *continas*, ready to consult the god Triglav about any sort of occurrence.

[12.] In the end, those temples were given over into the bishop's power, and on his command, they were pulled down and destroyed in such a way that you would have seen their timbers eagerly dragged off, not only by the faithful but also by the idol-worshippers. These timbers were not only useful for honouring the divinities of old and protecting the symbols of the gods; they were also useful for fuelling fires and cooking turnips! All those things that had been offered in the temples he sprinkled with holy water and returned to the inhabitants, in order that those things they had offered improperly he might distribute properly; he redirected things that had been delivered up for diabolic services toward the uses of men. For he did not wish to take any of these things for himself, although in that place very many gold and silver vessels, among other things, were kept. Truly, that seemed wondrous and very praiseworthy to the pagans, especially because he, who persuaded men to despise the world, spurned and had contempt

---

126 Here, and in the other two early Otto *vitae* as well, Triglav is identified as the most important god of the Pomeranians. See Moszyński, *Die vorchristliche Religion*, 73–5 and *Heiligenleben zur deutsch-slawischen Geschichte*, 240 and 398.

for those things *that mortals prize most highly*, namely silver and gold.[127]
He destroyed the statue of Triglav himself, but its three silver heads,
from which the name Triglav comes,[128] he later took away with him
from there; afterwards, he sent them to Pope Calixtus [II] of blessed
memory – with the appropriate giving of thanks to Christ – in witness
of his labour and of the conversion and belief of those pagans.[129]

[13.] In truth, I could not easily explain how great his zeal for discretion
was, when he then turned his attention to baptizing the men and women,
boys and girls. Indeed, though he invited everyone to secure the grace
of holy baptism, he himself furnished it only for men. For he preferred
that newborn infants and all women of any age or condition be baptized
by others, lest you might for this reason deny the reverence owed to
the priest – the priest who fulfilled his ministry in such a way that he
saw nothing shameful, he touched nothing inappropriate. Moreover, he
arranged that men and women be baptized separately, so that there
would be absolutely nothing that might upset or disturb the view of
those doing the baptizing or being baptized. Afterwards, he refreshed
liberally with food and drink everyone of middle rank and of the poor
who had been baptized, and he also gave them some clothes. He bestowed
rings and belts, sandals, gold embroideries and some other precious
gifts on the sons of nobles and the powerful, and he received some of
them from the holy font himself.

Truly, he provided everything that seemed necessary for completing
what had been instituted for this sacred mystery. He carried the water
on his shoulders. He ordered the barrels to be set in pits and made level
with the ground, so that those being baptized might descend into them
without difficulty. He omitted nothing, intentionally or unintentionally,
that might be consistent with honesty or faith in such business. And as
soon as he had purified this place and its pagan people of the filth of
idols, he constructed a church there, which he consecrated in honour
of the blessed martyr Adalbert. He believed that Adalbert, who had
previously offered his own blood to convert to Christ non-believers
in the same nation and of the same language, would without a doubt

---

127 Cf. Sallust, *The War with Jugurtha*, 41.1; Sulpicius Severus, *Dialogus Primus*, 5.5
    (*The First Dialogue*, 167).

128 Triglav means 'three-headed'.

129 Pope Calixtus II died on 13 or 14 December 1124, meaning he would not have
    received the gift.

lift up that young church with his services and intercessions.[130] He constructed and consecrated another church as well, before the gate of the same city, in honour of the blessed apostles Peter and Paul, so that the pagans converted to God might rejoice at the protection and services of the princes of the apostles, with whose teachings they had been filled.

[14.] Meanwhile, the Lord, *by a great and wonderful miracle,*[131] strengthened the tender faith of the pagans and praised his priest. For a certain woman had gone out into a field to gather grain on a Sunday – against the bishop's prohibition. But suddenly, her left hand holding the crops touched her right hand holding the sickle and became stiff; falling down, she died. Truly, everyone felt wonder and, especially, terror. It was given to them to understand clearly what sorts of punishments they would be given thereafter – on account of their more serious sins – considering that the Lord had punished such a transgression by no other means than a sentence of death.

Then, after everyone had been comforted in the faith of the Lord, the blessed priest came by ship on the Oder to a certain small city called 'Gridiz'.[132] Thereafter he sailed again to another site on the coast, which is called Lubin, and after very many in both places had converted, he made haste to see the inhabitants of Szczecin again.

[15.] There, after everything had been duly arranged, he foresaw that there was still not a little work for him in converting others. He said farewell to these people, who were just like dearest children whom he had begotten in Christ through the gospel.[133] Thus, he confidently approached those who had driven him away earlier, namely the inhabitants of Wolin. They, supported by divine grace, ran toward the arriving bishop, and they finally received him with the appropriate veneration. They said that they had erred, that they had sinned, they who had

---

130 Saint Adalbert (Vojtěch), bishop of Prague, had died a martyr's death in 997 while trying to convert the Prussians (*not* the Pomeranians), who lived further northeastward along the Baltic coast.

131 Isaiah 29:14.

132 The identity of the city is uncertain. See *Die Prüfeninger Vita,* 101, n. 149 and *Heiligenleben zur deutsch-slawischen Geschichte,* 162, n. 25, where both argue for Nowe Warpno.

133 Cf. 1 Corinthians 4:15.

presumed to provoke such a great priest of the Lord in any way. They humbly asked that he, called forth by the example of God – who did not want the souls of those erring to perish, but rather their sins[134] – *forgive them this trespass*[135] and show them, freed from the darkness of unbelief, the light of truth. Then, the bishop gave thanks with paternal affection and instructed them fully in the faith of Christ. And he had them prepared for the salvific bath with penance and fasts. Because he had observed them to be thirsty for the font of life and eager in faith, he rejoiced, rendered thanks to the Lord, and cleansed all those rejoicing people with the baptism of Christ. There, such a multitude of those to be baptized flocked to him that their number exceeded by far those whom he had baptized at Szczecin.

[16.] Without delay, they turned over to the bishop's hand a *contina*, which contained among other sacred objects the holy lance of Julius Caesar that they worshipped.[136] At that place and time, the Lord deigned to perform a great miracle for the glory of his name. For there, where (as we said) that *contina* was located, the overflowing river had made a marsh, and at that time, because the water surrounded the temple on all sides, it was possible to approach that temple in only one place, by a bridge that extended across the marsh. When that *contina* submitted to the power of the bishop after the pagans were converted to the Lord, the place dried up so suddenly that everyone who had been present was amazed, because it was most certainly evident that it had been done by the Lord; for it surely could not have been done in so short a space of time by human device. Then, after the marsh had dried (to everyone's great amazement, as we said), he had the depression, which the repeated overflowing of the water had made, filled with a piled-up mound [i.e., of earth]. Next, he erected an oratory there in honour of the blessed Adalbert and adopted as an associate for him the blessed George[137] – both so that the Christian people might honour the martyr as their own patron, and also so that the Christian people might more easily obtain the desired abundance of heavenly mercies through an increased number of intercessors.

---

134 Cf. 2 Samuel 14:14.

135 Exodus 32:31.

136 See above, p. 122.

137 Saints Adalbert and George share the same feast day, 23 April.

[17.] There too, a short time after,[138] the Lord deigned to work through his servant with the same strength, but in a different element, to show him joining (not undeservedly) with the saints and apostolic men – so that he who had been illuminated by preaching might also glitter with miracles. For, impelled by their sins, the people of the city had turned away little by little from the path of truth, which the holy bishop had shown to them. And this progressed all the way to the point of madness, such that they erected idols, which they had formerly cast down, and celebrated profane and detestable festivals of their sacred rites. Meanwhile, you would have seen dramatic games performed through the whole city, mixed together with all sorts of clamour and uproar.

Suddenly, the city caught fire. It was impossible to know from where it had come, but it was thought that the fire had descended from above, that it was an avenger here below of the impiety permitted against God. The aforesaid church [i.e., of Adalbert and George], although provided with divine strength, looked like it had been made very cheaply, since it was built out of brushwood and was completely covered over with straw. And so, when the city caught fire, flames invaded that church's roof and after that, raging, jumped to the sanctuary. Then, in a wondrous way, without any hard work from human labour but as if from heaven, the fire was repelled and stood still – as if it exclaimed, by the turning back of its attack, that it did not dare to consume completely the bishop's labour, which it had touched just partly with a view to a greater miracle. For truly, they said it was a greater miracle that the material that had caught fire, which was very thin and which was always accustomed to feed a fire, was extinguished without human device, as if it had not even been touched by fire.

[18.] There, another very great miracle also came to pass, which should astound you equally. The fire's flames, when they were growing high up, invaded the church's interior too, and whatever they were able to touch in there. They completely consumed the covering that overspread the exterior of the altar – except for the image of the crucified Saviour, which had been painted on it. For the flames consumed the other images, namely of the blessed Mary and St John, which had been painted on one side and the other. But as we said, only the image of the Lord remained completely unharmed, in this way having been fully preserved

---

138 This story is set in the period between Otto's first and second missions to Pomerania.

in undiminished condition and form, as if it had been cut out on purpose. Behold, this is what we said: that the Lord deigned to exercise the same strength, but in a different element, since he who a short time before had dried the marsh from an inundation of water, a short time later cast out the flame of the fire from that new church. Finally, he preserved his image unharmed from the heat of the fire, while others on one side and the other were burning.

[19.] In addition, the bishop built and consecrated another church, before the same city's gate, in honour of the blessed archangel Michael, and there he intended to locate an episcopal seat. A certain priest by the name of Adalbert, who had been *a partner on land and sea* to him and *a companion and consoler on the entire pilgrimage*,[139] undertook the care of this church while the bishop still lived.[140] Afterwards, he [Bishop Otto] departed from that place and went to visit the inhabitants of Kamień Pomorski. He repeated to them everything pertaining to Christian worship.[141] Then, he proceeded with his companions to 'Cloden', which is a very large village situated in the recesses of a certain forest.[142] There, *an innumerable multitude of men*[143] converted at the first word of his preaching and submitted their necks to the Christian faith. And there, the bishop constructed a church in honour of the Holy Cross, in a sufficiently suitable way that he raised a banner of the cross there, where he had preached the glory of the cross. Afterwards, he came to certain men, who out of fear of the duke of Poland *were wandering* always *in exile, without any fixed abodes*.[144] Nevertheless, they had built a few houses on the seashore, since this afforded them a place of escape whenever the same duke invaded that same province of the Pomeranians, as he was accustomed to do. And so, when the place was discovered – because the bishop passed by them – they offered themselves voluntarily in order to secure the grace of baptism, and confessing the faith of the Lord, they were baptized immediately, however many they were.

---

139 Sulpicius Severus, *Dialogus Primus*, 23.2 (*The First Dialogue*, 192).

140 This Adalbert would be the first bishop of the Pomeranian church (1140–63/64). See below, p. 149, for the author's explanation for why he was not formally designated as bishop prior to Otto's death.

141 He had preached there already; see p. 120.

142 The identity is uncertain, but *Heiligenleben zur deutsch-slawischen Geschichte*, 412, n. 107 suggests Kłodkówo on the basis of recent excavations.

143 Judges 6:5.

144 Sallust, *The War with Catiline*, 6.1.

[20.] After he had finished these things, he went to yet another very great and wealthy city, which has the name Kołobrzeg. There, after very many had been baptized, he constructed a church, which he consecrated in honour of the blessed Mary, forever virgin. He did this so that she might ask for perpetual help for this pagan people who now believed, she who had brought forth from herself the incarnate son of God himself for the salvation of believers. In this place, the bishop lost a certain deacon named Herman, a companion in his journey, who drowned in the river that flowed past there.[145] He left behind the holy bishop and his companions, who were filled with enormous sorrow. The bishop immediately celebrated the funeral rites, in the middle of the same church. There, pouring forth many tears from deep inside, he handed over the pilgrim's bones to be buried honourably, calling upon the Creator of all things not to deny the fellowship of the heavenly citizens to that man, whom he had caused to be without fatherland, home, properties and all prosperity.

But let us leave behind these sad things and return to the order of his deeds. The bishop departed from that place and came to preach likewise in another city, which was called Białogard, deriving its name in that barbarous language from the beautiful site of that place.[146] He preached and baptized, and after he had baptized everyone whom he found, he constructed and consecrated in the same place a church in honour of All Saints, as a consummation of all his labours.

This was the total of the baptized: in his first visit [to Pomerania], he baptized 22,165 people.[147]

[21.][148] After they had been baptized, he constructed and consecrated churches in diverse places (as we said). And he taught them to keep these things according to the institutes of the holy fathers: namely, that they abstain on the sixth day [i.e., Friday] from meat and milk in the manner of other Christians; that they be free on the Lord's Day from every evil work; that they come to church ready to hear the divine office; and that they devote themselves zealously there to prayers. They should observe the saints' feast days with vigils and all diligence, according to

---

145 The river is the Parsęta, which flows into the sea at Kołobrzeg.

146 The name means 'white city'.

147 The source for this number is unclear.

148 This chapter is taken from Bishop Otto's report on his first mission to Pomerania, a text that was also copied into *The 1125 continuation of Frutolf's chronicle*, 282–4.

what was shown to them. They should strive to observe most holy Lent
very diligently with fasts, vigils, alms and prayers. They should bring
their infants for baptism on the holy Sabbath [i.e., Saturday] of Easter
and on Pentecost with candles and the cope, which is called the white
garment, and accompanied by the godparents. And they should bring
them to church, clothed in that garment of innocence, on every day until
the eighth day from the same Sabbath, and they should try to be present
for the celebration of the divine office. He enjoined this as well: that
they not put their daughters to death (a sin which flourished especially
among them); and also that they not hold their sons and daughters at
baptism, but that they seek godparents for them, and that they also keep
faith and friendship with these godparents like natural parents. He also
forbade that anyone take his godmother in marriage or his own relative
up to the sixth and seventh generation.[149] Each should be content with
one wife. They should not bury dead Christians alongside pagans in
woods or in fields, but in cemeteries, as is the custom of all Christians.
Nor should they place clubs on their tombs. They should reject every
pagan rite and depravity. They should not construct houses for idols.
They should not visit a soothsayer, and there should be no fortune-
telling. Also, they should eat nothing impure, nor an animal that died
of natural causes, nor a choked animal, nor a sacrificed animal, nor the
blood of animals. They should not communicate with pagans, nor should
they take food or drink with them or from their vessels. In all these
things, they should not return to pagan practice. He also enjoined that,
when they are well, they should come to the priests of the church and
confess their sins. When sick, on the other hand, they should call the
priests to them and confess their sins and receive the body of the Lord.
He also established that they perform penance for perjury and adultery,
homicide and other crimes according to canonical precepts and that they
be obedient in every Christian duty and observance. Women, after birth,
should come to the church and receive a blessing from the priest, as is
the custom.

Prologue of the third book

Helped by the mercy of our Lord God, who orders and arranges us
and our words by his command, I have described in order the life of
the blessed bishop and the whole history of his pilgrimage. I will

149 This was a common way of calculating degrees of consanguinity in canon law.

undertake to set forth the few things that remain. *I ask this with good indulgence from the readers: that they weigh carefully the matters rather than the words and consider, with an impartial mind, if a bad word perhaps upsets their ears, that the kingdom of God stands firm not on eloquence but on faith.*[150] Who does not know, as a certain man said, *that salvation was not preached to the world by orators, but by fishermen?*[151]

Book III

[1.] So the holy bishop, after he had decided to return at last to his own diocese, his preaching finished, bade farewell to everyone he had instructed in the faith of Christ. He directed his journey toward Poland, which was separated from the territory of the Pomeranians by a certain *howling* and great *waste of a wilderness.*[152] After he had arrived there [i.e., the wilderness] on the first day of Lent,[153] he had priests sing individually the three offices for the three remaining days of that week, together with the office for that same day, because he foresaw that these would not be able to be celebrated in their proper order, both on account of the howling emptiness of the wasteland and the attacks of thieves. At last, having traversed the same wilderness, he arrived safe and sound at a city by the name of Ujście, which is located at the outermost limits of the Poles. His most numerous and most loved company of disciples was with him. From there, he directed his course to the duke of Poland, and it is extraordinary to relate with how much devotion and joy he was received. For the canons of the church of Gniezno went forth to meet him as he came, singing – with the delight of a rejoicing voice – that response from the Book of Wisdom that is appropriate for meeting a wise man: 'The Lord *conducted the just man through the right ways, and showed him the kingdom of God, and gave him the knowledge of the holy things, made him honourable in his labours, and accomplished his labours.*'[154] The prudent reader certainly understands how aptly this fits that person, especially after he had completed such laborious preaching.

---

150 Sulpicius Severus, *Vita Sancti Martini*, prologue (cf. *The life of Saint Martin*, 4).

151 Ibid.

152 Deuteronomy 32:10. See *The life of an unnamed* magistra *of Admont*, ch. 3, p. 157 and *The deeds of Count Ludwig of Arnstein*, ch. 5, p. 233 for other uses of this biblical passage.

153 Ash Wednesday: 11 February 1125.

154 Wisdom 10:10.

[2.] And so, the aforesaid duke kept him for many days in the highest veneration and honoured him with many great gifts. Then he was dismissed in peace, after farewells and kisses and other displays of charity, and protected by divine grace, he joyfully came to his own territories. For he celebrated Holy Thursday in his monastery of Michelfeld[155] and finally consecrated the chrism there according to the duty of the episcopal office.[156] On Holy Saturday,[157] he reached the city [of Bamberg], advancing all the way to the church of St Gangolf on the near side of the Regnitz river.[158] Thereafter, when he rose on the next day,[159] the clergy and people of the city gathered in the cathedral and awaited their bishop's arrival. When he entered, that assembly of clerics and monks, clothed in white, advanced toward him. Rejoicing, they received the priest of the Lord, whom they had missed and awaited for a long time, with a song of this sort, which clearly fit the person and time aptly: '*You have come, awaited one, whom we were expecting in the darkness; you have been made a hope for the desperate, a great consolation in torments.*'[160] Thereafter, he greeted the clergy and the people and everyone rejoicing in common.

And he stayed for four straight years in his own see.[161] During this time, he certainly did not shoulder any less of the responsibility for his children [i.e., the Pomeranians], though they were elsewhere. He directed many gifts to the princes of that land and many others to the churches he had constructed there: in gold and silver, books, sacred vestments and ornaments of every sort, together with saints' relics. He also sent a great deal of money for ransoming the Christians he heard had been captured by pagans, and he generously freed them from their chains, prisons and pillories.

155 26 March 1125.

156 Bishops were supposed to bless the chrism, the oil used for anointing, every year on Holy Thursday.

157 28 March 1125.

158 St Gangolf lay on the opposite side of the river from the cathedral, near the edge of town. He likely stayed there on Holy Saturday, rather than crossing the river to the episcopal residence, in order to align his return to his cathedral with Easter Sunday.

159 i.e., Easter Sunday: 29 March 1125.

160 From the Easter hymn *Cum rex gloriae*. See *Die Prüfeninger Vita*, 113, n. 24.

161 The actual length of time between his two Pomeranian missions was closer to three years. See *Die Prüfeninger Vita*, 116, n. 40.

[3.] From that time, the blessed man remained more firmly in contemplation of his Creator. He paid more attention than he had been accustomed to psalmody and prayer, and he committed himself more diligently to the prayers of God's servants, such that one time he had sixty Psalters sung for himself in that aforesaid monastery of blessed George [i.e., Prüfening]. He asked that this also be done for him in his other monasteries, and in the end, it is believed, he elicited much grace for himself from the prophetic spirit through psalmody and prayer. *Because so long as the sound of psalmody (as was also said before our time) is brought forth by the heart's efforts, the route to the omnipotent Lord is prepared for the heart in this way, such that the sound eagerly* unfolds *the mysteries of prophecy for the mind and pours in the grace of compunction.*[162] So it is that *when Josaphat* asked the prophet Elisha *about the future and the spirit of prophecy abandoned him, he had a musician brought forth, such that the spirit of prophecy descended upon this man through the praise of psalmody and filled his mind with the things to come.*[163]

And so, while the blessed man built with psalmody and prayers a route for the Holy Spirit to come to him, he realized that sometimes he was informed through inward inspiration about things happening in distant regions. For on one occasion, while the holy bishop was staying together with his clergy and faithful followers in the castle called Pottenstein[164] – which is known to belong to the Bamberg church – he rose suddenly from his sleep in the dead of the night and asked for his familiar Psalter, the one he had been accustomed to have frequently at hand. The chaplains were amazed and asked why he was seeking it at such an hour as this. He said that he ought to sing some Psalms for the soul of his brother, who had just died. And he declared that the one who would announce his death as a certainty would be standing outside in front of the doors. It happened, just as he had said, and at first light a man arrived, who announced that the bishop's brother had migrated from the world.[165] Nothing reports whether he foresaw this in spirit or knew it for certain from a vision; really, that does not matter, because

---

162 Gregory the Great, *Homiliae in Hiezechihelem prophetam*, I.15.282–5.

163 This story comes from 2 Kings 3:11–15, but the text here follows Gregory the Great, *Homiliae in Hiezechihelem prophetam*, I.15.279–82.

164 For this castle, see above, p. 115.

165 *Heiligenleben zur deutsch-slawischen Geschichte*, 174, n. 10 reports that Otto had three brothers, but we do not know which one is meant here.

it is of one and the same grace to recognize concealed things through a vision and to predict future things through the spirit.

[4.] Then, when the course of four years had elapsed after the pilgrimage we described previously, he arranged to visit the people of the Pomeranians again, for the purpose of going on pilgrimage and preaching.[166] Soon, ready to take a route through Saxony, he departed with the great sorrow and joy of his men; even though they rejoiced in Christ's glory and saving pagans, they nevertheless could not avoid grieving, like good sheep, about the absence of their good shepherd. And so, he travelled downstream on the Elbe River from Magdeburg by ship and landed with his men at the castle called Havelberg. There, although he had discovered a very great multitude of pagans,[167] he was forbidden to preach, because that great and eloquent man Archbishop Norbert of Magdeburg claimed that people for himself as they bordered upon his diocese.[168] The archbishop took the voice of preaching away from the holy bishop by certain secret machinations.[169] And although his companions exhorted him to preach to the pagans, the holy bishop, *careful to keep the unity in the bond of peace*,[170] through more profound advice – namely that one should not be seen to send a sickle into someone else's crop[171] – did indeed abstain from preaching in those regions. But after passing through the land of the Liutizi,[172] when he had arrived in the province called 'Wnzlov', his journey was finished.[173] He preached in three very famous cities: namely Usedom, Gützkow and Wolgast.[174]

166 He undertook his second mission to Pomerania in 1128.

167 The diocese of Havelberg had been founded in the Ottonian period after Saxon conquests in the region, but this region on the Eastern bank of the Elbe had fallen to the pagan Slavs again during the uprising of 983.

168 Norbert of Xanten, founder of the Premonstratensian Order, was archbishop of Magdeburg from 1126 to 1134 (see also *The deeds of Count Ludwig of Arnstein*, ch. 9).

169 The diocese of Havelberg had belonged to the archdiocese of Magdeburg since the Ottonian period, meaning that Archbishop Norbert was the prelate responsible for missionary work in the region. It is unclear what 'secret machinations' might have been involved.

170 Ephesians 4:3.

171 Cf. Deuteronomy 23:25 and *Die Prüfeninger Vita*, 117, n. 52.

172 The Liutizi were one of the pagan peoples inhabiting the region between the Elbe and Oder rivers.

173 The location of this region is uncertain but may be part of the island of Usedom on the modern Germany–Poland border. See *Die Prüfeninger Vita*, 118, n. 54.

174 All three are in modern-day Germany.

However, everyone whom he found was baptized, chiefly because he had converted very many of them to the faith before then through his intermediaries. So he built a church in each city for them and obtained an endowment for each church from Duke Warcisław, to whom we made mention above. Finally, the fourth city was Demmin, in which he stayed for very many days, and he did not cease from preaching and baptizing.[175]

[5.] Meanwhile, the inhabitants of Szczecin, on whose conversion the holy bishop had spent all his time on his [first] pilgrimage, had sunk back into their former dregs through the treacherous action of the [pagan] priests. They thought to build again the temples for the gods, which he [i.e., Bishop Otto] had destroyed a little while ago, and to destroy the churches he had constructed. Accordingly, the [pagan] priests, seeing that *the hope of their gain*[176] had been lost when the idols were abandoned, said that the gods had stood before them, terrible in expression and appearance, and had blamed them for the worship of Christ and their own neglect. For they said that the wrath of the gods had caused the pestilence, which had arisen by chance in those days and had attacked almost the whole city of Szczecin, because after the people had received the empty superstition of the Christians, they had abandoned the old faith. And so, the pagans gathered and broke into the church of the blessed martyr Adalbert, and first they threw down the bells, which had been hung before the doors of the church – although, truly, the bells remained so safe and sound for declaring the power of Christ that it was as if they had not been thrown down at all.

Meanwhile, a certain impious and detestable priest of their idols entered the church, raging, in order to destroy with reckless daring the altar that Christ's priest had built with the zeal of sacred purpose. There, he was made to tremble, and he stiffened; he was almost completely deprived of the services of all his limbs, such that he was amazed at his lack of control. As a result, he was corrected a little on account of this blow; he went forth and bore witness to the people that the God of the Christians was the strongest god. And he stated that his altar

---

175 The authors of the other two early *vitae* of Bishop Otto, Ebo and Herbord of Michelsberg, both have much more to say about missionary efforts in this region than the author of this text does. See *Heiligenleben zur deutsch-slawischen Geschichte*, 248–55 and 418–35. In these two *vitae*, Demmin is the first place he stops after Havelberg, which makes more sense geographically than the description here.

176 Acts of the Apostles 16:19.

was not to be destroyed, but that another was to be placed next to it for the [pagan] gods, so that the ones worshipping both would be able to keep both favourably inclined to them. The people acquiesced to these things, and setting up another altar next to the Lord's altar, they consecrated it to their idols. Afterwards, making sacrifices to God on one altar, but to demons on the other, the people accommodated both with equal zeal – except that the custom of their idolatry had been implanted in them and made them more inclined toward showing service to the idols. That story from antiquity was repeated, in which it is told that the people of Samaria, when they worshipped the gods of the pagans, nevertheless served the Lord.[177]

[6.] The bishop was absent, a great distance away. Having discerned these things in a wondrous manner, he wasted away, such that in him was fulfilled what the Psalmist wrote: *My zeal hath made me waste away: because my enemies forgot thy words.*[178] For we said, rightly, that they were his enemies, they who were forgetful of his words (that is, his former preaching); they had not submitted to God's justice, though they were willing to establish their own justice.[179] And so, because the bishop was wasting away completely on account of these evils, he arranged to visit the inhabitants of Szczecin again and to exhort them to penance and conversion. His familiars, very few of whom had remained in that town, warned him many times that if he wished to be mindful of his own life, he should not approach those people at all. They advised him that his would be unproductive labour, that there was no good hope in that people, that they bore a fierce spirit, that they were thirsty for the bishop's death and the blood of his men.

Truly, the bishop desired in every way *to be dissolved and to be with Christ.*[180] However, the same ardour had not been kindled in all his companions. Some of them, in particular, held him back with more profound advice, saying that it could be arranged that he sail – more opportunely for himself and more appropriately for his men – once that infidel people had quieted a little from the fury that had taken hold of them. After that, they said that it did not seem right for him to throw himself headlong into death; it would be useful for him *to abide still in*

---

177 Cf. 2 Kings 17:26–33.

178 Psalm 118:139.

179 Cf. Romans 10:3.

180 Philippians 1:23. i.e., to die.

the flesh,[181] if not for himself, certainly for his men, whose advantage he had to seek, especially following the example of the apostle.[182] Now the bishop was not moved much by this reasoning; nevertheless, he was compelled to delay for some time, because none of his men would agree to follow him. Hardly had a few days passed by, and he again wanted to set out. Since he observed that his companions were more apprehensive to make the journey, he prepared to depart alone, impatient of delay and inaction as long as the inhabitants of Szczecin persisted in their perfidy. And so, when an opportune moment arose, he secretly took some of his priestly vestments from his case, in which he stored his episcopal books and symbols of authority, and hurried *on the way, which leads to the sea,*[183] with no one aware or accompanying him.

Someone, seeing this, hastened breathless to the others and announced that the bishop was gone and had secretly taken certain things from the case.[184] When they heard this, they leapt up and as quickly as possible followed the old man, whom they found and restrained. They chided him that he had departed alone. As he struggled, they led him back to the site of the tent, which they had pitched away from the region of the sea. But they did not have the firmness to resist and oppose his desire and good plan for much longer. They all were so overwhelmed by his authority that they would have thought it impious if they had not acquiesced.[185] Therefore, they decided to go as quickly as possible and to die with him, if the situation so required, trusting not in their own strength but in God's grace. The bishop rejoiced and approved of each one's devotion. But in truth, he did not tell everyone to make ready, since they would be sailing into such great danger to their lives; this was to be for the few who seemed more excellent than the others. He ordered some to stay by the baggage, but others to pursue the assigned work. And so, he departed at last with a few proven people, whose faith and devotion were known to him.

[7.] Soon, he boarded a ship and crossed the sea with such great speed that you would have thought he had flown rather than sailed. And when

---

181 Philippians 1:24.
182 i.e., Paul, author of the letter to the Philippians cited here.
183 Numbers 21:4.
184 In his *vita* of Bishop Otto, Ebo of Michelsberg identifies this person as the monk Udalrich of Michelsberg. See *Die Prüfeninger Vita*, 122, n. 85.
185 Cf. Sulpicius Severus, *Vita Sancti Martini*, 25.3 (*The life of Saint Martin*, 27).

he arrived at the town of Szczecin,[186] where the news of his coming
had already preceded him, he withdrew into the church of the blessed
apostles, which he had built before the gate of the same city.[187] There,
he was with a very numerous and most beloved company of followers,
ready to pray to the Lord for their salvation and that people's ignorance.
Then, a crowd of armed men from the city forced their way in and were
prepared to seize the priest and massacre those who had come with
him. But one of the townsmen, to whom not only wisdom but also old
age had added authority, saw what was happening and grieved exceedingly. At first, he turned to the common people to ask why armed
people came together against unarmed ones; [he said] it was wrong
that those who had offered peace be met with arms, and finally, that
they ought not to destroy innocent men without cause, without
audience.

He spoke on, in the same vein, inflexible.[188]

In the end, the people acquiesced reluctantly to his words and somehow
held back their hands, for this day and hour, from the deaths of the
bishop and his followers. The next day, which happened to be a Sunday,
as he celebrated the solemnities of the Mass in the aforesaid church,
that infidel people arrived suddenly, with a great uproar. This time,
they were ready to kill the bishop and all his followers by a new and
unheard of method of death, for they regretted their error: namely, that
they had spared them the day before, even for the span of one hour.
But that man, adorned with the symbols of episcopal authority as he
stood at the holy altar, along with the two priests who served him at
the Mass in place of the deacon and subdeacon, proceeded through the
middle of the city as the people watched. Soon, in a wondrous manner,
the purple vestments of the bishop and of those same ministers, as the
sun poured in from above, shone in such a way that the unaccustomed
radiance of clothes and sun – and what is more likely, divine will – struck
the infidels with terror and put them to flight.

[8.] Then the bishop, ready to speak to the people, stopped *in a high
place of the city*,[189] in order that he might prove himself by deed and

---

186 Here, the author uses the word *urbs* for Szczecin instead of his usual *civitas*. See
       Die Prüfeninger Vita, 123.

187 See above, II.13.

188 Virgil, *The Aeneid*, II.650.

189 Proverbs 9:14.

character to have been established – with the Lord arranging it – in the lofty tower of apostolic office. In that place, at that time, a great multitude of men came together, ready to hear at last what he was eager to say. The bishop ordered his interpreter, a prudent man, who was then presiding over the same people,[190] to explain the reason for his coming, which was namely this: that he might call them forth to penance, they who had abandoned *the living and true God*[191] (whom they had come to know through his earlier preaching) and who had worshipped with undue veneration the idols of the pagans, which neither see, nor hear, nor speak.[192] And while the bishop's interpreter was arguing very eloquently about all these things, that impious priest of the idols came and, letting out a great cry, silenced the preacher's voice. Then, having turned to those standing around, he warned them to give thanks with a single voice to the gods, who had delivered into their hands the gods' enemies and the public enemies of the fatherland. For, truly, he bore witness that the others ought to die by various tortures – but that the bishop, who was the head of all this evil, ought to be chopped into pieces.[193]

After he said these things, he prepared to throw the spear he held in his hand (as was the custom of all of them) into the Lord's holy man, and he encouraged the others to do the same, saying, 'Now let him die, pierced by everyone's spears, he who strives for the ruin of all of us in every way.' But the wretched crowd of pagans, when they dared to raise their hands against the bishop, froze in their attempt, having surely experienced the strength of him, whose priest they wanted to kill. Then, indeed, they stood immobile alongside the crime's instigator, fixed to the ground as if made of stone. They did not have the strength then to let drop their hands, which they had audaciously extended on high, such that you would have believed they were bound in the air. *You are*

---

190 Adalbert, the future bishop of Pomerania, who was mentioned above (see p. 132). Otto is described at the start of his *Life* as being fluent in Polish, not Pomeranian (see above, p. 101), but these were both Slavic languages, meaning that Otto must have had at least some familiarity with the Pomeranian tongue. It is possible that Otto relied on an interpreter on this particular occasion because of the significance of this moment for the success of his missionary efforts. For bilingualism on the frontier, see Rossignol, 'Bilingualism in medieval Europe'.

191 1 Thessalonians 1:9.

192 Cf. Psalm 113:12–14.

193 Cf. 1 Samuel 15:33.

just, O Lord: and your judgement is right,[194] when you take good health
away from those who had come to take away another's good health.

'What,' the holy bishop said to his interpreter, 'are we to do in such
a sad state of affairs?' The interpreter advised – for the bishop was
accustomed to make use of him for such counsels – that he bless the
people with a raised hand and permit them to depart for home. Without
delay, he first said the two verses of the Psalmist – *Blessed be the name
of the Lord*[195] and *Our help is in the name of the Lord*[196] – as was customary,
and then he impressed that familiar sign of the cross on his mouth and
recited the solemn words of blessing above those who were standing
around him. Instantly, the pagans experienced the efficacy of his blessing,
and having soon recovered their former good condition, they returned
joyfully to their homes.

[9.] The bishop went off, hurrying to the church of the blessed martyr
Adalbert, accompanied by his disciples. Meanwhile, some boys whom
he had met when they were playing in the street *crowded around eagerly
from all sides to see him*[197] and followed the bishop from behind. They
marvelled at the appearance and demeanour of the strange men, as was
typical for boys their age. He spoke to them through the above-mentioned
interpreter and inquired if any of them had received baptism. And
because this one and that one said they had been baptized, the bishop
asked whether it was settled, in their opinion, that they would remain
in the faith they had received when being held for baptism. The boys
responded that this was their intention, to remain with the Christian
laws and in the catholic faith they had recognized once before. The
bishop warned those who remembered they had been baptized to be
separated from those who had not been baptized, and thereafter not to
mix with the infidels or have contact with them.

At these words, the Christian boys began to cast aside the pagan
boys and, while the bishop observed, to drive them back a distance – such
that they permitted none of them to stand in their midst. Thus did a
children's game present a beautiful spectacle to him on that day! Rejoicing
and giving thanks, he instructed those who were believers more fully

194 Psalm 118:137.
195 Psalm 112:2.
196 Psalm 123:8.
197 Virgil, *The Aeneid*, II.63–64.

in Christ's faith, and he guided the unbelievers to the faith by pious exhortation. In this, we believe truly that prophetic voice of the Psalmist to have been fulfilled: *Out of the mouths of infants and children you have perfected praise, because of your enemies, that you may destroy the enemy and the avenger.*[198] Because the praise of Christ was perfected in this way, *out of the mouths of infants*, it happened not long after that the hostile faction was revealed and at the same time destroyed.

[10.] After they had seen the wondrous things that had happened, the princes of the city sat with the rest of the multitude, deliberated with them, and decided to obey the bishop and believe in Christ – especially because he had inspired to the faith a certain very rich and powerful man named Wirtschak, who had actually had a great part in miracles. That man had travelled to the province of the Danes a short time before;[199] he was captured by them and thrown in chains for a great many days, having endured all those things that the condemned are accustomed to endure, such that he despaired completely not only for his return but also for his life. Unexpectedly at night-time, *a distinguished old man with white hair that gleamed like snow*[200] seemed to stand by the man and to promise him his life and his return. But thereafter, he would punish the man, if he did not obey the bishop and did not busy himself by commending the bishop's teaching to others. That man, who was bound fast at such a critical moment, wanted to promise even greater things; he began to swear an oath, and calling the name of the divinity to witness, he said, 'Lord God, who has made our people come to knowledge of your name through the same bishop, if I ever have contempt for his teachings (even the most extreme ones), if I do not undertake to commend everything he preaches to others, I have denied you.'

Now this was no empty sleep or idle dream, by which we are often deceived.[201] For *he was released*, then, *on taking this oath,*[202] and he departed, free from the chains and, likewise, the prison. When he had come to the

198 Psalm 8:3.
199 In their *vitae* of Bishop Otto, Ebo and Herbord of Michelsberg describe him as engaging in piracy at the Danes' expense. See *Die Prüfeninger Vita*, 129, n. 135 and *Heiligenleben zur deutsch-slawischen Geschichte*, 450.
200 Gregory of Tours, *De virtutibus b. Martini*, I.6 (*The miracles of the Bishop St. Martin*, 208).
201 Jerome, *Epistulae*, 22.30.6.
202 Jerome, *Epistulae*, 22.30.5.

sea, he boarded a ship he found, alone, without oarsmen or guide, driven by fear of the enemies whom he dreaded behind him. He judged it safer to trust himself to the waves of the sea than to experience again the inhumanity of those whom he had escaped once. And so, the ship was seized by a very strong wind and was brought headlong through the waves; it crossed the great vastness of the sea with wondrous speed and set him, unharmed, on shore. That man disembarked from the ship and arrived at the city of Szczecin. As everyone listened, he recounted Christ's mercy and strength and the story of his liberation – not without the appropriate admiration of praise.

Thereafter, he sat in the aforesaid meeting of the princes and alone persuaded almost all the people to obey the bishop, just as he remembered he had been divinely ordered to do. Afterwards, therefore, the entire assembly conceded to his judgement, and he was charged with this mission:[203] that he announce to the bishop the manifest wish of everyone and their unanimous consent for Christ's faith. That man went and called out the name of the bishop, which in their language sounds like 'father' (since you would say '*otta*' instead of 'Otto', having changed one letter for another).[204] He said, 'This city agrees to obey your teachings, and it spreads out the idols it worshipped to be trampled upon by your feet.' Then, he threw down at the bishop's feet the rod he bore in his hand, as a sign of this subjection.

That impious priest of the idols, dismayed and silenced, fled and undertook various plots afterwards against the bishop. But Christ, by his unavoidable power and strength, destroyed them along with the author of the wickedness. But we will describe this in another place;[205] now, let us describe what is left.

[11.] Therefore, after the bishop had received this embassy, which seemed to fit his prayers and to be advantageous for their salvation, he first began to weep for joy and to give immense thanks to God. Afterwards, he did not cease to restore the churches and to instruct the common people in Christ's faith. There was by chance at that time a man who had a nut tree, which that foolish pagan people had been accustomed to visit frequently, as if under the pretence it was sacred. By no reasoning could he be persuaded to permit the tree to be cut

---

203 Cf. Sulpicius Severus, *Dialogus Primus*, 23.7 (*The First Dialogue*, 193).

204 Miklosich, *Etymologisches Wörterbuch der slavischen Sprachen*, 228 (otŭ).

205 See below, p. 148.

down – especially since he judged it a sacred object for worship and also possessed the yield from its crop. Now the bishop *impressed upon him carefully that there was nothing sacred in a tree trunk*; they should trust in *the God, whom he served, instead of in that tree that ought to be chopped down, because it was dedicated to demons.*[206]

But that man yielded in no way to these lines of reasoning. Afterwards, he swore on his gods that while he lived, he would never consent to the tree being chopped down. By chance, when the bishop approached the tree to cut it down, that man preferred to strike him with the axe instead, but he was overawed by him and struck only air, not injuring him. Then, the bishop was asked by the faithful, who by chance were then present, that he be the first to show patience, as he persuaded others to show, and that the tree be left unharmed. The bishop should allow it to stand unshaken, if the error [i.e., of worshipping it] should be rejected. Convinced by them, he agreed to their requests. And so he permitted the tree to stand, lest it seem that he was avenging his injury. Indeed, he received from the aforesaid man the assurance he demanded: that, thereafter, the man would not offer veneration to it, nor would he believe it worthy of veneration by any sort of worship.

[12.] Thereafter, the holy bishop, who also wanted to visit the inhabitants of Wolin, departed with his followers and some other companions. But in this place, that impious bishop of idols directed his plots against the holy man.[207] For he had sent men ahead on a ship who, if they at some point had the opportunity, were to kill the holy priest. When the bishop encountered them and they wanted to rise up against him, some of the inhabitants of Szczecin, who were sailing together with the bishop, took up arms and began to stand firm in defence of the ship and to fight so fiercely that those who *were prepared against them*[208] were repulsed – not without ignominy.

Meanwhile, that man [i.e., the impious bishop of idols] was at home, *complicit in such a dreadful crime.*[209] Behold, he suddenly began to proclaim the mercy of the gods, boasting and saying that he had received a response from them: that on this day, at this hour, namely the one he had arranged with the murderers, a messenger would arrive, who would

206 Sulpicius Severus, *Vita Sancti Martini*, 13.2 (*The life of Saint Martin*, 16).

207 See above, the final section of III.10, p. 146.

208 1 Samuel 17:21.

209 Sallust, *The War with Catiline*, 34.2.

either carry the severed head of that old bishop or announce surely
that he had most certainly drowned with his men in the sea. He had
not quite finished these words, when – behold! – his head was suddenly
flung back and he began to let out awful and horrible sounds, such that
an innumerable multitude of men came together, roused by the news
of this event. In the presence of this multitude, he revealed, amidst the
horrible sufferings of his body, all the secrets of his malice. Finally,
telling of the severe sentence against himself, he said, 'Because I had
contempt for obeying the bishop, because I persuaded people to stray
from the faith he preaches, *lo I die,*[210] *fear God!*[211] Having said these
things, he died immediately. Moreover, so great and so intolerable a
stench filled the whole of that little house, in which he lay, that he left
behind certain evidence of the kinds of banquets to which he had gone
forth from his residence.[212]

And it happened that, at the very time when he had predicted that
the messenger would arrive concerning the bishop's death, a messenger
came to announce that man's sudden death to the bishop, who was
staying at Wolin. Another of the [pagan] priests, too, who had given
his approval to that man in both the bishop's murder and other evils,
ended his life not much later by a horrible death, raised on a cross.
However, concerning these things and others, which truly seemed worthy
of being miraculous, the holy bishop proclaimed the firmest silence to
his followers, teaching them to be confident in the Lord's goodness,
not to take pride in his actions.

[13.] We think it suitable to insert in this place another miracle, too,
which we learned happened in the same city of the people of Wolin,
since it comes to mind at present from our memory. A certain man was
working in the field on the feast of the blessed Lawrence.[213] The priest
who presided over that place came upon him by chance and reproached
him, because he did not have reverence for the sacred day, on which all
Christians were to be idle. That man, since he had been accustomed to
the works of paganism up to this point, disdained to listen to the priest's
words and did not cease from the work he had begun. Then, suddenly,
fire invaded his crop, and the greedy flames consumed all his grain

210 Genesis 25:32.

211 1 Peter 2:17.

212 Cf. Sulpicius Severus, *Vita Sancti Martini*, 24.8 (*The life of Saint Martin*, 26). This
     is a dramatic way of saying he went to Hell.

213 10 August.

found in the same field, leaving utterly untouched the labours of others. For it was necessary that the fire expiate especially his contempt for that martyr, who had offered his body to the flames, to be burned for the Lord.[214]

[14.] Also, a certain woman there, who had been struck with a sudden blindness, came to the church and in the bishop's presence lamented the sad occurrence of such a great calamity. He instructed her, as he was accustomed to do for very many others if anything adverse ever happened to them, to go ring the bell, which hung before the doors of the church. She departed, she rang it, and her blindness was immediately removed; the light, which had formerly been denied to her, was revealed to her uncovered eyes.

[15.] After he had duly finished these things, he returned home and was received with the highest exultation by everyone. He sent a ring to the Roman Pontiff Honorius [II] of blessed memory.[215] He asked that he [i.e., Honorius] send the same ring back to him after he had consecrated it, so that he [i.e., Otto] might invest through that ring someone recommended by knowledge and character with the episcopal see, which he had resolved to locate in those regions [i.e., Pomerania]. And afterwards, he held onto this ring, once he had received it back, but he was hindered by the varied course of events and, at length, by the moment of his own death; thus, he was unable to carry out what he had intended.[216] In the year of the Lord's incarnation 1139, in the thirty-second year of his ordination, in the second indiction,[217] on the day before the Kalends of July [30 June], he withdrew from human affairs.

[16.] After this, the bishop of the city of Würzburg arrived,[218] and the body of the blessed man was buried in great glory in the church of St Michael the Archangel, where he, while he still lived, had had a tomb prepared for himself.[219]

---

214 According to one tradition, St Lawrence had been martyred by being roasted alive.

215 Pope Honorius II (1124–30).

216 The delay likely was the result of a dispute between the archbishops of Magdeburg and Gniezno concerning the question of which archdiocese had authority over the region where Otto conducted his missions. See *Die Prüfeninger Vita*, 136–7, n. 201.

217 See above, n. 103, for the term indiction.

218 Bishop Embricho of Würzburg (1127–46).

219 This is the monastery of Michelsberg in Bamberg. His tomb is still there today.

THE LIFE OF AN UNNAMED MAGISTRA OF ADMONT (D. MID-TWELFTH CENTURY)

INTRODUCTION

Nothing, beyond what appears in the short text translated below, is known about the woman who is the subject of this *vita*. She belonged to one of the most important Benedictine communities in the south-east of the German kingdom: the double monastery of monks and nuns at Admont in the march of Styria (today a part of Austria). While the composition of the *vita* can be dated with some confidence to the period around 1170, or the years immediately following, the dates of the unnamed nun's life are much less certain. According to the *vita*, she was educated in Salzburg at the convent of Nonnberg and seems to have arrived at Admont in or around 1121, when Abbot Wolfold of Admont (1115–37) established a separate women's community there alongside the pre-existing male monastic house. From the beginning, she was the *magistra*: the head of the women's house, tasked with educating the other members of the fledgling convent. The text reports that this unnamed *magistra* lived to be quite old. However, there is no way of knowing exactly how long she lived after she joined the Admont community, and the text ends before describing her death.

Despite all of the uncertainty surrounding the woman at the centre of this *vita*, the brief text is a remarkably rich source. It offers its readers a deeply personal account of the anonymous nun's life, written by another Admont nun who seems to have known her quite well. Such a detailed glimpse into the inner workings of a twelfth-century convent is rare, and it is difficult to find the subject of any other medieval *vita* or *gesta* who comes across in his or her biography as being quite as lifelike, quite as convincingly human, as this unnamed *magistra*.

Context

According to the text, the unnamed *magistra* was born into a ministerial family belonging to the archbishops of Salzburg. Ministerials were unfree and were therefore of a lesser status than nobles and the other freemen in medieval society. This lack of freedom meant they did not have, among other things, the right to marry or to alienate property without their lord's permission.[1] Despite this unfree status, beginning in the eleventh century some ministerial families became quite influential within the archdiocese of Salzburg. The archbishops relied on them to assist in various administrative and military functions, and over the course of the twelfth century the leading families of Salzburg ministerials became the de facto lesser nobility of the archdiocese.[2] As a result, while this *magistra* did not belong to the highest strata of the medieval German nobility, she was certainly not of lowly status either. Her role as *magistra* in one of the leading convents in all of the German kingdom – one known for housing many high-ranking women during the middle decades of the twelfth century – leaves little doubt that she came from an important Salzburg family.[3] Nevertheless, the author of the *vita* makes no attempt to connect her to local or regional social networks, meaning it is impossible to draw any definitive conclusions about her background.

Archbishop Gebhard of Salzburg (1060–88) founded the Benedictine monastery of Admont deep in the Alps in 1074. Although this region was lightly populated and was surrounded by rugged mountains, the Enns River valley where the monastery lay was a vital transit route. As a result, the monastery suffered greatly during the years of the Investiture Controversy. But thereafter, it rapidly emerged as both a religious and economic centre within the region of Styria – and beyond. During the twelfth century, the male community played an active role in reform circles, and many Admont monks were sent to other Benedictine houses across the south-east of the German kingdom to improve monastic practices in other communities. The house of nuns at Admont enjoyed an equally strong reputation among the secular and religious elite in the region. Today, Admont is best known among scholars of the Middle Ages for its extensive library of medieval manuscripts, which remains

---

1 For more on this point, see the general introduction.

2 For Salzburg ministerials, see Freed, *Noble bondsmen*.

3 She was probably at Admont during the period when a half-sister and a nephew of Mechthild of Diessen (see *The life of Mechthild of Diessen (d. 1160)*, in this volume) were members of the community there. In addition, she was probably *magistra* when a Hungarian princess was also a nun there; see Lyon, 'The letters of Princess Sophia of Hungary'.

a powerful reminder of this community's standing and influence during
the twelfth century.[4]

Text and authorship

The text opens with a poem that uses the words *vita* and *gesta*, but in
the form this source has been preserved, it is anything but a typical
work of medieval biography. It begins with the unnamed *magistra* already
an elderly woman, and the bulk of the text concerns her final years.
Passing references to her birth and family background appear in the
middle of the text, not at the start as one would expect. The unusual
structure of the work, combined with its location in the manuscript in
which it survives, make it very difficult to know whether the *vita*, in
its present state, is complete. Regardless, its lack of conformity to the
standards of the *vita* and *gesta* genres make the text unique and interesting
in a variety of ways.

The opening poem makes explicit reference to a woman named *Gerdrût*
(Gertrude) as the author of the work. Recent studies have demonstrated
convincingly that many of the nuns at Admont were highly educated
women who both wrote and copied texts; male and female scribes
collaborated in the monastery on the production of manuscripts and
the composition of letters during the twelfth century.[5] As a result, there
is no reason to doubt the female authorship of the *vita*. The final five
lines of the poem are addressed to this Gertrude and therefore suggest
a second author, quite possibly the scribe, who has also been identified
as one of the Admont nuns.[6] In other words, three women – the unnamed
magistra, the author Gertrude and a second author/scribe – are the
figures at the heart of any attempt to understand this text.

The work's intended audience is difficult to discern. Scholars have
put forward various theories, in some cases identifying a pope or an
archbishop of Salzburg as a potential patron for the text.[7] The latter

---

4 For a more detailed account in English of the history of Admont in this period,
   see Lutter, 'Normative ideals, social practice, and doing community', and Beach,
   Women as scribes, 65–103.

5 See especially Beach, *Women as Scribes*, and Beach, 'Voices from a distant land'.

6 The most detailed discussion of this text, including the question of its authorship,
   is in Lutter, *Geschlecht & Wissen*, 87–92.

7 Lutter, *Geschlecht & Wissen*, 91.

seems more likely; Admont had been founded by an archbishop of Salzburg, and the *vita* praises this archdiocese and its prelates. However, it is also possible that the author(s) intended the text to be read principally inside the community of nuns at Admont, as a means of preserving the memory of one of the most important early members of the convent.

One of the only internal clues to the date of the text's composition is a citation – previously unidentified – from a letter of Bishop Eberhard of Bamberg to Provost Gerhoh of Reichersberg.[8] This letter was written in the early 1160s, and a copy survives in an Admont manuscript that has been dated to the closing years of the same decade.[9] As a result, the text must have been composed some time after the late 1160s. As discussed in the following section, the manuscript that preserves the only known copy of the *vita* was produced around the year 1200; however, this *vita* was added a short time later in a thirteenth-century hand. All of this means the work can be dated to either the final quarter of the twelfth or the first quarter of the thirteenth century. Given the author Gertrude's knowledge of so many personal details about the unnamed *magistra*, it seems most plausible to assign the text a date on the earlier end of this spectrum, to the period around 1175, with the second author/scribe then adding it to the manuscript a few decades later.[10]

This text focuses very narrowly on the *magistra* during her final years and provides few details that do not relate directly to this stage in her life. After the Bible, the author references the Benedictine Rule more than any other work, clearly embedding the *magistra* within the ideal of the monastic lifestyle. References to a few other sources suggest the author was very well-educated, but the author's intention was not to impress the reader with her own erudition; the text is not over-saturated with biblical and classical allusions. Nor was it her intention to transform the *magistra* into a saint, for the few wondrous events described in the text seem to fall well short of the miraculous. Instead, the text offers a moving account of this unnamed *magistra's* profound impact on the community of nuns at Admont in the middle decades of the twelfth century.

---

8 See below, ch. 5, p. 160.

9 Classen, *Gerhoch von Reichersberg*, 383, nr. 118.

10 The text has generally been assigned to the second half of the twelfth century. See Lutter, *Geschlecht & Wissen*, 88.

Manuscripts and editions

The text can be found within the hagiographical collection known as
the *Magnum Legendarium Austriacum (MLA)*.[11] While this compendium
of saints' lives survives in multiple late twelfth- and early thirteenth-
century copies from several different Austrian monasteries, the *vita* of
the unnamed *magistra* is extant in only one of these manuscripts, namely
the one from Admont. Its location in the codex is noteworthy; the
scribe squeezed it into a blank space, created by an erasure, on the recto
and verso of a single manuscript folio, using a very small hand. This
is a clear indication that the text did not belong to the official corpus
of the *MLA* as it was originally conceived.[12] Since the *magistra* was not
a saint, this is not surprising. The text was apparently added to this
hagiographical collection later, by an Admont nun who wanted to
preserve the *vita* of the *magistra* alongside the lives of Christian saints.
This sole manuscript copy of the text has been the basis for two modern
editions: one in the *Analecta Bollandiana* series and the other, much
more recently, in an appendix to Christina Lutter's study of twelfth-
century Admont.[13]

Notes on this translation

I have relied on Lutter's recent edition for my translation here. The
chapter divisions, which do not appear in the original manuscript, are
taken from both her edition and the one in the *Analecta Bollandiana*. I
have supplemented Lutter's edition with some additional references to
other sources that the author used in composing the text. The opening
poem, which in the original Latin consists of fifteen rhyming hexameter
verses, has been translated here to capture the sense and meaning rather
than the poetic style. The remainder of this short *vita* is written in a
straightforward prose style with few rhetorical flourishes, making it
an easy and enjoyable text to read.

---

11 For a recent overview of this collection, see Ó Riain, 'The *Magnum Legendarium
   Austriacum*'. This same collection also includes *The life of Bishop Otto of Bamberg*
   translated in this volume.

12 For a description of the text's location in the manuscript, see Lutter, *Geschlecht &
   Wissen*, 88–9. For a similar situation, see the introduction to *The deeds of Count
   Ludwig of Arnstein* also translated here.

13 'Vita, ut videtur,' 359–66, and Lutter, *Geschlecht & Wissen*, 226–9.

TRANSLATION

The resplendent life of a maidservant of God, or the shape of the
    triumph,
By which she conquered the world: this splendid writing tells
    of that.
And its virginal style recounts well the pious deeds
Of the elect virgin, so that they may be manifest to worthy people.
A virgin, out of virginal love, has written about the love
With which she loved Him who alone bestows love.
May each one speak by praising what seems good to them.
This I would say for my part: not rightly is reward denied
To Gertrude, the describer of the venerable life,
Which pleased the eternal King, and is for us to imitate.
Indeed, learned Gertrude, you ought to know *my intent*.[1]
What you fervently stated in Christ's name,
Has been made quite elegant, has been written with true praise.
O King of earth and sky, as you watch over the writer,
Preserve the readers, you who protect everywhere what is just.[2]

[1.] No one can recall ever seeing her rise from bed with the others,
or lying down. She preferred to stand, and when excessive weariness
pressed upon her, she slept while sitting. *Although*, as our father and
master St Benedict says, *human nature is inclined to be compassionate toward
the old and the young, ... and they should certainly not be required to follow
the strictness of the Rule with regard to food*,[3] she nevertheless maintained
the appointed feast days and night-time vigils inviolably from the Ides
of September [13 September] until Easter. If she had happened to break
them, she would have deemed it a sin. Truly, she carried the gospel of
Christ in her heart. She was not thinking about tomorrow.[4] Two cooked
dishes were sufficient for her daily refreshment in accordance with the
Rule; praising God, she was frequently refreshed from one dish.[5]

---

1 The two words *minen mût* ('my intent') are the only two words in the poem in
  German rather than Latin. *Mût* rhymes with *Gerdrût* (Gertrude) in the first half
  of the same line. See the introduction to this text for the issues of authorship raised
  by this opening poem.

2 I would like to thank my colleague Michael I. Allen for his helpful suggestions for
  how best to translate this poem.

3 *RB 1980: the rule of St Benedict*, 234–7, c. 37.

4 Cf. Matthew 6:34.

5 Cf. *RB 1980: the rule of St Benedict*, 238, c. 39.

Indeed, because (as the Psalmist attests) *all things are vanity: every man living,*[6] she was strong in the vigour of her spirit but was falling apart in her fleshly body. She had grown weak under her great number of years and labours. In a certain way, the grace of a seven-year-old child seemed to be in her. Nevertheless, never forsaking the convent, she properly followed along through all the rites. With the Lord cooperating, she had sought out the eight beatitudes.[7] Understanding and following them in all her desires, and by following them faithfully grasping them as well, she had exaltedly ascended the eighth step of humility. After she accomplished that, she was eager to pursue *only what is endorsed by the common Rule and the example set by her superiors.*[8] What the Lord says in the Gospel was clearly evident in this blessed woman: *A good person brings good out of the treasure of good things in his heart.*[9] Never was there anything in her heart except piety, except peace, except compassion; she proved this in her deeds, actions, words and sayings. She remained reverently in silence until the time for talking named in the Rule.[10] With how much dignity and kindness she spoke and advised us all! And all her conversation among us was about the past, the future, the glory of the faithful and the eternity of the saints.

[2.] Because she was considered second to none in religious habits and in the liberal arts too, she was sent several times to other places as an edifying example. She fled immediately from those places where everyone loved her for living piously and justly; she longed to conceal herself, hidden among us in the midst of rocks, because she took no pleasure in the false adulation of men.[11] She worked with good zeal for justice and truth – I should say, rather, for piety – and always with the most fervent love. She admonished very harshly those who transgressed and lived wickedly, upbraiding and rebuking them. But she supported those who recognized their sins and made amends, consoling them kindly and praying for them. Truly, *bold as a lion,*[12] she censured and rebuked

---

6 Psalm 38:6.

7 Cf. Matthew 5:1–10.

8 *RB 1980: the rule of St Benedict*, 200–1, ch. 7.

9 Luke 6:45.

10 Cf. *RB 1980: the rule of St Benedict*, 190, ch. 6 and 242, ch. 42.

11 The mention of rocks is likely a reference to the location of Admont, in a narrow valley surrounded by rugged mountains. Cf. *Passio Thiemonis*, 54–5, where the difficult landscape around the monastery is mentioned.

12 Proverbs 28:1.

for their evil works not only those like her and similar to her, or those lower than her; she also did not hesitate to assail even bishops, archbishops, and the powerful too, admonishing them constantly about rendering account. *Rendering evil for evil or insult for insult* to no one,[13] she rejoiced that she was worthy to suffer disgrace for the name of Jesus[14] and to be slandered with insults and blasphemies on account of the condition of the spiritual life.

Moreover, her speech (like the precept of the apostle) was *with grace, seasoned with salt*[15] that is, full of favour, pleasing, well-ordered, temperate and giving forth instruction to her listeners. In this, she was not forgetful of her beginnings, for she came forth in descent from the most illustrious ministerials of the church of Salzburg and passed some years of her youth there, having been educated in the castle above the same town.[16] For this reason, she especially loved St Rupert as if by hereditary right.[17] She served him with the highest devotion and gloried to have all his just and pious successors as lords and patrons.[18]

[3.] The Lord, who performing a miracle in a miracle once proved to his people *that he might suck honey out of the rock and oil out of the hardest stone*,[19] had determined to prepare a dwelling suitable for his servants among the Alps at Admont *in the howling waste of the wilderness.*[20] To the lord Archbishop Gebhard,[21] who was assisting him, he spoke through a certain mute: '*You ought to lay the foundation, God wants to finish it.*'[22] A congregation of monks was founded and built; they dwelled in unity[23] under the administration and dignity of three previous

---

13 1 Peter 3:9.

14 Cf. Acts of the Apostles 5:41.

15 Colossians 4:6.

16 See the general introduction for a discussion of ministerials. The *magistra* was educated in the convent called Nonnberg, which was located in Salzburg on the same hill as the archbishop's fortress.

17 St Rupert (d. 717) was an early missionary in the region around Salzburg, the founder of the Nonnberg, and the patron saint of the archbishopric.

18 The monastery of Admont was under the authority of the Salzburg archbishops.

19 Deuteronomy 32:13.

20 Deuteronomy 32:10. See *The life of Bishop Otto of Bamberg*, III.1 and *The deeds of Count Ludwig of Arnstein*, ch. 5, p. 233 for other uses of this biblical passage.

21 Archbishop Gebhard of Salzburg (1060–88), founder of Admont.

22 *Passio Thiemonis*, 55, which includes an account of Admont's foundation.

23 Cf. Psalm 132:1.

abbots.[24] But just as in ancient days, when *the people, still ignorant, were living in small thatched huts*[25] and *there was not an ordered system of religious worship* and service *nor of social duties*,[26] so also in that time the condition of this place [i.e., Admont] did not improve to their benefit until they were living with enclosed virgins and other piously chaste women.

When Wolfold of blessed memory succeeded as abbot,[27] he was inspired by the Lord and was the first to discuss the refuge of an inner building for enclosed women. From that place, the Lord's sanctification flourished upon himself[28] in the increase of the good flock. Our fellow sisters, the dependents of St Erintrude, conducted themselves most well;[29] they sent the one who was beloved to God to this place, into a convent of some female novices living together in common. She instructed them in the liberal arts and pushed them toward the increase of all good things. It is by no means worthwhile omitting – rather, it must be retained firmly – that she was thoroughly educated in Sacred Scripture, on which *she was meditating day and night*, sitting at the feet of the Lord with Mary.[30] Christ was never absent from her mouth, nor justice, nor anything else that pertains to the true life. To her credit, this is evident and manifest in our right order and spiritual rigour up to this day.

[4.] As we said before, she never ceased praying; she remained in divine contemplation, mild and moderate in so much, and listened to the command of her prelates, a whisper sweet with the Lord very often bursting forth from her. Nevertheless, she completed the business charged to her with a cheerful countenance and spirit, in a perfect spirit in all necessary work. For, whenever in the night-time she composed a letter and dictated to a scribe, she nevertheless maintained the observance of silence and never uttered any German words.[31] In addition, although

---

24 The meaning here is unclear. Admont had more than three abbots during its first few decades, before the arrival of the *magistra*, making this reference difficult to explain.

25 Paul the Deacon, *Historia Romana*, I.I.

26 Cicero, *De Inventione*, I.2.

27 Abbot Wolfold of Admont (1115–37).

28 Cf. Psalm 131:18.

29 The convent called Nonnberg (see above, n. 16) is meant here. Its first abbess was St Rupert's niece, Erintrude.

30 Psalm 1:2 and cf. Luke 10:39.

31 This is an intriguing statement on communication within the community and has caught the attention of scholars: see Beach, *Women as scribes*, 70 and Lutter, *Geschlecht & Wissen*, 98. For monastic silence more generally, see Bruce, *Silence and sign language in medieval monasticism*.

she kept perpetual silence after compline in accordance with the Rule,[32] nevertheless when the young girls asked her to tell them the verses and sequences – since she was full of charity and love – she took writing tablets and wrote for them the verses and sequences to be recited the next day.[33]

She was similar to Moses, wasn't she? Like him, her eyes were not dimmed.[34] In her old age – indeed, she was his same age[35] – she was not disturbed by the trembling of old age or by any grave illness. She lived in Christ, never employing earthly medicine for her body, and she took care to purge herself by blood-letting, as was customary. She considered sensible what the Psalmist says: *my strength, I watch for you.*[36] For the heavenly doctor, for whom no sickness is incurable, always provided for her in all ways. On one occasion when she was ill, he accomplished her cure in a wondrous manner. When everyone was resting during midday and she was sitting in front of a couch reading aloud, the middle vein on the top of her foot, as if cut open by a lancet, burst by itself with copious blood; immediately, she was made well.

She had few grey hairs, since God was foretelling the years of eternity for her. She reckoned one hundred twenty years of her life – as many as the one mentioned earlier had years of his life [i.e., Moses]. But, so that I may pursue the truth in all things and may not speak falsely about anything, more or less, she did not say this by asserting it true, because her age had disappeared from her memory; but, so she claimed, she had learned this computation through somebody's revelation in a dream.

[5.] It would be pleasing, above all, to know your paternal care.[37] Because frequently, after she had completed the vigils and fasts and was free from psalm-singing, when she was sitting or standing near a light, the garments on her head caught fire, such that her robe and veil were completely burned. With difficulty, we were able to free her from the dangers of the fire. Wondrous to say, she never suffered any injury

---

32 Cf. *RB 1980: the rule of St Benedict*, 242, ch. 42. Compline was the night office.

33 i.e., the biblical verses and the sequences (chants) that formed part of the daily office. See Fassler, *Music in the medieval West*, A41–2.

34 Cf. Deuteronomy 34:7.

35 See below for this comparison with Moses's age.

36 Psalm 59:9.

37 Scholars have suggested this is a reference to a male patron (the archbishop of Salzburg, perhaps, or the pope). See Lutter, *Geschlecht & Wissen*, 91. It may also be a reference to God.

either to a single hair or to the surface of her skin. We, foolish and
stupid, mocked her.[38] But she, more righteous than Noah, did not curse
us indignantly, but speaking kindly, blessed us.[39]

As for the rest, I know that you, lord, sit on the throne of apostolic
power, not exalted and elevated but humble and gentle toward everyone.[40]
For this reason, my confidence in speaking and writing these things
has increased. *Truly, another reason is the quality of the comparison, and
another is the simplicity of direct speech.*[41] *To what shall I compare her, or to
what shall I liken her?*[42] For she made known plainly in the end what
kind of reward there will be in the Lord's presence.

And so, as the day of her death drew near, she began to have a fever
in accordance with the debt of the flesh. Immediately, she was anointed
with holy oil and took communion with the body and blood of Christ.
Although she breathed as if near death and her soul was barely thriving
in her, nevertheless she had undiminished and complete comprehension
and uttered a response readily in deciding questions of divine truths.
After she received communion, she called over the priest who gave the
heavenly sacraments to her. As he approached, she was clapping her
hands, playing. When all of us were listening, she revealed to him the
mysteries she had seen around him and the ministries of the angels. 'I
saw,' she said, 'one after another in the order of the holy innocents, the
holy angels assisting the altar attendants at this sacred mystery, having
little heads shining as if silver with crowns.' Then, she seized his hands
and blessed him, saying, 'O how great, of what quality is the priestly
dignity! Why is that? Because the apostolic lord [i.e., the pope] and
his priests are thought to be better and higher from the power and
right of binding and loosing.[43] Without doubt, every honour is inferior
to the unique priestly character.'

[6.] To be clear, she did not see this angelic vision just once. When
she was first beginning to die, we all came together above her and sang
a litany. We invoked the name of St Rupert, her chosen and preferred

---

38 The feminine plural adjective *stultae* here is evidence that 'we' is referring to the
    other nuns of the Admont community.

39 Genesis 6:9 for Noah. Cf. Luke 6:28 for blessing those who curse you.

40 See the introduction to this text and n. 37 above for the question of audience.

41 *Letter of Bishop Eberhard of Bamberg to Gerhoh of Reichersberg,* 525C. See also Classen,
    Gerhoch von Reichersberg, 383, nr. 118. For more on this reference, see the introduction
    above, p. 153.

42 Lamentations 2:13.

43 Cf. Matthew 16:19.

patron, repeating it more often than the names of the other saints.[44] She joined with your companions, and gathering strength, she made known with signs, in so far as she was able, that a guard of holy angels was present and surrounding her.[45] The seven days after her unction with holy oil she spent mostly in a trance, her appearance changed, her eyes rigid, looking upward into heaven; then, over the course of an hour, she returned to a lively capacity. From that hour, she knew the present and future. She burst out in this voice, making this speech: '*Seek the Lord, while he may be found*,[46] serve him, for whom to serve is to rule; this is God, our God unto eternity and forever.[47] He is our king, who is before the ages.[48] *Serve the Lord with gladness*, and you will be repaid with a reward and neverending glory.'[49]

[7.] On another day after that, we thought that she was breathing her last and began to carry out the funeral rites devotedly. She was looking at us and signalling farewell to each of us individually with a lowering of her head. Directly, she began to speak: '*The grace of our Lord Jesus Christ be with you all.*'[50] She also looked surprised at the unusual state of affairs as we attended to keeping watch over her without the usual reverence. For us, this caused grief, not for her. 'In me,' she said, 'consider yourselves. Rest from every attack. Don't you know that the most beautiful youths enter and exit carrying walking sticks in their hands? I know this to signify to me the words of the Psalmist, saying "*Your rod and your staff, they have comforted me.*"[51] Also, some part among them is wicked on account of malignant spirits, *but finding nothing destructive in me*,[52] with the holy angels watching over me,[53] it [i.e., evil] *will not*

---

44 A litany naming a series of saints and petitioning them for comfort and support was a common form of prayer. For St Rupert, see above, n. 17.

45 The '*sociis tuis*' (your companions) here would appear to be a reference to God and his saints, but the explicit mention of St Rupert may also imply a connection to the archbishops of Salzburg.

46 Isaiah 55:6.

47 Cf. Psalm 47:15.

48 Cf. Psalm 73:12.

49 Psalm 99:2.

50 Romans 16:24 and elsewhere in the Pauline Epistles.

51 Psalm 22:4.

52 Sulpicius Severus, *Epistula Tertia*, 149 (*The Letter to Bassula*, 157). The borrowing from a Sulpicius Severus passage is noteworthy, since he is best known as the author of the *vita* of St Martin, who was the patron saint (alongside Mary) of the convent at Admont. See Lutter, *Geschlecht & Wissen*, 55.

53 Cf. Psalm 90:11.

however draw near me.'[54] When the hour then approached, in which she
was about to go to the Lord, with eyes and hands raised toward Heaven,
she said farewell to us with these words: 'My peace be with you and
yours with me.' Then, she ordered that the Psalter be brought to her;
she sought and found this verse: *'The lord is sweet and righteous, therefore.'*[55]
She explained this, saying: 'As often as you examine these words "sweet
and pleasant"[56] when reading, having pressed your lips on the same
place, praise the Lord; what thanks he will have, as if you embraced
him and greeted him with a pious kiss.' And then, with evening approaching, she asked that vespers be sung for her. We read them before her,
but directing all our senses to her, we did not pay attention to them.[57]

54 Psalm 90:7.

55 Psalm 24:8.

56 The Psalm reads *dulcis et rectus*, but the *rectus* has been changed here to *suavis*.

57 The text ends here in the manuscript. It is unclear whether there was ever more
to the *vita*.

THE LIFE OF MECHTHILD OF DIESSEN (D. 1160), BY ENGELHARD OF LANGHEIM

INTRODUCTION

At some point around the year 1200, a noblewoman asked the Cistercian monk Engelhard of Langheim to write a *vita* of the canoness Mechthild of Diessen, who had briefly been abbess of Edelstetten.[1] As Engelhard admitted in the dedicatory letter he wrote to this noblewoman (whose identity remains uncertain), he had little material with which to work in crafting his text. He had never met Mechthild, who had died four decades earlier, and he had gathered all his information about her during a meeting, lasting barely an hour, that he and his patroness had with unnamed informants.[2] Nevertheless, from this limited material, Engelhard wrote a surprisingly lengthy *vita* that interweaves many common hagiographical tropes with tantalizing details about Mechthild's life. According to him, she was a child oblate, given by her parents at the age of five to the double house of Augustinian canons and canonesses at Diessen in Bavaria. There, she rose to the position of *magistra*, the leader of the female community. At the time of Pope Anastasius IV (1153–54), she reluctantly agreed to become abbess of Edelstetten, a convent desperately in need of reform in Engelhard's version of events. She successfully improved the religious practices and commitment to the spiritual life at Edelstetten, but her time there seems to have been relatively short. Near the end of her life, she was anxious to return to Diessen, where she died on 31 May 1160.

---

1 In keeping with German scholarship on this canoness, I have chosen to use the name 'Mechthild' for her. However, in some other English-language scholarship she is called 'Matilda'/'Mathilda'. See, for example, Griffiths, 'Women and reform', 457 and Newman, 'Real men and imaginary women', 1197.

2 Engelhard wrote two other dedicatory letters for this work, one to the canons at Diessen (translated below) and a second to Abbot Herman of Ebrach (see Newman, 'Real men and imaginary women', 1197–8).

Although Mechthild was never formally canonized,[3] much of her *vita* reads like a typical saint's life. Engelhard filled the many gaps in his knowledge with biblical allusions, and he did not hesitate to compare Mechthild to a seemingly endless parade of women from both the Old and New Testaments. Indeed, his text is an exegetical tour-de-force in some places. Nevertheless, there are also numerous passages where careful reading offers glimpses into Mechthild's life and, more generally, into life within the convent at Edelstetten and the double community of canons and canonesses at Diessen. As this text reveals, neither Diessen nor Edelstetten was sealed off from the world, and the descriptions of Mechthild's interactions with people inside and outside these religious houses are a rich source for the thin grey line that separated the ecclesiastical and secular spheres in the German kingdom during the twelfth century.

Context

Although much of Mechthild's own life remains shrouded in obscurity, a good deal is known about her family and about the early history of the house of Augustinian canons and canonesses at Diessen. Her parents were Count Berthold I of Andechs (d. 1151) and the heiress Sophia of Istria (d. 1132), and they were also two of the founders of the religious community at Diessen. During the second half of the eleventh century, Berthold's ancestors had used a castle at Diessen as one of the main centres of their lordship in western Bavaria. By 1100 or so, the new family castle at Andechs, situated on the other side of Lake Ammer from Diessen, had replaced this older fortification. Similar to many other German nobles during this period, Count Berthold I and Sophia, in conjunction with some of their relatives, made the decision to transform the unneeded castle at Diessen into a religious house.[4] It received its first papal privilege in 1132, but the origins of the community probably lie in the late 1110s or early 1120s.[5] During subsequent decades, the

---

3 In the modern Roman Catholic Church, she is considered to be beatified. Two thirteenth-century women from her extended family, Elizabeth of Hungary and Hedwig of Silesia, were both canonized soon after their deaths. Mechthild's blood connection to these two saints has helped in the preservation of her memory up until today, especially in western Bavaria.

4 Arnold, *Power and property*, 153–8.

5 *Die Traditionen und Urkunden des Stiftes Diessen*, 64*.

house at Diessen emerged as an important site for the preservation of
the Andechs lineage's memory, and many of the twelfth-century members
of the family were prominent patrons of the community.[6]

Mechthild was probably born during the 1120s, meaning she would
have been given to Diessen as a child oblate during the very early years
of the religious community. Over the course of the approximately four
decades she spent at Diessen and Edelstetten, her family rose to become
one of the leading noble lineages of the day. By the time of her death
in 1160, one of her brothers, Count Berthold II (d. 1188), possessed
– besides the Andechs lordships in western Bavaria – additional rights
and properties in eastern Bavaria around Passau, Franconia around
Bamberg, Tyrol (where he would found the town of Innsbruck), and
Carniola in modern-day Slovenia. Another brother would become bishop
of Bamberg almost two decades after her death.[7] The next generation
saw the Andechs lineage rise even further into the upper ranks of the
imperial nobility when Mechthild's nephew Berthold III became duke
of Merania in 1180. By the time Engelhard of Langheim wrote her *vita*
around 1200, her lineage was one of the most powerful in the whole
of the German kingdom. This suggests that at least part of the impetus
for the anonymous countess's request to Engelhard may have been a
desire to elevate the lineage's status still more by emphasizing the
saintliness of one of its early members.

Family networks may also have been a factor in Mechthild becoming
abbess of Edelstetten, but here the evidence is more problematic. Very
little is known about the early history of this community of canonesses.
In fact, Mechthild's *vita* is the best source we have for its twelfth-century
history. The earliest known charter from the community dates from
1276, and even it survives in a later copy; only a necrology from
Edelstetten gives hints at the situation in the earlier period.[8] Nevertheless,
it is plausible that one of Mechthild's relatives, perhaps her own sister
Gisela, wanted her to become abbess in the mid-1150s in order to
reform the community. Gisela had married one of the counts of Berg,
a noble lineage from the region near Edelstetten, and one of her sons,
Bishop Otto II of Freising (1184–1220), may have been one of the

---

6 For the relationship between the religious community and the lineage of its founders,
see Borgolte, 'Stiftergedenken in Kloster Dießen'.

7 For her brothers Count Berthold II, who later became margrave of Istria, and
Bishop Otto II of Bamberg (1177–96), see Lyon, *Princely brothers and sisters*, 77–80.

8 Seitz, 'Zur Person der Gisela', 360.

people who pressed Engelhard to write the *vita*.[9] All of this is speculation, however; the sources do not permit definitive conclusions about why she was chosen to reform Edelstetten – or why she left that community and returned to Diessen before her death.

The only extant text that confirms any of the details in Engelhard's account of Mechthild's life is a letter of Pope Anastasius IV from 1153–54, in which he insists that Mechthild be obedient and accept the position of abbess to which she has been appointed; as the pope explains, he had already given the bishop of Augsburg permission to censure her if she refused.[10] The sharp tone of this letter is striking and suggests that Bishop Conrad of Augsburg, in whose diocese Edelstetten lay, had already been working for some time to convince Mechthild to become abbess of the community. The reasons for Mechthild's reluctance are unclear, but the letter – combined with the fact that Mechthild returned to Diessen near the end of her life – strongly suggest that she had little interest in being abbess of the religious house. Indeed, it is noteworthy that Diessen, not Edelstetten, was the community to which Engelhard wrote one of his dedicatory letters. Her death is recorded in one of the Diessen necrologies of the early thirteenth century under 31 May; a hand of the later thirteenth century added the year 1160.[11]

Text and authorship

The author of this text, the Cistercian monk Engelhard of Langheim (c. 1140–1210), is known from other works; he wrote a book of *exempla* and various letters besides his *vita* of Mechthild.[12] He briefly served as abbot of a Cistercian monastery in Austria, but he otherwise spent his adult years in Langheim in Franconia, not far from Bamberg. Like Diessen, this was a monastery with close ties to the Andechs lineage, and some of the thirteenth-century members of the family would even

---

9   Seitz, 'Zur Person der Gisela' and Pörnbacher's introduction to Dobereiner, *History der heyligen Junckfrawen*, xii. Wüst, 'Die Schwabegger (898?–1167)', 442 argues against the idea that Mechthild's sister Gisela played a role in reforming Edelstetten.

10 *Die Traditionen und Urkunden des Stiftes Diessen*, 105–6, nr. 3.

11 Borgolte, 'Stiftergedenken in Kloster Dießen', 271: *Mathildis abbatissa de Otilinesstetin bone memorie obiit.*

12 For Engelhard's career, see Newman, 'Real men and imaginary women'.

be buried there. As a result, it is plausible that the unnamed countess who commissioned the work knew Engelhard through Andechs family networks, at least by reputation, when she asked him to write the *vita*.[13] However, as Engelhard himself admits, he was not well-suited for the job. He neither knew much about Mechthild nor made any real effort to embed her in the spiritual milieu of the Augustinian canons and canonesses – a milieu with which he was probably unfamiliar.[14] Instead, he painted a picture of Mechthild as the ideal Cistercian monk or abbot.[15]

Engelhard's lack of knowledge is evident throughout most of the work, which offers few specifics about Mechthild's life.[16] However, Chapters 21 and 22, and perhaps Chapter 24 as well, do not fit neatly into this overall assessment. These chapters include a striking amount of detail and preserve conversations that Mechthild supposedly had with her father – in her mother's presence – and with Provost Hartwig of Diessen (c. 1132–1173). Based on their placement in the text, these conversations apparently took place after she returned to Diessen from Edelstetten, meaning they belong to the late 1150s. But Mechthild's mother had died in 1132 and her father in 1151, making them a historical impossibility. The anomalous nature of these passages concerning Count Berthold I, his wife Sophia and their daughter raises the question of why these stories were included in the *vita* at all. According to the text, the conversations between Mechthild and her father revolved around the tithe for the estate of Oberding in Bavaria, which the count agreed to grant to Diessen at his daughter's request. Thus, the canons and canonesses at Diessen are the chief beneficiaries in the story and the ones with the most to gain. Although there is no evidence from other sections of the *vita* that Engelhard of Langheim used Diessen sources to write his work, the religious house's own interests are clear in the discussion of this donation.[17]

---

13 Some scholars have speculated that the unnamed countess was from the Orlamünde lineage, but the evidence is not definitive. See Newman, 'Real men and imaginary women', 1197–8.

14 For Augustinian canons and canonesses, see the general introduction.

15 Newman, 'Real men and imaginary women', 1198–9.

16 This is probably the reason why Wattenbach, in his *Deutschlands Geschichtsquellen*, vol. 1, 466–7 has little positive to say about the text as a historical source. He briefly summarizes it, focusing on the unusual story about her hair at the end.

17 For a more detailed discussion of these chapters of the *vita*, see Lyon, 'Cooperation, compromise and conflict avoidance', 102–10.

In this context, it is worth noting that on 17 March 1248 Duke
Otto II of Bavaria (1231–53) issued a charter for Diessen, in which
he granted the religious community the right of protection over the
church at Unterbrunn in western Bavaria. According to this document,
the duke of Bavaria had decided to make this gift 'in recompense for the
tithe at Oberding, which my illustrious father Duke Ludwig of Bavaria
and I took away from the house of canons a long time ago'.[18] Thus, this
charter suggests a property dispute may have been the reason why the
conversations between Count Berthold I and Mechthild were inserted
in the *vita*. Moreover, the unusual theme of these chapters is perhaps an
indication that Engelhard did not write them; they may have been added
later at Diessen in an attempt to strengthen the religious house's legal
claims to the Oberding tithe at a time when that source of income had
been lost. The overall style of these chapters would seem to confirm
this, as they are not as reliant on biblical allusions as other chapters.
More work on this subject needs to be done, but the evidence suggests
that the text translated here includes both Engelhard's original *vita* and
some material added subsequently at Diessen, after the canons there
had received a copy of his text.

Manuscripts and editions

No one has thoroughly researched the manuscript tradition of this
work; indeed, there is not even general consensus on how many medieval
manuscripts of the *vita* survive.[19] To date, one of the key manuscripts
for the *vita* has been a thirteenth-century codex from Diessen, today
in the Bavarian State Library in Munich, which contains – among other
texts – several saints' lives.[20] The first of these lives is a polished version
of Mechthild's *vita*, including all the chapters (with chapter titles) and
the two dedicatory letters that have been translated here. The same
manuscript also contains additional material for her cult: a sequence,

---

18 *Die Traditionen und Urkunden des Stiftes Diessen*, pp. 149–50, nr. 26.

19 I am immensely grateful to Prof. Martha Newman, who shared with me some of
    her thoughts on this topic, based on her own research into the manuscript tradition
    for Engelhard's works. Some of her findings are available at: https://notevenpast.org/
    medieval-nun-writing/ (accessed 20 July 2016)

20 Munich, Bayerische Staatsbibliothek, Clm 1076, 1r–29r.

hymns and an office.[21] All of these point to the importance of this codex for the spiritual life at Diessen in the later Middle Ages. This manuscript, alongside other sources for Mechthild's cult at Diessen, formed the basis for the Latin edition of the *vita* found in the *Acta Sanctorum*.[22] A facsimile of a 1574 German version of her life has also been published recently.[23]

Notes on this translation

I have relied on the *Acta Sanctorum* edition for this translation, but in tandem with the thirteenth-century Munich manuscript originally housed at Diessen. From this manuscript I have drawn occasional improvements to the text, but the *Acta* edition has, for the most part, proved to be dependable. In one way, this translation does not follow the manuscript: I have placed the two dedicatory letters at the beginning, as they appear in the *Acta Sanctorum*, rather than at the end after the *vita* itself. Although Mechthild was never formally canonized, she is frequently referred to as *sancta* in the text, a word I have translated as 'saint' to maintain the text's intent of praising her holiness. Throughout my translation, I have included numerous biblical citations that were not identified as such in the *Acta Sanctorum* edition.

This is a beautifully written text. Engelhard of Langheim was a gifted author who was capable of seamlessly interweaving biblical passages into his narrative of Mechthild's life. One of his favourite literary touches was to use present tense verbs, rather than past tense ones, when he wanted to lend immediacy to the events at key moments in the text. I have tried to preserve this element of his style, alongside many others, as frequently as possible in this translation. Although this text is more deeply immersed in the hagiographical tradition than the others in this volume, that should not dissuade readers interested in twelfth-century German noble society from engaging with it. Engelhard's work is a rich source for the connections between monastic culture and secular culture in the German-speaking lands in the years around 1200.

---

21 One hymn follows the text; the other material was inserted into the codex before fol. 1.

22 Engelhard of Langheim, *Vita B. Mathildis Virginis*.

23 Dobereiner, *History der heyligen Junckfrawen*.

TRANSLATION

[Dedicatory letter to the canons of Diessen]

Engelhard, poor and small, sends in no small measure greetings in the Lord to the lord provost and all the brothers in Diessen. I have served you, though you did not know my service. I do not know whether you want it or not – would that you bear it patiently! I revealed your treasure [i.e., Mechthild]. Forgive me, I beg, as you reflect on this, because it is good to conceal the king's secret but also honourable to reveal God's glory. You might be uneasy about this, because it does not concern me. This was yours, and perhaps you object with Esau that I have snatched away your blessing. If I should do this again, you would rightly complain: '*for*,' he said, '*this is the second time he has taken advantage of me.*'[1] I have laboured for you this one time in writing the life of the blessed Mechthild. Would that I may deserve the father's blessing on her account, and she may be a Rebecca for me, *lest he shall bring upon me a curse instead of a blessing.*[2] Would that God give me another Mechthild, on whose account I may deserve a second blessing, by writing truth, praising God, putting forward her example, and extolling the miraculous.

These things were done for your Mechthild, nay rather ours, about whom I was asked much but taught little. I wrote what I wrote, and I would have done more, if I had known anything more or better. I would have preferred to be with you, to become another Apollos among you, acting faithfully for the saint, and you would have been Priscilla and Aquila to me, teaching me what I do not know, in order to write these things with strength.[3] Still, there is space for you to earn a well-deserved blessing: fill in my omissions, correct my errors, erase my lies, and fashion glory from my labours in your charity. Christ is God's strength and God's wisdom:[4] he is strength for the sick, wisdom for the foolish. Take up his office yourselves in my place by improving both: by supporting the sick and correcting the foolish. And reflect upon this. That he is the bread, saying, *Those who eat of me will hunger for more.* And

---

1 Genesis 27:36. Esau sold his birthright to his younger brother Jacob, who later used deception to obtain from their father a blessing that should have rightly been given to the eldest son.

2 Genesis 27:12. In his deception, Jacob was helped by his mother, Rebecca.

3 Aquila and his wife Priscilla were early converts to Christianity, who later taught another early convert, Apollos, about the faith (Acts of the Apostles 18).

4 Cf. 1 Corinthians 1:24.

also, he is the spring: *Those who drink of me will thirst for more.*[5] Next, that he is wisdom: *Those who explain me shall have everlasting life.*[6] And I will place last what is first. That he is the stone: *Those who work with me*, it is said, *shall not sin.*[7]

[Dedicatory letter to an unnamed countess]

Brother E[ngelhard], formerly called abbot, now however Christ's pauper in Langheim, [offers] the prayers of a sinner and a pauper's service to the illustrious lady, Countess N.[8] Asked by you to write a life of the blessed Abbess Mechthild, I scarcely have the courage to agree, because I know how difficult it is for the words of an unlearned man to please the learned. There are those who want to fix everything according to weight and measure and plan in the manner of God,[9] and to display everything so established; I would have preferred that those men had seized hold of this work and had taken from me the chance and opportunity to bring false information. But because they refuse, occupied with laws and decrees,[10] I who am fond of talking in a rustic manner will undertake the life of the blessed woman, invoking the Holy Spirit, the author of her sanctity, so that he may confer upon me knowledge of the good things he gave her to do. I do not touch on everything of hers, because I do not know everything. For, as you know, I sat with you scarcely one hour, at which time I collected the chapters as they were recited to us. When she was alive, she did not want her things or any others to be known. Although by the Lord's example she commanded that there be silence concerning her, her virtues were unable to lie hidden, but her strength shouted. May the saint's piety be present for me, may it help me who is undeserving of her merits, so that if I am displeasing to the masters and wise ones of the world with my writing, I will be pleasing to him for whom the saint proved herself. She who did not want to be praised in life, because she was afraid of it, permits praise of her piety after death, because the pious woman is not afraid.

---

5 Ecclesiasticus 24:29.

6 Ecclesiasticus 24:31.

7 Ecclesiasticus 24:30.

8 See the introduction to this text for more on this countess.

9 Cf. Wisdom 11:21.

10 'Leges vel Decreta', seemingly a critique of those churchmen who study canon law.

The life of the blessed Mechthild in Diessen begins[11]

1. Mechthild, offered to Diessen, lived a holy life.[12]

Mechthild, noble in flesh but more noble in mind, took her origin from imperial blood.[13] But she considered her descent to be more from God on account of her piety. She had converted her whole self to this [i.e., piety], she strove after this, she was zealous in this, such that she did not know any other father than God, nor another mother than that church of Diessen, where she had been offered: specifically, its *magistra* at the time.[14] Indeed, she drew her blood from Diessen, from where she drew her sanctity too. The daughter of the prince of the land, having been betrothed to the son of the heavenly God in the same monastery by a solemn offering, made such a great effort to please her husband that she hated the earthly and loved the heavenly. She knew that she could not be subject to two lords, that the virgin seeking unworthy lovers cannot be loved by the noblest man. She had heard from David: *Listen daughter, and look, and incline your ear, and the king will long for your beauty.*[15] And so it happened. She listened in fear, now she sees in exultation; she bent her ear, exhibiting humble and cheerful obedience, and this kindled the king's desire for her.[16]

She entered the monastery at the age of five. She did not place a foot outside of it, nor her tongue, nor her heart, and no profane word was ever heard from her mouth. The sweet infant managed her childish things so maturely that she reproved those mature in age, not by word but by example.

---

11 This opening is taken from the manuscript: Munich, Bayerische Staatsbibliothek, Clm 1076, fol. 1v.

12 The title of this first chapter is also taken from the manuscript, fol. 1r. The *Acta Sanctorum* edition has instead '*Quo fuit genere nata*'. The other chapter titles are, with only minor variations, the same in the manuscript and the edition.

13 Mechtild is later described as a relative of Emperor Frederick I Barbarossa (see ch. 17, p. 196), and one of Frederick's own charters refers to her brother Otto as a relative as well (*MGH DD F. I*, 4:50–1, nr. 840). Though they were not close relatives, there was a kin connection through Mechthild's mother, Sophia: Weller, *Die Heiratspolitik*, 702–4.

14 See *The life of an unnamed magistra of Admont*, translated in this volume, for more about the office of *magistra*.

15 Psalm 44:11.

16 For the significance of obedience for the monastic life, cf. *RB 1980: the rule of St Benedict*, 186–9, ch. 5.

2. When she had grown, she abstained from meat and wine.

She grew in body, she grew in mind, and she grew in virtue, even more than in age. Often, she ventured on account of her strength to put forth her hand toward strong things,[17] to control her flesh by abstaining from meat: not so that she might reject God's creation, which is good, but so that she might not nourish the sins of the flesh by eating meat. She also abstained from wine, *in which there is luxury*,[18] so that she might often drink in drunkenness that wine that cheers the heart of man,[19] and she might say in the cheerfulness of her heart, *A cluster of henna blossoms my love is to me.*[20] Lastly, she frequently received that flesh of the paschal lamb [i.e., the Eucharist], of the lamb taking away the sins of the world,[21] in forgiveness of her own sins, eating it with the mind rather than the teeth, making herself an earthly temple for it, both in her heart and body. This was not sufficient in her eyes; she further anticipated greater things, with the spirit sustaining the infirmity of her sex. And she thought little of baths, hearing with Peter, *He who has had a bath needs only to wash his feet.*[22] I would even deny that she washed her feet, lest she heard that thunder: *If I do not wash you, you will have no part with me.*[23]

3. She did not use bodily medicine.

She was frequently sick and said with Paul, *For when I am sick, then am I* stronger and *powerful*; gladly, therefore, did she glory in her weakness, so that the strength of Christ might dwell in her. She was determined and tested, because *strength is made perfect in weakness.*[24] For this reason, she never gave earthly medicine to her body; thus was she similar to Agatha, and a companion to her.[25] For although the sword was absent at her death, nevertheless she was wounded daily with the

17 Cf. Proverbs 31:19.

18 Ephesians 5:18.

19 Cf. Psalm 103:15.

20 Song of Songs 1:13.

21 Cf. John 1:18. During the Mass, the *Agnus Dei* is always sung at the start of communion.

22 John 13:10.

23 John 13:8.

24 Cf. 2 Corinthians 12:9–10.

25 St Agatha, a virgin martyr. She refused medicine, and St Peter appeared to her in a vision and healed her wounds. Cf. *The life of an unnamed* magistra *of Admont*, ch. 4, where the *magistra* is also described as refusing earthly medicine.

sword of the word of God.[26] She drew it all to herself: what she heard in speech, what she read in texts. She crucified her flesh along with vices and desires, fearing the supplications of hell, striving for the promises of heaven.

4. That she was obedient beyond the measure of man.

She did nothing by her own decision. She hung upon the word of the *magistra* for everything, such that what she [i.e., the *magistra*] prohibited, the other never undertook; what she ordered, Mechthild never disregarded, never delayed to do. She was so obedient that she had appropriated for her own use the ancient miracle of obeying, and she abandoned any imperfect work whatsoever as soon as she heard the voice of that one calling or ordering her. Because she had been taught to write and was accustomed to do so, it was very frequently discovered at the sound of the calling *magistra* or the bell that she had not finished the letters she had begun. Thus did she hear the Lord's praise about herself: as soon as she heard me, she obeyed me.[27]

Also, comparing herself to a strong man – about whom Solomon said, *an obedient man will speak of victories*[28] – our Mechthild spoke of victories, by conquering her heart, conquering her sex, conquering the devil. And having been made in God's spirit, she was one spirit and one heart with God, since indeed (with Paul as witness), *he who is joined to the Lord is one spirit.*[29] Then, in her mind, she stood above everything as if on a mountain in the heavens; she saw and looked down upon all things under her, singing and chanting in her heart that song of purity, that song of charity: *I despised the kingdom of the earth and every ornate thing of the world, on account of the love of my Lord Jesus Christ, whom I have seen*[30] with proper faith, sought with firm hope, and loved with perfect charity. And thus our Mechthild, *in the midst of young damsels playing on tambourines*[31] sang *of the ways of the Lord, for great is the glory of the Lord.*[32]

---

26 Cf. Hebrews 4:12.

27 Cf. 2 Samuel 22:45. Cf. *The life of an unnamed* magistra *of Admont*, ch. 4, where the *magistra* is also described as knowing how to write.

28 Proverbs 21:28.

29 1 Corinthians 6:17.

30 *Regnum mundi et omnem ornatum*: a chant sung as part of the monastic office.

31 Psalm 67:26.

32 Psalm 137:5.

5. That she was patient in her weakness.

She joined strength to strength, obedience to patience. She bore every whip lash of weakness from God, of adversity from her neighbour, of temptation from the devil. She complained about none of these things, nor did she become indignant or resist them. For when she was tempted by the devil, she set herself against him with all her strength, and she rejected and despised him. She never had anyone as an enemy except him. Greater than every jealousy, she overcame the jealous ones [i.e., the other canonesses] – if there were any – with charity. She dismayed them with her strength, she overwhelmed them with her authority, she laid them low with her humility (as she would have done even to herself), if any of them attempted anything against her. For the most noble one of them all made herself a maidservant to all of them, placing herself before no one, comparing herself to no one. She made herself into a broken vessel,[33] but a useful one, and into an honour for everyone who was in the house of God. Nevertheless, if anyone at any time said anything that could offend, as is accustomed to happen, she strove to disregard it with deaf ears; she closed her ears, following the Prophet, lest she hear of bloodshed, and averted her eyes, lest she see vanities.[34] She had imposed such strict silence upon herself that you would have believed her mute; indeed if she did speak, you would have thought you were conferring with an angel.[35]

6. That she would avoid lying.

She guarded against lying. She hated it so much that no flesh would accuse her of it. She strove to be excellent in conscience so that, following Job, her heart would not rebuke her so long as she lived.[36] For this reason, she was beloved to God and to men, and because many people entreated her with devotion, she was tested by their little gifts. Guarding herself as a turtledove for his turtledove,[37] she despised presents, rejected flatteries, and fled conversations. As a result, it was only reluctantly that she allowed her princely brothers to see her – and so briefly that it was sufficient for her to sit with them for a quarter of an hour. For

33 Cf. Psalm 30:13.

34 Cf. Isaiah 33:15.

35 See *RB 1980: the rule of St Benedict*, 190–1, ch. 6 for the importance of silence in religious communities.

36 Cf. Job 27:6.

37 According to the medieval bestiary tradition, the turtledove would not remarry or take another lover after the death of its first partner. See *Bestiary*, 163.

this reason she became more dear to them, and she therefore refused their conversations. She knew that sin could not be absent when speaking too much.[38] Because she responded reluctantly to questions, she showed in herself that *a wholesome tongue is a tree of life.*[39] On account of this, they did not call her 'sister', but they cherished and honoured her by calling her their 'lady'.[40]

7. How, although severe to herself, she was pious and merciful to others.

She possessed nothing of her own, and accordingly she said nothing was hers. She made her things common to everyone, and accordingly she allowed herself to possess nothing separately in preference to others.[41] She was so pious, so merciful to everyone, so patient, so compassionate to all, that she believed anyone else's pain was hers; in short, by Paul's example, *she rejoiced with those who rejoice, she wept with those who weep,*[42] she was weak with those who were weak, and she burned at the sins of others.[43] Grey from these feelings, a youthful saint from these emotions, she managed her life blamelessly in old age, pleasing to the greater and to the lesser. To everyone she returned what was owed: subjection to prelates, honour to her elders, love to her juniors. But also, when making a request to the maidservants, she commanded that they not call her 'lady' but 'sister'. And so, while she fled, she did not escape honour; while she shows favour to everyone, she reluctantly has everyone's favour.

8. That she is elected *magistra* in Diessen.

A shining and burning light, she wanted to be hidden concealed under a bushel. But what she wanted, she could not have; she was placed upon a candlestick, so that she might give light to everyone entering the house.[44] That house in Diessen was deprived of its *magistra*. Everyone felt sorrow and grief – but most of all Mechthild, who then for the first time felt herself to be an orphan, because (as was said before) she did not know that she had another mother and valued that other one

---

38 Again, see *RB 1980: the rule of St Benedict,* 190–1, ch. 6 on silence.

39 Proverbs 15:4.

40 This is presumably a reference to her brothers in the Andechs lineage. She had three: Count Poppo of Andechs and Giech (d. 1148), Count Berthold II of Andechs, margrave of Istria (d. 1188), and Bishop Otto II of Bamberg (d. 1196).

41 Cf. *RB 1980: the rule of St Benedict,* 230–3, chs 33–34.

42 Romans 12:15.

43 Cf. 2 Corinthians 11:29.

44 Cf. Matthew 5:15.

little.[45] Discussions about replacing her [i.e., the *magistra*] with another kept them busy, but every point led to this: who mixed the useful with the sweet? What might each say more usefully, what might each hear more sweetly, than 'let Mechthild rule us, govern us, order us'? The Lord made his word short.[46] Result follows speech, happiness follows result, constancy follows happiness.

Mechthild becomes *magistra*; she grieves, she refuses, she cries out in protest, she who had refused no order, no request before. She is compelled on the strength of her obedience; being obedient, she does the work of the Evangelist, teaching *and arguing persuasively about the kingdom of God* with faith, with fervour, with sweetness.[47] Previously she had been attentive to saving only her own soul. Now she is attentive to saving many, restraining her body and reducing it to servitude, lest by chance she be found worthless while preaching to others, lest they say to her as if in secrecy, *Doctor, heal thyself.*[48] Before, she had fasted often, she had been on her guard even more often, and she had prayed as often as possible. She thinks she had done nothing; she is equipped for the first time now. Seizing the arms of God's army, the spiritual arms, the arms of God's power, she becomes another Judith, ready to fight with Holofernes.[49] She becomes Esther, ready to destroy the wickedest enemy, Haman.[50] Finally, she becomes Miriam, ready to go before the people of God *with tambourines and dances.*[51] She exhorts those under her, *Sing to the Lord, for he is highly exalted.*[52] Praising the name of the Lord with a song, she glorified him in praise. She began to work and to teach with Jesus.

First, she entered the chapter with everyone. She was seated at her work. Firm in her discipline, she intermingled all things with piety, knowing according to the Apostle that *bodily discipline is only of little*

---

45 Cf. ch. 1 above for similar language, but also ch. 21 below, where reference is made to her birth mother.

46 Cf. Romans 9:28.

47 Acts of the Apostles 19:8.

48 Luke 4:23.

49 Cf. Judith 13:6–8, where Judith cuts off Holofernes' head with his own sword.

50 Cf. Esther 9, where Queen Esther convinces her husband, the king of Persia, to execute Haman, who had plotted to kill the Jews.

51 Exodus 15:20, where the prophetess Miriam, Aaron's sister, and the other Israelite women celebrate the defeat of Pharaoh's army.

52 Exodus 15:21.

profit.[53] There was no distinction in diet, no distinction in clothing,
except that she wore more common things, and she could not be distinguished from the others except by her clothing – not that it was
dirty, to be sure, but it was more common than everyone else's. A sign
of her judgement was the humility and cheerfulness of her expression,
which was so noble, so remarkable, that she showed herself an angel
in it. So serious, so mature was her expression that immodesty and
levity dared nothing in her presence. In short, she led herself and hers
[i.e., her sisters] in such a way that that house was a school of Christ,
joined to God through love to such an extent that, following the Prophet,
no one's mouth would speak the works of men.[54] And each one coming,
hearing and withdrawing bore witness that *God is with you.*[55] Today
Mechthild, as if living in body, is an example of holiness to them.

9. That she is elected abbess in Edelstetten.
Our Mechthild was gold, which had passed through fire. It seemed
pure to everyone, even transforming gloriously into the crown of the
highest king. It was produced with hammers, but what it was producing
was better still. The work she had done already did not suffice for God.
He calls her again to work, to gain for himself people worthy of
acceptance, pursuers of good works, and to call those who were not
the people of God, the people of God.[56]
There was a house among the ancient churches, noble in its persons,
rich in its resources [i.e., Edelstetten]. The abbess had died, and monastic
discipline had likewise departed, either before her death or with it.
Truly, it is the customary and just judgement of God that, when discipline
is neglected, properties and goods are most certainly destroyed. *In those
days there was no king in Israel,*[57] and each person did what seemed right
to him. The house had fallen into decay, its resources had been ruined,
its discipline had been taken away.[58] As for its restoration: those who
cared about it and had the heart for it thought that God might have

---

53 1 Timothy 4:8.

54 Cf. Psalm 16:4, which Engelhard may be confusing with Isaiah 37:19.

55 Zechariah 8:23.

56 Cf. Hosea 2:24 and Romans 9:25.

57 Judges 18:1.

58 Cf. *The deeds of Margrave Wiprecht of Groitzsch; The life of Bishop Otto of Bamberg;*
    and *The deeds of Count Ludwig of Arnstein* for similar language regarding monastic
    communities in need of reform.

glory in this place of God, discipline might bloom again, vices might cease, virtues might be planted anew. They asked, through whom might that be done? *No one was found worthy, who would open the book*, except *the lion of the tribe of Judah*,[59] and his maidservant Mechthild, the *magistra* in Diessen.

'Let them choose her,' the princes say. The bishop recommends her. 'We will be obedient in this,' the sisters say. 'We choose her, we ask for her,' everyone says.[60] The election takes place; the result is exultation. 'Praise and glory to God' is shouted. They pray for favourable things for the one elected, for peace for the house, for abundance in properties, for discipline in habits. God was present for the doing of these things: for their beginning, their advancement, and their completion with a blessed finish.

They send the announcement of the election in her favour. Papal authority commands it.[61] The prayers of the princes are joined together with the humble and devout petition of the sisters, the supplication of the whole household, and also the bountiful promise of the province to be served. All these things, in the company of messengers, were recommended in letters, strengthened with witnesses, and approved by the people.

They come to the place [i.e., Diessen] and open the message; the letters give testimony about the messengers, whose nobility had even more of an effect than what was written. The news flew through the house. Grief takes hold of everyone, because they were reluctantly about to lose the treasure they had discovered, the best pearl, through whose love the love of God had become strong in them. They did not know any other loves except only God's love and Mechthild's. The petition came to her, she blushed, she refused, she cried out in protest, saying, *'They have made me the keeper in the vineyards: my own vineyard I have not kept.*[62] It is enough that I have not guarded the one under my own authority, rather than I neglect that one too after this one.' However, episcopal authority prevailed, aided by the eloquence of the messengers

---

59 Revelation 5:4–5 (i.e., Jesus, the only one who would open the book with the seven seals).

60 The bishop here is likely Bishop Conrad of Augsburg. The 'princes' cannot be identified.

61 See the introduction to this text for Pope Anastasius IV's letter of 1153–54 concerning her reluctance to become abbess.

62 Song of Songs 1:5.

and the petitioners, such that she yielded; God's will was done more than hers. Nevertheless, the sisters and the household persisted in their sadness, recognizing the extraordinary loss to the progress each had in her presence.

Another Rebecca, she acquiesces, she walks with the children of Abraham, she comes to Isaac ready to bear not a few daughters for him, she meets him at the well of living and seeing.[63] She finds him there, possessing his soul in patience.[64] Accordingly, the patience of Rebecca leads toward laughter, who is Isaac,[65] and takes a walk to the well of living and seeing Scripture. For the living man has no other laughter except the laughter from the promise of God's word. But he does not see, unless God uncovers his eyes, so that he might consider the wonders of God's law. Thus, another Rachel, she proceeds to water her father's sheep. *For she fed the flock,*[66] this one of animals, that one of men. And behold, Jacob drew out water for her from the well, bringing water to the sheep with her, and made them to be led back to pasture.[67] And was she not Sephora, whom Moses defended from the violent shepherds, so that he might give water together with her to the flock, and might afterwards drive it to pasture?[68]

Now these things happened to them as an example for us.[69] Instead of those three – I mean Isaac and Jacob and Moses – Mechthild had Christ feeding the flock with her, with that bread, which descends from heaven and gives life to the world. And he also gave water from that spring, which flows forth from Paradise and afterwards is divided into four branches, because he himself is distributed into four principal virtues.[70] Toward this proceeds Lady Mechthild with the Queen of Sheba to hear the wisdom of Solomon, ready to show herself a friend,

---

63 Cf. Genesis 24ff. for the story of Isaac and Rebecca, especially 24:62 for 'the well which is called of the living and the seeing'.

64 Cf. Luke 21:19.

65 'Rebecca' means patience (Isidore of Seville, *Isidori Hispalensis Episcopi Etymologiarum sive Originum Libri XX*, VII.6.35), and 'Isaac' means laughter (Cf. Genesis 21:1–7). For a comparable example of the type of exegetical work that Engelhard is doing here, see Richard of St Victor, *The twelve patriarchs*.

66 Genesis 29:9.

67 Cf. Genesis 29:1–12 for this story.

68 Cf. Exodus 2:15–17.

69 Cf. 1 Corinthians 10:11.

70 Cf. Genesis 2:10–14.

a dove, beautiful, not by her own merits, but by the gift of Solomon's grace.[71] She proceeds, I say, with the rejoicing and exulting [sisters of Edelstetten], who would lead her forth, and with the weeping and grieving [sisters of Diessen], who would send her away. Who may lose a mass of gold and not suffer pain? Who may receive the gleaming pearl and the precious gemstone with equanimity? Picture Mechthild in your own mind like that, but reflect that it is more painful for those who had lost her.

But why should I lengthen the path that is already long enough, and why should I not lead this one forth on her way? May I present her to them [i.e., the sisters in Edelstetten]? The awaited one comes, and the blessing of the Lord with her. She is received with a song of joy, with kisses of exultation. The daughters rush into the embraces of the new mother of their household. Also, the whole body of followers is bowed before the lady's countenance. She is brought away to rest, but there is no rest, where she sees work to be done; nor is there rest, where she sees advice to be given, without work, about grave injuries. The strong woman clothes herself in the spirit of a man, she whose value is found not nearby but far away, at the farthest reaches.[72] She works as if she did nothing before, and the fruit of happiness followed her work.

10. How she lived in office.

Previously, she had no reason to fight with her fellow man, nor was she compelled to spend time on earthly matters. Now, everything hung at her command, and from Mary would have been made Martha, if she had not chosen the best part for herself at the feet of the Lord.[73] From there, the Lord answered for her, providing her with some relief for her responsibilities: men working with her on the outside and sisters on the inside, all of them faithful and prudent in conducting their business. They pledged themselves to help her with her responsibilities and deferred the fullness of power to the lady.[74] She hastened to be

---

71 Cf. 1 Kings 10 for the Queen of Sheba's visit to King Solomon's court.

72 Cf. Proverbs 31:10 and *The deeds of Count Ludwig of Arnstein*, ch. 6, p. 234, where the same biblical passage is used for a very different purpose.

73 Cf. Luke 10:38–42, where the sisters Mary and Martha welcome Jesus into their house. Mary, who sits at Jesus's feet, is frequently understood to represent the spiritual life, while Martha, who works around the house serving the guests, is frequently understood to represent the active life.

74 *Plenitudo potestatis* was a term typically reserved for papal authority over the whole of the Roman church.

called 'Sister Mechthild', without the addition of 'Lady', despising
everything lofty in title. But the custom of the house and the rule of
the monastery required that she be called 'Lady' and 'Abbess'. She had
to be raised to this title and blessed solemnly by the bishop. She certainly
would not have consented to this, if she had not feared diminishing the
house in its rights and refusing God's gift to her.

Therefore, she consented. She was blessed, and was raised up by the
blessing. Raised up, I say, through grace, raised to glory – not so much
the glory of the title as the glory of perfected virtue. You would have
seen that the more complete is joined to the complete in her, the more
perfect to the perfect, such that he who did not know with how much
rigour she had lived previously might have thought that she was atoning
for past delights with a new punishment of the flesh. But she had
mastered the flesh to such an extent that she desired nothing hostile
to the spirit. She served as a handmaid to the Lord, not unwillingly, or
under compulsion, but she wanted this voluntarily, delighted by the
sweetness of virtue. Therefore, she sang in the ways of the Lord, since
the glory of God is great; she said to God in her prayers, *I rejoice in
following your statutes, as one rejoices in great riches.*[75] She did this, she
taught this, and she drew her flock after her with the same affection.
She was like the woman of the Gospel, who put yeast in three measures
of corn until all of it was leavened.[76]

Nevertheless, this was not easy in the beginning, for it was hard
for them [i.e., the sisters of Edelstetten] to abandon the things to
which they had grown accustomed; it was hard for them to want, more
than forbidden liberties, to prohibit those forbidden liberties. But these
things were prohibited, because the Lord worked together with the
abbess and strengthened her speech with accompanying signs. You
ask: with what signs? The first sign that the saint gave was herself: a
noble young woman, lordly in appearance, lovely in sight. So excellent
was she in her manners, so excellent was she in her movements, so
excellent in eloquence, so excellent in her companionship that no flesh
would reprove her. Nor did rumour dare to speak falsely about her,
because, as St Ambrose bears witness, the greatest dignity is that with
which the virgin is entrusted.[77] As excellent as Mary the mother of

---

75 Psalm 118:14.

76 Cf. Matthew 13:33.

77 This is probably a reference to Ambrose's *De Virginibus*.

God was, so too was her attendant, Mechthild, who imitated her in every observance of divine law; imitated her, I say, as far as that divine birth, which was Mary's privilege alone, and which separated her from his consorts in the fullness of grace. But he who was Mary's son: this one is Mechthild's bridegroom. He was so sweet to her, that she believed there was nothing that was not sweet, she reckoned there was nothing that was not agreeable, with which he would have been able to please her.

She was so effective at persuading people that she softened the hardest hearts, and she corrected every trivial thing toward perfection by saying a beneficial word. The one who had been corrected would say with Job, *The things that before my soul would not touch, now, through sorrows are my meats.*[78] Thus had she made them fearful of God, thus had she caused them to repent for their past life, such that they heard from the Apostle, *What fruit did you have then in the things of which you are now ashamed? For the end of those things is death.*[79] And in heeding her commands, she was the embodiment of the fear of God for them, so much so that they were able to say with Job, *I have always feared God as waves swelling over me, and his majesty I was not able to bear.*[80] After this, the willing ones were persuaded, and whatever had been twisted or bent, she put back in line, she recalled to the rule. She fixed all things in weight, measure, and plan,[81] saying to herself those lines of poetry,

A measure exists in all things, as do, in short, prescribed limits;
Go beyond or fall short of them and you cannot be right.[82]

Mechthild strove for what was right, such that she sang mercy and justice to the Lord, but with the Lord she exalted mercy above justice. She regulated everything, yet she also distinguished individual things in such a way that the strong ones sought more work for God and the weak ones did not run away. She said, in the spirit of discretion, what Jacob said: 'If I cause my flocks to be overdriven, in one day they all

---

78 Job 6:7.

79 Romans 6:21.

80 Job 31:23.

81 Cf. Wisdom 11:21.

82 Horace, *Satires*, I.1.106–7 (*Satires and Epistles*, 5). Note that this whole section is rather abstract but is explaining how she forcefully reformed the community at Edelstetten.

will die.'[83] Exhorting them boldly, she said what Solomon said: '*Whatever your hand finds to do, do it with all your might, for in the grave, where you are going, there is neither working, nor planning, nor wisdom.*'[84] And consoling them, she added, '*the sufferings of this time are not worthy to be compared with the glory to come, that will be revealed to us.*'[85] Also: '*For this slight momentary affliction is preparing for us an eternal weight of glory beyond all comparison.*'[86] And she also admired this: '*No eye has seen, no ear has heard, no mind has conceived what God has prepared* for those loving him.'[87] 'These things,' she said, 'are so great and excellent that it is easy to endure vigils, fasts and any adversities whatsoever on account of them.'

Her life and speech proved this, joining hand to tongue, work to word; nay rather, she placed a finger over her mouth, so that deeds might surpass words, and she might not teach the others what she herself had not done more of and first. She led the way with so much pious compassion that not by her words or by the title of her office was she considered their mother, but by her work and integrity. She exhibited so much confidence to everyone with her that their consciences hid nothing from her. Indeed, they were naked to her, like Adam and Eve: naked, I say, in heart, not body; in purity, not indiscretion; not in shamelessness, but innocence.[88]

11. That she closed off the opened cloister.

Now, she turned her thoughts towards producing greater fruit, towards prohibiting men access to the glory of the bridegroom, so that the truth of their chastity might be witnessed by these men from the outside – and so that the enemy might not have anything to say about them for the sake of disparaging them. She speaks to the sisters about this, she hears some speaking against it, but she does not heed them. She insists on speaking to them about the purpose of chastity, the powerful vow established by profession, the fragile sex, the multi-form enemy, and how it was not safe for women to join with him on the field of battle. But, according to Martin's judgement, there is enough to praise

---

83 Cf. Genesis 33:13.

84 Ecclesiastes 9:10.

85 Romans 8:18.

86 2 Corinthians 4:17.

87 1 Corinthians 2:9.

88 Cf. Genesis 2:25.

if they secure themselves inside fortresses.[89] Moreover, it is most filthy
if men frequently visit women, or women men. And she also plucked
many flowers of Scriptures for the purpose of urging chastity. Most
smelled the scent of life from these, such that they desired enclosure
for themselves; some received the scent of death, such that they refused
to be enclosed in any way.

The word came forth, it was received as if sent by God, and it was
committed to God by prayer. The bishop is summoned, the word previously concealed is made known. The [sisters'] wishes are sought; different
ones are found. But in the end, except for a few, all are converted after
the abbess. They render thanks and praise to God; those wanting to
remain are enclosed, those not wanting to be enclosed are sent away
of their own accord.[90] Then, at last, the garden of the Lord flourished,
and its *plants are* just as *a paradise of pomegranates with the choicest fruits
of the orchard.*[91] Those conversations that previously tended to be held
with *milites* were turned toward the angels, and in the clefts of the rock,
in the hidden places of the wall were dwelling doves,[92] who were happy
by themselves, engrossed in the wounds of Christ and in the crowd of
angels. They hastened with longing to paradise, carried by the joyful
delights in their hearts, and they invited the bridegroom to the garden
with tears, so that *he may feed his flock among the lilies,*[93] where each
might say to him with her individual strengths, '*How sweet are thy words
to my palate, more than honey to my mouth;*[94] to speak, however, about the
earthly is more bitter than absinth.'[95]

Thus flourished the garden of the Lord, which Mechthild had sown
for him with the help of the Holy Spirit. It was beautiful to see, sweet
to taste, pleasant to smell, but delicate to touch. For she had planted
new things, and she took careful precaution, lest they be incautiously
disturbed by worldly speech. Afterwards, she was glad to admit spiritual
and learned men, irrigators, asking each one to pour out his bowls
and to cool her plants with the word of God, to maintain the gardens,

---

89 I have been unable to identify a source for this reference.
90 In other words, the bishop seems to have asked each of the sisters if she wished to
remain with Mechthild in the reformed community or to leave it.
91 Song of Songs 4:13.
92 Cf. Song of Songs 2:14.
93 Song of Songs 2:16.
94 Psalm 118:103.
95 Cf. Proverbs 5:4.

the gardens planted with spices. Thus did Mechthild work, making
daily offerings, saying to God, 'Make perfect the vineyard your right
hand has planted, and may the wild beast of the field be absent from
it for a long time.[96] May your good spirit work good in it.' Therefore,
the daughters of God, separated from the sons of men, strove to be
above men, sitting with Mary at the feet of the Lord, and listening
to his word.[97] Their mother above them rejoiced that they were
praised by the voice of God, because they had chosen the best part for
themselves.

12. How she was frequently in church.

I was not silent before about the zeal she had, the fervour. But now,
as if starting anew, just as the eagle restores its youth in God's service,[98]
she began to seek high places – not, as it were, to walk above the earth,
but to say with Paul, *'Our conversation is in heaven.'*[99] She was frequently
in church, uniting her mind most truly with God, in conversation with
the angels, in cohabitation with the saints, rejoicing that she was near
their relics. If someone had sought her elsewhere, she would not have
found her; but finding her in that place [i.e., church], she would not
have dared to disturb her. The bridegroom would have stood above her
[i.e., the one seeking Mechthild], restraining her and saying, *'I entreat
you, daughters of Jerusalem, that you not rouse her, that you not awaken my
beloved, until she should wish it.'*[100] She presented herself so excellently
in the hour of prayer that another, who wanted to divert her from God,
seemed to do injury to him. And he seemed to say to Mechthild, 'Who
touches you, *touches the apple of my eye.'*[101]

For this reason, she clung to God, and she gloried in being one spirit
with him. She said, *'His left hand is under my head, and his right hand
will embrace me.*[102] And so *in peace I will both lie down and sleep.'*[103] How

---

96 Cf. Psalm 79:14–16.

97 See above, n. 73, for the story of Mary and Martha.

98 According to the medieval bestiary tradition, eagles, when they grow old, fly close
    to the sun until their wings catch fire and then dive into water, restoring their
    youth. See *Bestiary,* 118–9.

99 Philippians 3:20.

100 Song of Songs 8:4.

101 Zechariah 2:8.

102 Song of Songs 2:6.

103 Psalm 4:9.

sweetly she slept, sheltered in the shelter of God's presence from the confusion of men, protected in God's dwelling from objecting tongues![104] Oh, happy soul, how often it was given to you to arrange in your heart the means of ascent *in the vale of tears*,[105] and to go from strength to strength, and finally to see the God of gods in Zion, and to say with Paul, *'But we all, with unveiled face, beholding the glory of the Lord, are transformed into the same image from glory to glory, as by the Spirit of the Lord.'*[106] How often it happened that you covered your face like Moses,[107] because of your cheeks wet with tears, receiving from your father with Axa *the upper and lower springs*[108] – and as if saying to those who ask, *'The king brought me to his banquet hall and raised the banner of love over me.'*[109]

You went forth so excellently from the sight of the Lord, full of thanks, splendid and wise, because you had been speaking with the Lord.[110] You accomplished more by contemplating and praying in Christ, with God's strength and wisdom, than by reading from the page, or by hearing the masters in school. How often in your bed at night did you seek him whom your soul loved, nay rather whom it loves? For *love is eternal.*[111] And even if the house of love, your flesh, ended in death, truly your soul, in the middle between flesh and love, with the help of love and the testimony of truth, always lives. Rejoice and be glad now, *daughter of Zion*,[112] because you see the king of glory through the mirror and the mystery. But however much we are living in the flesh, we are not fighting after the way of the flesh:[113] that you were permitted to see. Nevertheless, you lifted yourself above yourself, saying in your heart, *Oh that I had wings like a dove! I would fly and be at rest.*[114] You strove for those hidden places in the wall,[115] the wall partly destroyed,

---

104 Cf. Psalm 30:21.

105 Psalm 83:7.

106 2 Corinthians 3:18.

107 Cf. Exodus 34:33–5.

108 Judges 1:15. Axa was the daughter of Caleb; she asked him for springs, because he had given her only arid lands when she married.

109 Song of Songs 2:4.

110 Cf. Exodus 34:29.

111 1 Corinthians 13:8.

112 Matthew 21:5 and John 12:15.

113 Cf. 2 Corinthians 10:3.

114 Psalm 54:7.

115 Cf. Song of Songs 2:14.

the sparkling gemstones falling from it; in the middle of those stones walked that blessed Lucifer (with Ezechiel as witness), until, no longer blessed, he burned from God's fire, because he kindled another fire, namely envy.[116] And from there he fell, and according to John he dragged *a third of the stars of heaven* after him.[117] From the princes of light were made the princes of darkness; against them is our battle, not against flesh and blood.

Our Mechthild meditated on these things – nay rather, God's Mechthild, because if we came to know her according to the flesh, yet now we know her so no longer, and she acknowledged no man according to the flesh.[118] She said, *it is good for me to be near God, to put my hope in the Lord God.*[119] She forgot those things that are in the past, extending her thoughts to the foremost things, thirsting for higher things, grasping eternal things in her mind. She frequently focused her eye on that angelic material, cleansing her eye from the dust of earthly desire, rubbing it with the antimony of heavenly wisdom,[120] so that she might see wisdom itself and arrange everything, with the individual orders of the heavenly virtues arranged in wisdom and distributed in this material. Oh, how desirable it was for her to reflect on wisdom, reaching boldly from one end to the other, and distributing all things sweetly, building from living stones that Jerusalem, which partly reigns, partly lives in exile as yet, and from exile receives daily the ones who return, rebuilding those hidden places of Jerusalem's wall in holy souls![121] She considers those many rooms in the father's house:[122] rooms granted for good works, provided for everyone, overflowing with delights, with perpetual joys, mingled together with the angels, separate in glories – but united with the chain and glue of charity. *To go from strength to strength*[123] was delightful for her; to go, I say, in spirit with desire around that temple, which is in heaven, to offer the incense of praise to God, and also to give glory to every order of angels from the offering of her heart. She brought forth praise for those blessed souls, for each one singularly, seeking intercession, preparing her share of happiness with them.

---

116 Cf. Ezekiel 28:12–19.

117 Revelation 12:4.

118 Cf. 2 Corinthians 5:16.

119 Psalm 72:28.

120 Antimony was used to colour eyelids, eyebrows and eyelashes black.

121 Cf. Nehemiah 2–3.

122 Cf. John 14:2.

123 Psalm 83:8.

Who do you think was there for each blessed soul with Mary, the lady of virgins, the queen of virgins? Oh, how often she sighed to her, speaking to her, and comforting herself in bed with her, away from the sinfulness of the world, from the snares of the devil, from the defiles of his dwelling! She considered this one [i.e., Mary] to be a unique comfort, the first to be contemplated, and the model and order for her life; through her, she approached the spirit, her spirit's guide. But she also consulted the instructress, sacred Scripture, so that she might follow this rather than her own sense to the contemplation of God. Safe to advance with these leading the way [i.e., Mary and Sacred Scripture], she entered into the holy of holies, contemplating with a pious heart that wonderful tabernacle, a copy of that one which was shown to Moses. And it was said, 'Look, make everything carefully according to the copy that was shown to you.'[124] The golden altar before the eyes of the Lord is wondrous, and under the altar are the souls of those who were slain [i.e., for the word of God];[125] and there was also the throne of God, at which sat those twenty-four elders in their seats;[126] and too four animals, having six wings, and full of eyes everywhere;[127] then, also, those 144,000, singing a new song;[128] and also the bosom of Abraham,[129] protector of the souls of the saints; and finally, that *great multitude, which no man could number, of all peoples, and tribes and tongues, standing before the throne, and holding palms in their hands.*[130] Our Mechthild was accustomed to contemplate these and similar things. She was more learned in her seeing than I in my speaking, and also more blessed in her experience than I, inexperienced, in my knowledge.

It is pleasing to follow our abbess to this place, inside into the king's reception hall she has entered; but I cannot bear to endure the brightness, on which she is nourished. My eyes are repelled as if by blindness, and I shout after her back, *'Enter into the joy of your Lord,*[131] for you are very worthy. And remember me, when you are well, so that you may suggest to your bridegroom that he remember me.'[132]

---

124 Cf. Exodus 25:40.

125 Cf. Revelation 6:9.

126 Cf. Revelation 4:4.

127 Cf. Revelation 4:6–8.

128 Cf. Revelation 14:3.

129 Cf. Luke 16:22

130 Revelation 7:9.

131 Matthew 25:21.

132 Cf. Luke 23:42.

13. That she lay down in straw without feathers.

This was her work,[133] or rather her idleness that was not idle in the church. It was sweetest for her to be employed in this during the day, but she also spent very much time at night doing this, or rather all her time. For this reason, lest the bed might caress her, and she might be slower to rise, she slept not on feathers but on straw. She would have rejected bedcovers too, if she had not shunned praise, and she would have willingly slept naked upon the ground, or upon stone. Nevertheless, milder to her sisters everywhere than to herself, she provided couches, little pillows and bed linens, and clean clothing, saying that nothing harms souls in this, provided the sisters are not considered proud or prone to excess. She recommended this approach for all sorts of things; however, she denied it to herself on account of the bodily benefits that came from not sparing the body. Nonetheless, she kept an eye on the others, demanding from none of the sisters more than each was able. As was said, she loved cleanliness with poverty, and so that she might give satisfaction to the honest man, she did not want to seem a pauper but to be one. Therefore, she had a sack of straw instead of feathers under her; this sack, covered with linen cloth, showed her ostentation and did not have value.

But what did she care about? She cared about her heart, preparing it fully for the Lord, seeking in her bed the one her soul loved. But not finding him, she rose and wandered through the city, seeking the one she loved. That city, I say, which is on high: Jerusalem, our mother. O, how often the sentries who guarded the city found her, and she asked them, '*Have you seen him, whom my soul loves?*' She passed right through them and found him whom her soul loves.[134] She had him as a companion, she prepared herself as a companion to him, and was one spirit clinging to him. What do I say she was? She is preferably a lover: then in hope, but now in fact; then in her soul's desire, now in fullness. Not the fullness that produces disgust, but the fullness that the delight of delighting promises everlastingly. Moreover, she said with Isaiah to the Lord, nay rather to her bridegroom, '*My soul yearns for you in the night; in the morning my spirit longs for you.*'[135] Thus, she slept,

133 A reference to the previous chapter.
134 Cf. Song of Songs 3:1–4.
135 Isaiah 26:9.

in order that she might say, '*I am asleep, but my heart is awake.*'[136] She kept watch with her bridegroom, so that, while sleeping on straw, she might dream of the palace of Heaven, and might believe the dream, and might reflect upon the straw, along with everything that world might admire. For this reason, she soaked her bed with her crying and wet her covers with her tears.

She was accustomed to arrive early for the communal vigils, so that, even if she did not precede those *princes*, the angels, I say, who are accustomed *to being joined with singers*, she would nevertheless be the first to be found *in the midst of the young girls playing tambourines.*[137]

14. Although she avoided honour, she did not escape it.

These works of light came into the light; they could not be covered, just as *the city placed upon the hill* could not be covered.[138] They had admirers, all of whom were honest in heart, and all who passed by along the way praised them [i.e., her works], so that her reputation for virtue might fly across the earth and arrive at the court.[139] The sight of her person was wonderful, because she was noble, because she was beautiful, because she was young – and her reputation was so much more agreeable, since she was younger, so much more pleasing, since she was a woman. For nobility of the flesh is accustomed to produce ignobility of mind in very many people, and they sin so much more freely, since they think that they are blamed or admonished more slowly. But who does not find fault with this, who does not judge this, who does not condemn this – not in public, but in out-of-the-way places? Where two or three have gathered together, their share is amongst them;[140] with two it is the third, with three it is the fourth: this is the share of nobles who act ignobly. But it was otherwise with Mechthild, who although she avoided the praises of men, could not escape them. According to Jerome, *Glory follows the virtues as if a shadow, and deserting the ones having a desire for them, desires those disdaining them.*[141] This saying of the holy man was shown true in our Mechthild, who – however

---

136 Song of Songs 5:2.

137 Psalm 67:26.

138 Matthew 5:14.

139 Cf. below, ch. 17, pp. 195–98.

140 Cf. Matthew 18:20.

141 Jerome, *Epistulae*, 108.3.4.

much more she spurned to be honoured – so much more was she honoured; and she was elevated so much more before the Lord, since she was more humble in his eyes and insignificant in the presence of his judgement. She showed to be true the Lordly and evangelical voice: *Everyone who exalts himself will be humbled; and he who humbles himself will be exalted.*[142] She learned exaltation humbly by experiencing it inside herself. She saw the humiliation in others who exalted themselves. Seeing it, she helped. She washed her hands in the blood of the sinner; she washed the sinner with compassionate weeping, with tears of remorse, with sighs of pious pain.

15. How compassionate she was.

She had so much compassion that she disregarded no one's pain, ignored no one's plight or misfortune; as soon as she had discovered it, she burst into tears, took refuge in prayer, and entrusted to God's mercy, through her crying, what was to be done. In this way, many were comforted when she prayed for their pain to subside, their dif-ficulties to be diminished, their health, either of body or soul, to return. Thereafter, the fame of her sanctity increased, such that they honoured her, not as one living in exile until now on earth, but as one reigning already in heaven. They did this, but she mistrusted their judgement because of this praise and considered their favour a torment, turning over in her own mind what the Prophet said: *O my people, they that call you blessed, the same deceive you, and destroy the path of your steps.*[143] Behold, she went far off, fleeing, and she lodged in the wilderness.[144] She persisted in her tears, and her eyes ran down with David's flowing streams and Jeremias's *streams of water.*[145] If she saw the church afflicted, she poured forth flowing streams in tears, suffering by having compas-sion for everyone's misfortunes. If affliction touched any individual, she made *streams of water* by crying for each one. If anyone had sinned, she wept for him. If a brother or sister were tempted, she did not cease to weep until the temptation ceased, and the soul was ripped from the snare.[146]

142 Luke 14:11.
143 Isaiah 3:12.
144 Cf. Psalm 54:8.
145 Cf. Psalm 106:33 and Lamentations 3:48.
146 Cf. Psalm 123:7.

She fed herself with the bread of tears, and she received tears in measure for her drink.[147] She made an ointment for herself from the difficulties of the poor, from the wants of the destitute, from the bereavement of widows, from the sighs of the oppressed, from the misfortunes of orphans and the abandoned, from the imprisonments and shackles of captives, from the dangers and shipwrecks of those traveling and sailing, and finally, from everyone placed in every tribulation. With this ointment, I say, she came with those women in the Gospel to anoint Jesus. But when they did not find him, because he had been resurrected already in glory, she did not waste that ointment; she used it on his body, that is the Church.[148] She anointed everyone who was afflicted, as it is said, with the unction of mercy, the grease of compassion, the oil of kindness, the ointment of clemency. At this she shed tears, so that she might assist in these things, and so that she might be praised – not by men, but by him who looks into her heart. For her *ear caught a whisper of it*,[149] and like the voice of a gentle breeze she listened to the whispers of her bridegroom, speaking to her in the Song of Songs, *your breasts are better than wine, smelling sweet of the best ointments.*[150] And she had been accustomed to prepare other ointments of the same kind: one that she might pour with Mary Magdalene upon his feet, crying to the Lord for sinners, and another that she might pour upon his head to give thanks for his good works.[151] But that second one is better than the first, not that the first one is despised, because *an afflicted spirit is a sacrifice [to God]*;[152] the latter one, however, is pleasing, and may be more pleasing, because it may be *a sacrifice of praise.*[153] The third, which is the best, our Mechthild preferred both physically and emotionally. She preferred compassion for her neighbour and good work for the poor, while not denying the others; she knew to make those other ointments, and not to neglect this one. For that reason, she was made pleasing to God, beloved to her beloved; she was heard favourably on account of her reverence, she who exhibited nothing rough to anyone, because she

147 Cf. Psalm 79:6.
148 Cf. Mark 16:1–6.
149 Job 4:12.
150 Song of Songs 1:1–2.
151 Cf. Luke 7:36–50.
152 Psalm 50:19.
153 Psalm 49:23.

was indeed serious and mature, but mixed in every way with sweetness and pleasantness.

16. How much she wept on account of one idle word, and that she did not laugh.

History compels me to say what I surely would not have said on my own, if I had not had a witness to what was said and someone inciting me to say it: the matron, noble both in her descent and in her truthfulness.[154] But why do I doubt? What is impossible for God? She [i.e., Mechthild] was never seen laughing, nor heard to say an idle word.[155] However, at the end of her life there was laughter for her, as I will tell in what follows, when I come to it.[156] Moreover, on the subject of idle words, she even repudiated herself; she repudiated herself in her conscience beyond what was normal. It happened in this way:

One of the sisters stood before her, carrying something in her hands. She dropped what she carried to the ground, and the abbess borrowed an expression familiar to the common people: 'Damn it!'[157] As she said it, she burst into tears, weeping and wailing, as if she had smashed the churches of Rome. For many days, she humbled herself because of this, with fasts and vigils, adding to the days of penance. What are we to say to these things, we who speak in violation of the prohibition [i.e., against idle words]? We who criticize our neighbour with our talk? We who shoot arrows in secret at her who is blameless? We who make our tongues as sharp as swords? She had heard in the Gospel, *every idle word that men speak, they will render an account for it on the day of judgement.*[158] She had heard this, and she anticipated the day of judgement, more readily and happily her own judge. She had heard from the wise one, *Anger is better than laughter: because by the sadness of the countenance, the heart of the offender is corrected.*[159] She was angry at herself, but she was never seen to become angry at others.

And how, you say, did she correct excesses? Or did no one sin there, but were they all like the angels of God in heaven? It is a sin not to disclose the sinners; it is the greatest sin, as the Lord said to Eli, *because*

---

154 This is presumably a reference to the countess, his patroness.
155 Cf. *RB 1980: the rule of St Benedict*, 200–1, ch. 7.
156 See below, ch. 25, p. 213.
157 In Latin, she says, '*Calca desuper*'.
158 Matthew 12:36.
159 Ecclesiastes 7:4.

*he knew that his sons made themselves vile, and he did not chastise them;
therefore I have sworn to Eli, that the iniquity of his house shall not be expiated
with sacrifices or offerings forever.*[160] Mechthild avoided this, censuring
them, but rebuking them with compassion and restraint, so that she
who had sinned might not ascribe anger when she was punished, but
justice – and moreover, so that no one might dare to resist her, so that
no one might test her. She who was judge had so much dignity that
the light of her expression did not fall upon the earth, but they heard
her sentence as if from one thundering from heaven. Like Ecclesiastes,
she counted laughter to be foolish and said to pleasure, 'what can you
do for me?'[161] While she sat with Job, encircled by a crowd of sisters,[162]
she was nevertheless a consoler of those grieving, just in judging, kind
in consoling, strict in action, and with the Apostle *all things to all people.*[163]
In many things she was, according to Solomon, *as if ignorant.*[164] Nevertheless, she neglected nothing, because she was devout. She knew to change
anything else but not to be changed herself; with Hannah, *her countenance
was changed no more.*[165]

O reader, you have in this woman many marks of virtue. If you
review them, you will discover examples of her sanctity from infancy.
She was working in the vineyard from the first hour of the day, not
giving a reward as her reason, for she had chosen no other reward for
herself except the Lord's grace. You have her sanctity; it was proven
by her deeds, blessed by her merits, obtained by her labours, but not
yet made manifest in miraculous works.[166] She did not lack these things
while living; in so many more ways, she does not lack them dead.

17. Going to court, she drank wine three times from water.

It happened that she was summoned to go to the royal court. This
was necessary to bring benefit to her monastery, and it would have
been immensely damaging if she had not gone. She wanted others to
handle this business, but Frederick, then emperor,[167] asked for the abbess.

---

160 1 Samuel 3:13–14.

161 Cf. Ecclesiastes 2:2

162 Cf. Job 42:11.

163 1 Corinthians 9:22.

164 Ecclesiasticus 32:12.

165 1 Samuel 1:18.

166 The next two chapters concern her first miracles.

167 Emperor Frederick I Barbarossa (1152–90).

It was his right to demand that she come and conclude the matter herself. He said, 'Let my relative come to Regensburg:[168] it is a solemn matter, to be handled in no other way than solemnly before the princes and the court.' She went, albeit reluctantly, having with her an escort appropriate to her rank, but larger than she would have preferred. For her, solitude was more delightful than the royal court.[169]

You would have seen this other Judith, after so many fasts, not showing a paleness of expression but appearing gracious in everyone's eyes.[170] And if her proven virtue had not rebuked the foolish, there would have been fools in attendance who thought that she had been idle with delights rather than labouring with fasts. What she did at home found approval there, because she held fasts to be delights. For this reason, her expression, because of a drunkenness of spirit, was more similar in appearance to roses than ashes. With Daniel and his allies, she rejected royal foods, content to eat beans.[171] She was so distinguished as she stood near the emperor! He saw her beauty and did not ignore her virtue, deferring to the saint more because of her sanctity than because of her descent and blood. He was most especially delighted that someone so distinguished shared his descent. He was amazed that this most saintly woman had come forth from people who were not saints, as if she had come forth a rose from thorns. He proclaimed this about her, and he rejoiced in her visit. And after he had heard from her the reasons why she had come, he arranged and completed everything for her.[172]

Mealtime came, the household's dinner. Supper was prepared for the abbess in the evening. While there was meat for the others, Daniel's food was served to the abbess.[173] She took in the sight and smell of everything indiscriminately, along with the others. But when everyone divided everything for tasting, she did not partake in the tasting of the food – except the beans.

---

168 See above, n. 13, for her imperial blood.

169 Between Mechthild becoming abbess in 1153–54 and her death in 1160, Emperor Frederick I Barbarossa held court in Regensburg four times: September 1153, October 1155, September 1156 and January 1158. There is no way of knowing which of these courts Mechthild attended.

170 Cf. Judith 8:6–7.

171 Cf. Daniel 1:8–17.

172 The reason why she went to court is unknown; there is no extant imperial charter for Mechthild or Edelstetten.

173 I.e. beans, see above, n. 171.

There was a *miles*, her butler, a very mature man, who knew what ought to belong to God and what to the world.[174] He did not forget to know his lady's will. Advised beforehand, and proceeding solemnly with his companions, he brought to the abbess water that he had drawn secretly from a well. For, like all the others, she was given wine to drink at every opportunity. But when she tasted it [i.e., the well water], she was amazed that she had been deceived or disregarded, contrary to custom, for the well water did not taste like well water but the best wine. Immediately abstaining from it, she beckoned very modestly to her butler; she disclosed his disobedience, and she privately made him take away the wine and bring well water.

He sent his attendant, he drew from the well, he brought it into the house. He sets it before her, and again the abbess drinks wine from the well. She rebukes the butler for his stubbornness. He swears that he saw the servant drawing the water, and that he offered nothing to her except the water he had drawn. Then she said, 'Drink, and prove yourself wrong.' Like another *wine steward*, he drank.[175] He sang the praises of this wine, saying, 'Bavaria produced no wine like this; Austria grew none; France or Alsace sent none; Cyprus or Greece gave none comparable to this.' The abbess restrained the man as he was praising it and demanded well water a third time. He runs, he draws it himself, he brings it to her. He asserts that he drew it himself. Nothing wanted to be tasted but wine.

The abbess wanted this to be kept secret, but the magnitude of the thing could not lie hidden and came into the open. You see how the Lord cherished his beloved, how, when all of his people had an abundance of wine, he did not want her alone to drink water. But he supplied the wine to her from *a bundle of myrrh*,[176] which was he, so that the beloved of the beloved might rejoice in such a great banquet. In the presence of the princes, whose notice it could not escape, it was honoured as a miracle. But she was impatient of honour; she suppressed the talk and desired that it be suppressed. But the more it was hidden, the more it was disclosed by the Lord's example.

---

174 For the term *miles*, see the general introduction.

175 Elsewhere in this chapter, Engelhard uses the word *pincerna* for the butler. Here, he uses *architriclinus*, the word used in John 2:8–9 for the wine steward who is the first to drink the water miraculously changed into wine at the wedding feast at Cana.

176 Song of Songs 1:13.

Therefore, she fled from court, not wanting to be burdened by gossip. But she left behind her a scent worthy of God, just as she effected contempt for delights, love for fasting, honour for God and disdain for the world. Lady Mechthild, along with the Lord Jesus, had *this beginning of miracles* – in both cases, so I believe, while Mary dwelled with them and reminded them, *'they have no wine.'*[177] This same one [i.e., Jesus] made wine from water for the one he loved [i.e., Mechthild]; he accomplished it for the many there who loved and believed in him. She claimed for herself as a result of this no praise or honour, secretly or publicly; she washed her hands of it, saying that she had no share in this deed. It was the Lord, maker of all things, and nothing was done on her account or by her, but on account of others, if anything extraordinary happened. Thus, she sent virtue back to the Lord of virtues, just as the springs and rivers run back to the sea, where the origin of everything is: since, indeed, *all the rivers run into the sea, but the sea is not yet full.*[178] And Mechthild had the miracle returned to the place from which it had come, so that it may start again; start, I say, and not falter again.[179]

18. Concerning a woman, possessed by a demon, who was cured.

Now, the Lord continued to act with her, and those living under her were made joyful. There was a woman, the daughter in flesh of a certain man. A demon possessed her. Her father had procured for her a place in the monastery, separated from the sisters, not as a sister but as a *prebendaria.*[180] He requested this; he did not pay for it. This sort of demon was especially wicked, and it was similar to the one from the Gospel, because it would not depart except through prayer and fasting. For that reason, the disciples were unable to expel that one, and the sisters were unable to expel this one.[181] Although they had frequently prayed for her, the demon was nonetheless still with her. The demon made her see suffering, wander naked, shout incessantly, revile herself with a tormenting spirit, seek a place to throw herself down into either

---

177 Cf. John 2:1–11 for the wedding feast at Cana, where Jesus performed his first miracle by turning water into wine.

178 Ecclesiastes 1:7.

179 Cf. Ecclesiastes 1:7.

180 This term refers to someone who was associated with a religious community and was entitled to food, lodging and burial but was not a full member of the monastic house.

181 Cf. Matthew 17:14–20, for the story of Christ curing the child who could not be cured by the disciples because of their unbelief.

fire or water, and combine things dreadful in sight and sound, so that he might destroy her. The demon, severe to everyone, had outlasted everyone's severity [towards it], such that – I hate to say this! – it was difficult to help the sick woman, or even to see her or listen to her.

Mechthild understood what had to be done in these circumstances. The spirit revealed it to her, and inspired by hope and faith, she approached the demon. She prayed and ordered it to depart. She commands it – as it cries out in protest, as if it were struck by whips – not to stay there any longer. The demon roars, gnashes its teeth, reviles her greatly. With the Lord Jesus helping his bride, it departed, showing as it tore itself to pieces how much and how great was its malice. The girl was cured. She was a witness to the abbess's virtue, and she served God as long as she lived with a life of sanctity and justice.

The abbess wanted this to be kept secret, but the other declared it a miracle. She said this, because the same Lord Jesus is in heaven, who had been on earth to perform miracles, and he is the same one who, unseen, does what sight revealed. This was done, so that she might be celebrated by many and might bring forth many celebrated signs. She concealed these signs in such a way that she attributed them to prayer and claimed nothing for herself concerning the strength of her virtue. But as she laboured in this work, her merit did not lie hidden, and from her fruits they recognized her. Returning from her with good health and help from tribulation, they bestowed honour on God because of her when they gave thanks.

She who had been cured was also mute (which I had almost neglected to mention). But with the Lord arranging it and Mechthild praying for it, she destroyed the demon and received speech; finally crushing Satan under her feet, she proclaimed praise of the Lord Saviour with her eloquent tongue, and imitated and praised the life of St Mechthild.

The sisters saw that they were not deceived, but that they had *their reward in sanctification, their end in eternal life.*[182] They had already experienced beforehand the greatest part of her spirit a hundred times, because God had given it to them on account of their contempt of the world and imitation of Jesus Christ. Therefore, they strove for the heavenly with all their strength, desiring to be unloosed and to be with Christ, for this was much better. All of them were hastening with desire, fervent with zeal and labouring with love. All of them were hastening, but Mechthild was hastening on ahead more quickly than the others.

182 Romans 6:22.

But she did not enter before the others; she sent many ahead of her to the bridegroom's marriage bed. She would have preferred to have been found there by them than to have been preceded by them, preceded in the blessings of sweetness, seeing that she was eager to exit her body and be present with Christ. She saw that the world was formed in evil; she saw this, I say, not so much in what people said but rather in what they did. She saw complete vanity under the sun, and she stretched with her mind beyond the sun. 'Oh,' she said, 'when will I come and appear before the face of my God? When will this that belongs to mortal life be swallowed up, when will this that is corruptible be clothed in incorruptibility? Who will free me from this mortal body?' And she received an answer from the spirit, a joyful and pleasing apostolic response: *Thanks be to God, through Jesus Christ our Lord.*[183] Those voices of her heart were heard, were heard clearly in heaven; they entered into the holy, and help was sent to her from the holy.

19. That she had foreknowledge of her death and returned to Diessen.

Now, she knew that she would die in a short time, and she did something similar to what the patriarch Joseph did, who commanded his sons to carry his bones.[184] She remembered that she had been offered and betrothed to Christ at Diessen, and she desired a tomb there with her sisters. Gathering her sisters [i.e., in Edelstetten], she says she is very sick. She indicates that the dissolution of her body is imminent and that it is necessary for her to return to Diessen, either to die there quickly, or to recover in a short time. They agreed, hoping for her life thereafter, at the same time seeing no signs of death in her.

She went, not doubting she was about to die, or rather to cross from death to life. She enjoined what belongs to this life to protect the sisters, especially the ones who had seen her and had learned by her word and example. She said, '*I am innocent of the blood of all of you, for I did not shrink from declaring to you the whole purpose of God.*[185] I leave you: whether I will return is uncertain; it is certain, however, that the Lord renders to each according to his own labour.'[186] And kissing everyone, and commending them to God, she departed for Diessen.

---

183 Romans 7:25.

184 Cf. Genesis 50:24.

185 Acts of the Apostles 20:26–7.

186 Cf. Psalm 61:13 and 1 Corinthians 3:8.

She was received sadly, because she was sick. But she was looked after with all care and kindness, not as a guest but as a dearest mother and as lady of the place. Her pain increased, but day and night God's bride considered nothing else with her heart and tongue except praise of God. Like *a well-trained young cow* (so that I may explain this in a positive way) *that loves to thresh*,[187] not knowing what else to do in a time of sickness, she showed her compassion. She kept to her practice in vigils and fasts – except not so many, since she could be persuaded to restore herself a little bit.[188] She calls the sisters, and mustering strength in her flesh, she greets all of them with the power of her spirit, with sweet talk. Thereafter, she addresses them, beginning her speech in this way:

'*I have eagerly desired to eat this passover with you*,[189] because passover is joyful to me, delightful, and always desired; passover, I say, that is, death. Behold, sweetest ones, I enter onto the path of all flesh; now I assemble with my fathers, and with Adam I return ashes to ashes. This is inflexible; everyone flees it, and no one has the power to escape. I am conscious that nothing belongs to me. But he who judges me is the Lord, the same one who is merciful, tender-hearted and just. If he should decide to save me, I will be freed continuously. If he should see my labour, he will see that there was nothing I avoided in my desire to please him. I laboured in everything, not I, however, but the grace of God with me. With his *support I fought the good fight, I finished the race, I kept the faith*.[190] I do not doubt but that *the crown of righteousness* is left to me,[191] which the Lord delivers to me, the Lord who is the crown, who is the end, who is the reward for the battle.

'Consider, dearest ones, *this slight, momentary affliction*, which *is preparing an eternal weight of glory beyond all measure for us*.[192] We do not contemplate those things that are seen, but those that are unseen. For the things that are seen are of this world; however, those that are unseen are eternal. Indeed, I despised the charming things of the world, I did not fear obstacles, and now I have an end to both in the return of delight, the fullness of glory, the eternity of happiness. I was able to walk that

---

187 Hosea 10:11.

188 Cf. *The life of an* unnamed *magistra of Admont*, ch. 1.

189 Luke 22:15

190 2 Timothy 4:7.

191 2 Timothy 4:8.

192 2 Corinthians 4:17.

202NOBLE SOCIETY

wide and spacious path, leading to death, with mortal men. Now may be the end of pleasures, but the beginning of torments, from which I might not escape; I might fall from punishment to punishment through eternity. Now my soul is freed *from the hunters' trap*, I say the trap of the wicked spirits in us, and of those dragging us to sin; but *the trap is broken*, and thanks be to God, I am freed.[193] Behold, *the ruler of this world is coming, and he has no power over me*,[194] because I never presented myself as a companion, familiar or friend to the world.

'*The bosom of Abraham* receives me,[195] Christ's marriage bed expects me, and Mary, the mother of my Lord, hurries to meet me with the virgin saints. The chorus of patriarchs and prophets, the council of the apostles, the glorious army of martyrs, and also the innumerable army of all the elect: they rejoice and dance at my arrival. Heaven rejoices, Paradise exults, and the Lord Christ himself invites me to dinner and a banquet. Behold, I come, I give thanks. I will be with them, who are redeemed by the Lord, who come into Zion giving praise. And eternal happiness will be upon their heads. They will obtain joy and happiness – pain and sorrow will flee. Oh, happy me! I would escape the judgement of God, eternal suffering, the punishment of hell, the inextinguishable fire, the immortal worm, the chains on hands and feet, the torments prepared for sinners, and the hammers continually striking the bodies of the impious. Through God's grace I escaped *the lion's mouth, the power of the dog*,[196] the dreadful faces of the torturers, death itself, Satan and the devil. Far off from me will be that Behemoth, Leviathan,[197] the ancient serpent, the twisting dragon, the asp and basilisk, *the wild boar from the forest, and the beasts of the field*.[198] The same one is called by many and diverse names, by which the cunning contriver is signified in his great and infinite wickedness. Consider that you conquered this one for me in Christ – how much grace there will be, how immense will be the glory, because of the magnitude of the enemy!

'And behold, paradise is opened to me, the entrance of Heaven stands open, and that heavenly Jerusalem, which was founded on sapphires, its rampart jasper, its towers built with gems, and every precious stone

193 Psalm 123:7.
194 John 14:30.
195 Luke 16:22.
196 2 Timothy 4:17 and Psalm 21:21.
197 Cf. Job 40:10–28.
198 Psalm 79:14.

the structure of its walls.[199] The streets of Jerusalem will be covered
with pure gold, and through all its rows of houses "Alleluia" is sung,
and a chorus of virgins, singing a new song there, follows the Lamb
wherever he may go. I am joined together with these; I am one of those
rejoicing and singing in the fullness of joy, in the abundance of the
feast, the crumbs and trifles of which I was accustomed to collect and
eat with the dogs under the lords' table. Indeed, the fullness of joys is
in the heavens, and from there come those sayings of Scripture, with
which we are consoled on earth; from there comes that voice, the voice
full of joy: *"For behold, I am about to create new heavens and a new earth;
the former things shall not be remembered or come to mind. But be glad and
rejoice forever in what I am creating; for I am about to create Jerusalem as a
joy, and its people as a delight. I will rejoice in Jerusalem, and delight in my
people; no more shall the sound of weeping be heard in it, or the cry of distress."*[200]
Quick, sweetest ones, hurry to enter into that city: and oh, fortunate
me, *if one of my offspring will remain* in there![201] I mean you, not the
offspring of my flesh, but of my heart, because I gave birth to you
through Christ's message of salvation.'

20. That she reminded the sisters about the gift of charity.

'To go there [i.e., the heavenly Jerusalem] is to love, for no one may
enter it except through charity. Nor is there another joy in it other
than charity. For me, this is not dull to say; moreover, it is necessary
for you — because it is necessary that you correct yourselves on this
side, so that you may pay greater attention to serving charity. You
attack and harass one another with insults, you keep your anger for a
long time, you quarrel for no reason, and you make for yourselves a
log from a piece of straw, hatred from anger.[202] Do I praise you? In this,
I do not praise you. I praise you, because you are eager for the divine
office, ready to fast, quick to vigils, prepared for obedience, virtuous in
your abstinence, and watchful for every good. I do not praise you,
because you have tensions amongst you and jealousy. What is it to
praise God, and disparage your neighbour? *The fountain does not pour
forth sweet and bitter water from the same opening*, as James said,[203] nor

---

199 Revelation 21:19.

200 Isaiah 65:17–9.

201 Tobit 13:20.

202 Cf. Augustine of Hippo, *Letters*, nr. 211 ('Letter of Aurelius Augustine to the
    consecrated virgins', frequently considered a source for the Augustinian Rule).

203 James 3:11.

does God receive praise of him alongside disparagement of a neighbour. What good is it to fast from food, which God created for the faithful in order to receive thanks, and to eat the flesh of your sister or brother with accusations and slanders? What vigils bring profit, during which the mouth sings to God, but the heart plots evil against a sister, or retaliation for evil? What is the use of having obedience for man alongside contempt for the Creator? What does it bring to keep the flesh safe from luxury but not to keep the heart safe from jealousy, the tongue from insult?

'Certainly, I praise you for these things, which are good, but I do not praise the jealousies and controversies that exist amongst you. You are virgins; you should not boast loudly. There were those, who were condemned, who did not have the oil of charity in their vessels; to them, as they were pleading, was said, "*I do not know you.*"[204] But let it not be that this is said to you. Turn yourselves away, dearest ones, from that saying of Jerome: the most evil venom of jealousy is compared to the viper offspring, which certainly kills its mother.[205] This alone is what I fear for you. I warn you, finally, to correct this, and I most certainly hope that you are saved, that you do not remain outside with the foolish virgins, but that you enter inside with the wise ones to the Bridegroom.'[206]

This warning was received with thanksgiving; correction was promised. Everyone who held anything against her exhibited correction immediately. She calls all of them to her, one by one she kisses them, and commending each to God, she rests a little.

21. That the tithe for her father's entire property in Oberding was given to the church of the holy Virgin Mary in Diessen.[207]

Her pain increased daily. God's bride considered nothing else with her heart and tongue except praise of God.[208] She wanted to refresh the male and female servants of God, her brothers and sisters serving God in Diessen, with some sort of financial support, not just in life but

---

204 Cf. Matthew 25:1–13, for the story of the wise and foolish virgins.

205 I have been unable to identify a source for this reference. In the medieval bestiary tradition, baby vipers bite their way out of their mother's body, killing her in the process. See *Bestiary*, 186.

206 See above, n. 204.

207 For the possibility that this chapter and two of the subsequent ones were written by someone other than Engelhard of Langheim, see the introduction to this text.

208 This same sentence can be found in ch. 19, p. 201 above.

also in death, not just in word but also in example. She turned to her parents, her father, Berthold, and her mother, Sophia.[209] The blessed Mechthild said in a calm voice before everyone, 'O father, remember that you sent me as a young girl into this church, in which, with the grace of the Holy Spirit guiding me, I made such progress that, even though I was unworthy, I nevertheless could not avoid the title of *magistra*. After that, as you know, I flourished until recently in Edelstetten with the title of abbess. Therefore, it is evident to your paternal care that I would have been able to lead a rich life with you in the secular state, if my contemplative life had not been more pleasing to God than an active one. Certainly, it is well known to everyone who knew the situation that I would have lived more luxuriously in Edelstetten than in the world, if I had wanted, because in that place I would have had so many more companions who were free from restraint.

'Now, therefore, because I was a young girl and a *magistra* in Diessen, I judge it proper that I, a maidservant and your daughter, deserve to be buried here with you. Now, my father, if you had betrothed me to a mortal man, you would have given to him, with me, a part of your property in the name of a dowry, yes? And thereafter, the same man would have considered himself not just a son-in-law but indeed more like an heir to all your property, yes? But in truth, because the King of Kings and Lord of Lords Jesus Christ chose me, your daughter, for himself as his bride, you decided not to give any marriage gifts to my sweet Husband – your Creator, Redeemer and Saviour – for me and for your own soul. Therefore, pious father, know that the church at Diessen, founded by you and other of my relatives, in which God preordained that my worldly bedchamber would be, is located in a woody, fruitless place that is full of water. Therefore, dearest father, give to my immortal Bridegroom – not from what is yours but from what is his – that which he chose for himself at the initial creation of the whole world.[210] I say, I beseech, give in the name of a marriage gift to me – and thus justly and fitly to my Bridegroom, who is making the request – the tithe for your property, which you are known to possess, within the limits of Oberding near the Isar river.'[211]

209 See the introduction to this text for more about the reference to her parents in this chapter.

210 Cf. *The deeds of Count Ludwig of Arnstein*, ch. 2, p. 230.

211 Oberding is situated north-east of Munich, not far from Freising. For the significance of tithes in this period, see Eldevik, *Episcopal power*.

The father of this bride of Christ understood his beloved daughter's request. Having received advice from his relatives, he joyfully and affectionately fulfilled her request. He said, 'O daughter, compared to all others, your relationship is dearest to me. Because of my love for you, I confer to this church of St Mary in Diessen the tithe for my entire property within the limits of Oberding near the Isar river, and with everyone present bearing witness, I make this gift upon this altar of St Mary, the Virgin Mother of Jesus Christ.'[212] Mechthild, the blessed bride of Christ, responded to this in a voice full of happiness, 'O my father, now I rejoice for you, because you have satisfied my request in every way.'

Then, the blessed Mechthild turned to Provost Hartwig and the community of brothers and sisters.[213] With knees bent on the ground and hands held high, she prayed tearfully to God, saying, 'Lord Jesus Christ, receive now to yourself the gift that has been bestowed, and keep it safe for your male and female servants, who serve you devotedly here, for their profitable use.' After she said these things, her father joined her, saying, 'O sweet daughter, beloved to God, I ask that you pray to God with me that, if any of my descendants should attempt to obstruct the gift now given through me (may this not happen!), this person ought to be punished here [i.e., on earth] with a most worthy punishment, and not be tormented perpetually with Cain at the Last Judgement.'[214] When this prayer was finished, the voice of holy spirits was heard in the sky, answering and shouting with the sweetest voice, 'Amen.'

22. On that wondrous occasion when she ate meat once, drank wine, and smiled once.

Blessed Mechthild learned the day and hour when the tithe from within the limits of Oberding, which was collected in her name for the church of the Virgin St Mary in Diessen, was brought to Provost Hartwig. Before all the brothers and sisters, she delivered a most excellent speech, saying, 'O lord and father in Christ, now I rejoice, because I see that my dowry, as proof of my betrothal, has been brought. Just as I feel it refreshing the present life, so too I hope boldly to be refreshed eternally in the future in the heavenly fatherland.'

---

212 This is common language in twelfth-century documents recording gifts to monasteries.

213 Hartwig was provost of Diessen from c. 1132 to his death in 1173.

214 This is an unusual turn of phrase and suggests the author does not want any descendant of Diessen's founder to suffer forever. For more on this chapter, see the introduction above.

After this, the brothers and sisters were called in the customary way, by the sound of the bell, to their refectories. Provost Hartwig left the community of brothers and sped to the sisters' refectory. Speaking to the blessed Mechthild with these words, he said, 'O daughter in Christ, beloved to God and men, the food is now prepared, which was collected through your sweetest intervention for us and for our successors for the refreshment of our bodies. And so, it befits your most pious devotion that it be eaten today in charity with the flesh and drunk with the wine. By the authority of him, who visibly changed the water placed before you into wine,[215] I teach, I entreat, I order you: by the virtue of holy obedience, from all the food that today and afterwards will refresh us and our successors, from that same food, you should joyfully be refreshed in the present hour.' Upon hearing this order, the blessed Mechthild groaned, and smiling quietly, she said, 'O father and lord, *even in laughter the heart is sad, and the end of joy is grief.*[216] Now, therefore, I do not know what I will do; only this alone I know, that I never want to be found disobedient.' At these words, all the sisters prostrated themselves at her feet and gave immeasurable thanks to her – not on account of the collection of the tithe, from which they profited, but rather on account of her sacred refreshment, for which they all rejoiced.

Then, the *magistra* of the community gave a sign that the sisters ought to rise from the table and ought to head toward the church with a Psalm, in the customary way.[217] Blessed Mechthild, trembling as she sang with the sisters, heard a voice in the air saying, 'O blessed Mechthild, you should know that today you have not eaten with Esau, who was rejected, but with Elijah, who was taken up into the air.'[218] Hearing this voice, she gave thanks silently to God. The sisters did not hear this, but observing her, they asked why it was that she directed her mind inwardly and did not sing the Psalm with the others. Blessed Mechthild responded to this with the Prophet: '*My secret to myself, my secret to myself.*'[219] At this response from her, all of the sisters were amazed and thought about what they could do. After they had debated by turns

---

215 See above, ch. 17.

216 Proverbs 14:13.

217 This passage indicates that Mechthild did not return to the position of *magistra* at Diessen after she came back from Edelstetten.

218 Cf. Genesis 25:29–34; 1 Kings 19:4–8; and 2 Kings 2:11.

219 Isaiah 24:16.

among themselves, as it is said, the *magistra* of the community of pious sisters spoke: 'Lest we debate for a long time in this way amongst ourselves, let us call the lord provost, if that pleases you.' When they heard this, they all said, 'O lady *magistra*, it is pleasing to us that you call the lord provost, so that through his help, we may learn what blessed Mechthild's secret is.'

At these words, Provost Hartwig was called; when he came, he began to ask why he had been summoned. The *magistra* answered him for all the sisters, as was proper, saying, 'O venerable lord and father in Christ, when we rose from the table today in the customary way and headed for the church, we perceived that our lady and sister, blessed Mechthild, had some sort of conversation with holy spirits. When we inquired piously to her, why that was and what had been spoken, she responded: *"My secret to myself, my secret to myself."* You should know, lord and father in Christ, that you were called on account of this response from her.'

Having heard this, Provost Hartwig ordered blessed Mechthild to be summoned to him. When she had been called, Provost Hartwig said to her, 'O daughter, beloved to God and to men, if you respect me as lord and venerate me as father, I say to you with the Prophet Malachi: "If I am your father, where is my love? If I am your lord, where is my fear?"[220] Therefore, on account of paternal love and fear of the master, tell me why you responded to your beloved co-sisters, when they asked you what you were doing, *"My secret to myself, my secret to myself?"*'

To this Mechthild answered, 'Father who must be loved and lord who must always make me fear, my spirit is melted because of what you have said in this way.' And she immediately placed herself prostrate at Provost Hartwig's feet. Provost Hartwig received her hand and raised her piously, taking her for a moment apart from the rest. He learned from her what the angelic spirits had said to her: 'O blessed Mechthild, you should know that today you have not eaten with Esau, who was rejected, but with Elijah, who was taken up into the air.' Scarcely had she finished this excellent speech, with tears, when Provost Hartwig said, 'O blessed Mechthild, beloved to God and men, may you be blessed now and in eternity.'

Without delay, he ordered that both of the communities, the brothers and the sisters, should sing with devotion – for the praise of God, who announced wondrous things today in blessed Mechthild – this

220 Cf. Malachi 1:6.

Psalm: *All ye works of the Lord, bless the Lord.*[221] Behold a wonderful thing! After the last verse of this Psalm had just been sung, blessed Mechthild's father, Count Berthold, stood at the doors of the church. He began the same last verse again, saying with tears, '*You are blessed in the firmament of heaven, and worthy of praise, and glorious; you are exalted above all for ever,*[222] you who made in my daughter so many wonders from her virtues.' After he said this, Provost Hartwig, blessed Mechthild and everyone else received him honourably. Upon their greeting, he returned thanks to everyone and joined with them, saying, 'Listen, I pray, and understand how I came to be here; weigh it carefully with me. On this night, *around the time the cock crows,*[223] while her mother and I were talking about my daughter, a certain voice sounded in my ears, saying, "O Count Berthold, rise and hurry to your daughter." And rising with haste, just as you see, I came. Now, therefore, o Provost Hartwig, what has happened? Tell me.'

Provost Hartwig responded to this, saying, 'I hear, and I understand that God did not want you to be ignorant of the wonderful things that recently happened to my lady, your daughter, God's bride: blessed Mechthild. You were partly aware, and you will become fully aware of the things that happened.' And sitting together, he told him everything. After Count Berthold had heard all of this, he responded, saying, 'God, who made me come here for such a great solemnity, may my devotion be offered to him now and forever, and may there be perpetual praise of him now and forever.' Scarcely had Count Berthold finished his words when the blessed Mechthild added, '*I sleep, and my heart is watchful.*'[224]

O, with how sweet sounding a voice did the bride of Christ bring forth the secrets of her heart! Because just as it is the duty of all brides to care for their bridegrooms, so is it also much more appropriate that the true bride of Christ contemplates in her watchful heart the love of her bridegroom, Jesus Christ. He had love for her, while clothed in flesh on her account. When he was hanging on the cross, he fell asleep, and in the sleep of physical death, through the opening of his side, he yielded up blood and water from the font of his heart for us. Mindful of that love, blessed Mechthild said, 'O lord and father in Christ, venerable Provost Hartwig, I who am wretched pray that you give this to me by

221 Daniel 3:57 and cf. Psalm 148.
222 Daniel 3:56–7.
223 Tobit 8:11.
224 Song of Songs 5:2.

your prudent administration. From the tithe collected in my name for this church of Diessen on account of my father, who is present, set aside a portion of very great size for Eucharistic hosts, so that they may be distributed to all the neighbouring churches plentifully and perpetually. And indeed, it will bring joy to me and salvation to everyone enjoying the remaining parts of this tithe, if ⌈from those parts was made⌉ that mystical bread, which descended from Heaven into the womb of the virgin and hung on the cross, and if that bread was baked in an oven (witness the Prophet Hosea), so that it might be made suitable for us to eat.[225] Therefore, so that we may be refreshed by the same bread also in the kingdom of Heaven, may your grace, pious father Provost Hartwig, fulfil for me what I have requested, and let it be confirmed by the consent of all my co-brothers and lords of this church of canons.'

When she completed this petition, all said in one voice, 'O blessed Mechthild, we are all pleased with what you have just requested, and we ask that it be done.' At this, the pious and charitable Provost Hartwig, imposing silence on the brothers with his hand, said, 'O blessed Mechthild, beloved to God and men, you have uttered a pleasing word, because you have excited all our hearts to fulfil your desire. Therefore, so that I may guide the affection for your desire to the desired effect, in the name of the Father, the Son and the Holy Spirit, I decree it. I order all our officials, every year in perpetuity, to designate from the tithe in Oberding, from within the limits of that place, the best part of the grain – a very abundant quantity of it – specifically for Eucharistic hosts, just as the blessed Mechthild has requested. And just as that salvific Eucharist, having been fashioned in the same form of bread, is to be denied to no one who is penitent and likewise to no one asking for compassion, so also this material bread is never to be refused to anyone. Truly, all the supporters of the most Christian faith understand that, through this salutary decree, the dowry of the blessed Mechthild, betrothed in the church of Diessen, is confirmed most solemnly in the presence of God and men.'

23. That she restored an eye that had been punctured by an awl.

There was one sister, who was practised in writing on parchment. While she was making holes for the lines, drawing the awl along incautiously, she pierced her eye, stabbing her pupil, and blood and tears

---

225 Cf. Hosea 7:7.

came forth continuously.[226] The pain elicited a shout, and everyone ran to this sister. The trouble is twofold on account of the mother's incurable weakness and the sister's blindness.[227] Indeed, she [i.e., the sister] was useful and beloved to everyone, and for this reason her pain caused all the more grief. This commotion awakens the mother, and she is called and led in. The eye streamed with tears, and the blood still flowed like a river. There was no hope of the eye recovering, no hope of her seeing again. The only thing they desired for her, since she was suffering, was that the pain might cease. [Mechthild] orders her to approach and touches the eye with her hand. And the hand of the Lord was present, chasing away the pain, returning health and the brightness of light. The blood stopped and her health became strong, such that never had she seen more clearly, never had she considered it sweeter. Our Mechthild did this while dying, bearing witness that she did not die but crossed from death to life, and took care of the living for a better life.

24. Concerning Provost Hartwig's exhortation over the ailing woman.

Meanwhile, people outside [of the community of canonesses] heard that the ailing abbess was now being prepared for death. Provost Hartwig hastened breathlessly, and the brothers rushed in with the greatest weeping and wailing. Everyone moaned and groaned over her, each individually, and mourned solemnly in common. They knew that through her the Lord had given health to the house, and rarely were the things to come similar to the things that had gone before.

Then, Provost Hartwig began to speak, consoling the abbess and exhorting the community: 'I see you, o mother, in the greatest weakness of body. Nevertheless, I do not yet despair for your life. The Lord is capable of restoring you to us for the health of the house, which depends completely on you. We mourn you; we grieve over you. We know that you desire Christ, whom you love. You have secured the rewards that come to the worthy, and if they are delayed, they will not be diminished. Rather, have compassion for us, whom you are deserting. Behold those whom you have won in two places for Christ by the example of your sanctity. Behold the brothers and sisters whom Christ acquired through you. All of them belong to your crown; they shine like jewels in your splendour. Behold all the neighbours who smell the odour of sweetness

---

226 Medieval scribes frequently used an awl, or a similar tool, to make small holes in the parchment to indicate the margins or the horizontal lines for the text.

227 The end of the chapter suggests Mechthild performed this miracle when she was very close to death.

from you in your works; they gained certain knowledge of these in the words they heard from you and also in the discipline of your habits, which they saw. In all these things you acquired glory for Christ, and there is nothing he would deny to you when you pray.

'We pray, therefore, that you ask for your life to be extended; we need this more than you do. Who else, when you have been taken away, will protect us with prayers, favour us with advice, strengthen us with counsels, relieve us with remedies? Your family are princes. Thanks to you, they all have had a place grateful to them. They have given their support, they have turned away every adversary, they have bent to your name. While you have lived, they have kept our peace. They have honoured everything of yours because of you. They dared to do nothing wicked. They, who hated peace, were peaceful to yours. We desire your life; but if it is more pleasing to Christ that you depart, go free from care, certain about the crown, glorious from the victory.

'And you,' he said, 'o sisters, behold the path that we run to the end: for this reason we direct our steps, so that we may end this life with death. Would that we were ended by this death, we who live wickedly! Would that another everlasting death did not follow, in which the sinner dies in spirit for eternity, but never dies completely! For she who is new to humiliation lives always and is not brought to the finish; she is destroyed and is not brought to perfection. She possesses for eternity what the despairing one suffers, and what she who despaired escapes.

'Hey now, sisters! I should have said, "you blessed ones", whom the Lord received to himself. He does not want you to be called his servants but his brides, because he does not want you to fear him but to love him. If he should be feared, he is pleased by filial fear, or rather wifely fear, not servile fear. You see before you your leader, running and finishing the course now, and beating on the door of heaven. Behold, it is opened to her now. She is happy, whom the Lord escorted along the proper paths. He showed her the kingdom of God and gave her knowledge of the saints. He honoured her in works, and he completed her works – guiding her with his help, showing her the kingdom with his counsel, giving her knowledge with wisdom, honouring her in works with constancy, completing her works with perseverance. And you, daughters, equip yourselves with the same strength, follow in your mother's footsteps, so that running with her, you may attain the reward, and you may attain by her merits the kingdoms of the heavens, with her bridegroom and yours providing, who lives and reigns forever. Amen.'

25. How angels and demons were observing her death.

Holy angels, demons, and the sisters were observing the saint's death. Then, suddenly, she began to weep most bitterly. After weeping, she did what no one had ever seen her do before: she laughed with great happiness.[228] In this way, she repeated three times her weeping and laughter; she was not demented of mind, as often happens, but had the best sense. Nevertheless, she revealed to no one why she had done this. Each is free to speculate about this. It seems to me (not that I am wise) that the cause of the weeping was the demons the saint saw, who were reckoning and weighing her evil deeds. The holy angels, however, were outdoing them by reckoning her good works on the other side, and on account of this, she was rightly laughing. She rejoiced, just as she had wept when she dreaded that the wicked ones might be the victors.

And so, three times this was done, because in three ways good or evil is brought about: by thought, by word, and by deed. The hostile demons weigh these one by one. First, they place the deeds on the scales. If the bad outweigh the good, they claim for themselves the soul that works wickedly; if the bad weigh less than the good, the defeated ones flee. Nevertheless, they still bring forward the case concerning words, which they also lead to the scales; defeated by these, they take flight a second time. Finally, they do not pass over the last thought without examination. If they should be defeated there, they have no further right to the soul. Moreover, just as evil spirits desire to destroy souls, so do the good spirits dare to take souls by force, such that they do not allow anything, which might be annihilated by penance, to be led into the midst of the evil spirits. And just as the good spirits pile up the good, so do the evil spirits pile up the evil. I believe that it was granted to this saint to see this for herself, but it was not granted to her to talk about it. This was done, so that she might be happier, and for this reason more free from care, in exiting from her body. And so that she might deliver another, troubled by her weeping but less holy, she did not deny there was faith too with laughter.

26. That, while dying, she was gladdened by a vision of St Mary.

Her continuing joy demonstrated this,[229] for she was so happy afterwards that she lay as if she had been invited to a banquet and had feasted with the angels. For she saw our lady St Mary, she saw her and

228 Cf. above, ch. 16, p. 194, where her avoidance of laughter is discussed.
229 i.e., what was mentioned in the previous chapter.

greeted her, saying, '*Hail Mary, full of grace, the Lord is with you,*[230] and therefore are you blessed.' She grew faint, and smiled, and rejoiced with great delight. The sisters offered her the image of St Mary; she turned it away with her hand, directing her eyes to the vision, which she saw in spirit, as if she were saying, 'I greet St Mary, not in image, but in truth.' And just as *the end of* fools' *joy is grief,*[231] so *will the hope of the righteous be gladness.*[232] And just as the death of sinners is most low, so is the death of saints most precious in the sight of the Lord, as is proven in this saint. She proved in herself the saying, *A patient man will hold back for a time, and afterwards joy will be restored to him.*[233]

You would have seen that she had become silent at Jesus's teaching, and no word had escaped her mouth. She had circled the walls for seven days, and then she had shouted, and she had destroyed the walls with her shout, and she had trampled death to death, and she had not felt the bitterness of death before the sweetness of life.[234] Then she laughed, she who had not laughed before, and she saw fulfilled that statement of Baldad the Suhite: *God will not reject a blameless person, nor take the hand of evildoers. He will yet fill your mouth with laughter, and your lips with shouts of joy.*[235] She had escaped every strait. She saw that she was to be carried across to life, perfected in merit and certain of reward, by the calling of Christ and by the conduct of the angels. These things were the reason for her laughter; these things were the substance of her joyful shout. These things could have been done in secrecy, except that God had prepared the remembrance of her among men by blessing her, just as he had prepared glory for her with him, so that she might carry us to a similar form of living.

27. She gave thanks to Conrad.

She still had not yet faded away completely. She breathed. She spoke in joy to everyone, and they were amazed. She exhorted each one individually by consoling them and comforting their hands in God. She gave thanks to everyone for their great service. She saw Conrad, faithful and devoted to her, who from a *miles* in her parents' household had

---

230 Luke 1:28.
231 Proverbs 14:13.
232 Proverbs 10:28.
233 Ecclesiasticus 1:29.
234 Cf. Joshua 6:1–21.
235 Job 8:20–21. Baldad was one of Job's friends.

become a *conversus*.[236] He did every kind of work for the monastery. Speaking to him, she filled him with much consolation and instructed him with salutary words. 'You,' she said, 'assistant to me and faithful servant in the Lord, you have served well with me in the workshop of the house of God. Behold, I have run to the end, and today I secure the reward.[237] There remain *for me the crown of righteousness*[238] and the rest of eternal life. Have confidence that they remain for you too, that you will not be kept waiting for long, because to a great extent you have prepared the crown for me. If I have accomplished anything by prayer, meditation or reading, it is because you have rendered me unencumbered, and the constancy of your labour was my rest. So now, your reward will be with my reward. Stand now, therefore, stand firm like a good *miles*, firm as a faithful athlete. Certainly, it is work, but short and modest work for future glory, which has no measure or end. I see our glory now, not only through faith but also through something of substance. I see our crowns, about to be handed over for our labour, crowns of such great delight, of such great glory, that no one's senses, no one's tongue could describe them to you. Continue doing good things, increase daily your rewards and glory in heaven, just as he who hoards treasures disdains nothing in profit.' She said these things, and beginning again, did not cease from praising God, as long as she had the strength to move her tongue.

28. That she took communion, unseen by human eye.

When she was healthy, she frequently took communion, eating the lamb *with bitter herbs*,[239] because she never took communion without weeping and bitter tears. And she combined a drink of the blood of Christ with her tears. She had taken communion in the bed where she lay in pain, and she had received both the sacrament of holy unction and the absolution of her sins (in accordance with the advice of St James

236 *Conversus* is usually translated as 'lay brother', someone who lived apart from the monks or canons and typically performed menial chores for the religious community for the sake of his soul. However, *conversus* could also be used to refer to someone who had joined a religious house as an adult, not as a child oblate, and who was illiterate. The necrologies from the community at Diessen list three different *conversi* named Conrad, under the dates 6 March, 18 October and 9 December. Borgolte, 'Stiftergedenken', 262, 282 and 287.

237 Cf. 1 Corinthians 9:24 and above, n. 190.

238 2 Timothy 4:8. Cf. above, n. 191.

239 Exodus 12:8.

the apostle).[240] Living among men, she did what men did. But now, about to reside with the angels, she took communion by angelic hands.

As the end approached, she did not have any voice left. She revealed by her bodily movements the presence of his majesty; she was bending reverently, opening her mouth agreeably, swallowing in her throat gracefully, also mimicking the act of drinking, and bending frequently. When they saw this, the sisters and those who were present were amazed. Producing this miracle, she soon released her soul, communing with the saints communing in joy, and departing with them, away from the sacrament to the reality of the sacrament, and away from the matter of faith to the face of beauty [i.e., God].

A miracle was seen there: not signs of death in the dead one, but the splendour of life. More similar to the rosy appearance of one living, she showed that her spirit had mixed together with the roses of the martyrs. But the body was left behind, mimicking the whiteness of the lily, and the virgins bore witness that their companion's soul was uncorrupted both in spirit and in flesh. Rejoice now and be joyful, Mechthild, daughter of Zion, not a captive of Babylon; sing with David a song to the Lord in your land, because you could not sing strongly in a foreign one. Say, *You have loosed my bonds. I will offer you a thanksgiving sacrifice,*[241] because you have fled *from the iron furnace* of Babylon,[242] and you dwell in light with the children of light.

29. That, with her passing, there was pious weeping, but more pious joy for everyone.

The funeral rites are celebrated. In that place, there was not much crying, for her glory had dried up the tears. Rather, they were rejoicing on account of her manifest virtue. If any were weeping, they were weeping for themselves – to her, not for her. Her body, previously weakened by fasts, wasted away entirely with the onset of her illness; there was nothing left behind to be devoured by worms. The skin, stretched out over her bones, elicited this saying from Job: *My bones cling to my skin and to my flesh, and only my lips are left around my teeth.*[243] Was she not dissimilar to that one who *runs stubbornly* against God *armed with a thick shield? He has covered his face with fat and has gathered*

---

240 Cf. James 5:14.
241 Psalm 115:16–17.
242 Jeremiah 11:4.
243 Job 19:20.

fat upon his sides.[244] Nothing of this sort was in Mechthild. Her spirit had guided her limbs to carry it without difficulty to where it wanted to go, and it had directed them not to want anything from the spirit, except that it cross from death to life. And so it was done.

Nothing of spiritual glory was absent from the funeral rites: Psalms, hymns and spiritual songs were sung. A very great number of candles were lit, but they were extinguished by a frequent and violent wind. But God performed a miracle, such that, although men were unable to stand before the blowing winds, the candles burned unceasingly. And whenever they seemed to be extinguished, they burned anew, invisibly set alight. H*e who commanded the winds and the sea*[245] did not want his bride to be deprived in death of the light she always loved.

30. Concerning a certain Conrad, who was cured of a serious headache in that place.

God wanted to show that she lived after death by giving a sign in a brother, who would have died if the dead one had not come to his aid. His name was Conrad: not the one we mentioned before,[246] but a free man, a *conversus* in spiritual love, who was so sick in his head that the business of death occupied him daily,[247] but especially after crying on the death of the abbess. What was he to do? He and death were separated by only one step. He took courage, having received faith, and approached the dead one, thinking of the example of the woman in the Gospel: *if I may but put my hand on the hem of his garment, I will be made well.*[248] He touched the saint's head, and he gained health for his own head. And because he did not suffer pain from then until his death, he thereafter gave his own witness and testimony of the abbess's virtue.

31. Concerning the glory of her funeral rites.

A multitude of common people was present to celebrate her funeral. A salvific offering is made on her behalf; everyone makes it in her memory, commending the saint to God, and commending themselves to the saint before God. The neighbours who were present were wailing with tears. Widows and orphans were lamenting their plights, as if Dorcas were present and lay dead, and they were showing Peter the coats and

---

244 Job 15:26–27.

245 Matthew 8:26.

246 See above, ch. 27, p. 214.

247 Cf. 2 Corinthians 1:9.

248 Matthew 9:21 and Mark 6:56.

garments she had made for them.[249] Sick people who had been cured
by her were present. They acknowledged their illnesses and that they
had escaped those illnesses through her, but they confessed that they
had always concealed this, lest the saint be burdened. Indeed, she had
threatened that if they should reveal this, they might relapse into the
same evils. These threats ended with her death. It was an agreement
only up to that point; afterwards, they were permitted to say what they
wanted. A great many then appeared and spoke: one said that he had
been blind and had seen; another that he had been deaf and had heard;
another that he had been paralyzed and regained his health. Many others
had escaped diverse and innumerable infirmities through her. Also, sick
people came to her funeral; a great many were cured. I do not record
the number of them for the reason that, out of the negligence of those
present, it was not written down. Also, if jealousy had been present, it
could not have been concealed in the presence of this obvious miracle.

She was buried with honour, placed in Diessen before the altar of
St John the Baptist, her spirit rejoicing in the Lord, and her body placed
there as testimony against those who act contrary to her life. Act now,
God's saint, know our creation and yours too. Know that you could
have done nothing without divine help. Acquire this same divine help
for us for doing good, if we are unable to approach your reward, to
near your towering glory, or if we are unable to avoid punishment
through you, who is joined to God and incapable of nothing in the
Almighty. You reign with God. Give, so that sin may not reign in our
mortal body. He who gathered for you the hundredfold fruit with the
virgins, may he gather for us sixtyfold with the chaste ones; nay, rather
thirtyfold with the married ones who please him.[250]

May the lily adorn you, in the crown of glory and the wreath of
exultation; may the violet become for us a witness of your penitence
and humiliation. May you sit as bride with the bridegroom on the
throne of the kingdom, may you sleep in his lap, a peaceful consort and
partner in the marriage bed; may it be sufficient for us to have escaped
suffering, and to become the last ones in the kingdom of heaven. May
you, a virgin, follow the lamb with the virgins, wherever he may go, and
may you sing a new song. May we, however, avoid that woe of torments
through prophetic lamentations. Finally, may you sit with Christ as

---

249 Cf. Acts of the Apostles 9:36–41, for the story of Peter raising the woman Dorcas
    from the dead.
250 Cf. Matthew 13:23.

judge of the living and the dead. May we take position with the ones
on the right in the rank of the blessed, we who are about to gain the
kingdom with your prayers, because we cannot by the righteousness of
our own merits. May he grant it, who lives and reigns forever. Amen.

32. The hair of the deceased, having been cut off, was powerful against
thunder.

I hasten now to the end. There remains one thing to say, which
history forbids me to leave unsaid. By Paul's advice, she had taken
good care of her hair; as he said, *if a woman takes good care of her hair,
it is a glory to her.*[251] Hearing and obeying this, lest it might seem that
she had disregarded any of his commands, she thought to observe this,
acquiescing to the word of the learned one – not to the beauty of her
body. For she had her hair covered in such a way that it was never
seen. It was more because of the labour than because of its good look
that her hair was not cut, because no part of her served licentiousness;
everything served the burden of her body, everything served the courage
of her spirit, and her eye was plain in everything.

After she died, they cut her hair, preserving it for relics: the goodness
of faith does not deceive, for the sick are often cured at the touch of it.
Moreover, it is a most certain remedy against storms and lightning.
By rising and threatening winds, they hang the saint's hair up in the
air; and in this way the storms settle down and the thunder ceases, as
if the Lord Jesus orders them, as once he did at sea, so now on land.[252]
It was very commonplace in this monastery, and very well known in
the province, that showing St Mechthild's hair would ward off storms.
Since her death, the storms there have not been harmful, though they
often were before.

Let us pray to the saint that she defend us from the storm of temptations
by the merits of her sanctity, that she protect us with her prayers from
the fiery snares of the devil. May she also, by her spirit of justice and her
spirit of ardour, inflame us, so that we may have fervour for God, through
love, and a moderate mind for our neighbour, through discretion. May
St Mecthild obtain for us the grace of the Holy Spirit. May she drive
away anger, restrain jealousy, extinguish hatred, press hard upon pride,
heal the conscience, cut down luxury, bestow chastity, grow faith, pile
up hope, and increase charity, so that we may see God, who is charity,
in that goodness of the elect, he who lives and reigns forever. Amen.

251 1 Corinthians 11:15.
252 Cf. Luke 8:22–25.

THE DEEDS OF COUNT LUDWIG OF ARNSTEIN (D. 1185)

INTRODUCTION

In many ways, the opening years of Count Ludwig III of Arnstein's life seem to have been typical ones for a twelfth-century German count. Thanks to a series of marriages in the preceding generation, he grew up in a region where many of the neighbouring counts and lesser lords were tied to him by kinship. When his father died while Ludwig was still young, Ludwig succeeded him as count and gathered a band of loyal followers around him in his castle of Arnstein. He also arranged a good marriage (or so it appeared at the time) to Guda, the daughter of another count. But when Ludwig and Guda failed to have any children, the count chose to pursue a path that was decidedly less typical. With his wife's consent, he renounced his rights and properties, invited a group of Premonstratensian canons to transform his castle into a religious house, and embarked upon a religious life. He was not unique in deciding to give away his property while a young man in order to found and join a monastic community; across Europe, other lords were also driven by the reforming spirit of the early twelfth century into seeking out religious houses where they could atone for the sins of the aristocratic lifestyle. Nevertheless, Ludwig's decision was hardly a common one, and it is not surprising that the monks at Arnstein chose to preserve in writing the memory of their exceptional founder.

The text translated here combines an account of Ludwig's life with a history of the Premonstratensian community at Arnstein. As it shows, Ludwig did not disappear from the world of the secular nobility after joining his religious foundation. On the contrary, his reputation amongst the local laity seems to have grown after he bound himself to the Premonstratensians. People flocked to his side, offering properties to Arnstein and asking Ludwig to help reform other monastic communities in the neighbourhood, for there was much spiritual capital to be gained by following a count who had dedicated himself to the religious life.

Ludwig must have been quite old when he finally died in 1185, but as the vivid description of his burial attests, he remained until the end a prominent figure in local society.

Context

The setting for most of this work is the Rhine region, specifically the eastern bank of the river between Mainz and Coblenz. As the text explains, the castle of Arnstein was situated on the river Lahn, a tributary of the Rhine, and most of Ludwig's properties were clustered in the area around the confluence of these two rivers. This region had long been of central importance to the economic and political life of the German kingdom, and there had been lords exercising comital jurisdiction in the vicinity for more than two centuries before Ludwig's time. However, as is typical for the lineages of counts that appear in the surviving sources from the German kingdom around the year 1100, it is impossible to determine Ludwig's genealogical connections to most of the earlier lords in this vicinity. His castle of Arnstein may take its name from a Count Arnold who was active in the region around 1050, and counts with the name Ludwig had been appearing in sources from the area since the 1060s – but a definitive family tree cannot be reconstructed.[1]

Ludwig was not the only German nobleman of the early twelfth century to decide to convert his castle into a religious house. For example, two of his contemporaries, the brothers and counts Godfrey and Otto of Cappenberg, had done the same only a few years earlier.[2] Like Ludwig, Godfrey and Otto had also chosen to turn their fortress into a Premonstratensian house. This was a new form of the religious life, one of the products of those calls for spiritual reform that had become so loud during the decades around 1100. The order's founder was Norbert of Xanten (d. 1134), who had spent time as a wandering preacher before establishing a religious community at Prémontré in 1120; there, he and his followers strictly adhered to the Rule of St Augustine for regular canons. In subsequent years, the popularity of Prémontré's form of spiritual life spread rapidly, and other houses of canons were soon founded along similar lines. Thus, Count Ludwig of Arnstein was at the cutting edge of aristocratic/monastic

---

1 Krings, *Das Prämonstratenserstift Arnstein*, 3–8.

2 *The life of Godfrey of Cappenberg* has also been translated into English: see *Norbert and early Norbertine spirituality*, 85–119. For this phenomenon of castle conversion more generally, see Arnold, *Power and property*, 153–8.

culture when he chose to invite Premonstratensian canons to establish his new religious community. They were one of the most dynamic and exciting religious orders of his day.[3]

As the text translated here notes, Ludwig was called a *conversus* after giving away all his property and joining the community of Premonstratensian canons at Arnstein. This term is not an easy one to define. It is sometimes translated as 'lay brother', someone who lived apart from the monks or canons and typically performed menial chores for the religious community for the sake of his soul. However, *conversus* could also be used to refer to someone who had joined a religious house as an adult, not as a child oblate, and who was illiterate.[4] Ludwig's status seems to have been closer to the latter, but as the text makes clear, he was also permitted to play an unusually active role in promoting his community's interests. In other words, there was almost certainly a level of juridical flexibility in his status, because it was frequently advantageous for the house of canons at Arnstein to have a member who was familiar with the ways of the secular world.[5]

His wife Guda's status in the wake of his religious conversion is equally difficult to summarize neatly.[6] As the text makes clear, her consent was necessary before he could found a new religious community on the site of his castle, but she seems to have been reluctant. Eventually, she agreed, and she ended her life living as an enclosed recluse near the house of canons at Arnstein. Some scholars have suggested that a mid-twelfth-century manuscript from Arnstein may have been her personal prayer book, but this is only speculation.[7] Indeed, it is difficult to say anything definitive about Guda's situation, because the text's author writes her off the stage with remarkable speed, not even noting when she died. This suggests that later generations of canons at Arnstein may have been anxious to bury the truth about her role in their community's early history. Monastic conversions like Ludwig's, when there was a spouse involved, were often complicated affairs.[8] As is the case with many monastic narratives, what this one does not say is, in many ways, more interesting than what it does say.

3 For more on Norbert and the Premonstratensians, see the general introduction.
4 Constable, *The reformation of the twelfth century*, 77.
5 Crusius, ' ... *ut nulla fere provincia sit*', 18.
6 For women and the Premonstratensians more generally, see Wolbrink, 'Women in the Premonstratensian Order', and Krings, 'Die Prämonstratenser und ihr weiblicher Zweig'.
7 Krings, *Das Prämonstratenserstift Arnstein*, 226–30.
8 Elliott, *Spiritual marriage*, 157–62.

Text and authorship

Internal evidence indicates that the text, in its oldest extant version, was written at the Premonstratensian house in Arnstein. Its opening line – 'Here begins the prologue of the deeds of Count Ludwig, *our founder* [added emphasis]' – is only one of numerous passages in the text that allow it to be localized to Arnstein. The genealogical sections at the beginning, which mention nobles active in the period between 1198 and 1219, help to narrow the date of the text's copying to these years. Whether the entirety of the text was written during these two decades is impossible to determine, however. The fact that the text draws on privileges for Arnstein from the years 1156 and 1163 but makes no mention of any later charters for the community may be an indication that parts of the text were composed much earlier than the period around 1200. Indeed, more than four-fifths of the text concern the years prior to 1164 – before jumping ahead two decades, in the final section, to describe Ludwig's death and burial. One possible explanation for this gap is that Ludwig, who was probably born around the year 1100, was no longer as active in the closing decades of his life; however, it is also possible that much of the text had already been written by the mid-1160s. In that case, a later author, or perhaps the scribe of the oldest extant copy, might have added a few additional details – bringing the genealogy into the thirteenth century, for example – while otherwise relying on an older text.[9]

The form of the text, which combines the memorializing of a monastic founder with a discussion of his foundation's most important properties and rights, was a common one in monastic narratives of this period. Count Ludwig's life is unquestionably the central theme of the work, but the canons at Arnstein also used this text to preserve as many key details about their house's history as they could. Thus, listing their territorial holdings in a source about their founder was a way to lend antiquity and an aura of religious authority to their property rights. Similarly, the extensive discussion of Ludwig's kin connections in the opening part of the work served a pragmatic purpose for the religious

---

9 Widmann, in the introduction to his Latin edition of the text ('Die Lebensbeschreibung des Grafen Ludwig von Arnstein', 244), sees the oldest surviving version of the work as a later copy, not the original. Krings, *Das Prämonstratenserstift Arnstein*, 10, argues instead that the text was composed c. 1200 and that the oldest extant copy probably is the original. Wattenbach, *Deutschlands Geschichtsquellen*, vol. 1, 417, suggests the text was written shortly after 1190 by Provost Gunther of Arnstein, but he offers no evidence to support his position.

community during the thirteenth century; it provided them with a list of potential patrons for their house, patrons who could be reminded by way of this *gesta* of the fame and spiritual reputation of their ancestor Ludwig. In other words, this work served a variety of functions for the community at Arnstein.[10]

Another prominent feature of this text is the numerous allusions to other sources. It is laden with extensive biblical, classical and post-classical citations; on at least one occasion, the author even seems to have tried his own hand at writing original verse.[11] Many of the biblical and other textual allusions were used to gloss over aspects of Ludwig's story that the monks of Arnstein were clearly reluctant to tell in too much detail, including his activities during his youth and his wife Guda's apparent unwillingness to give up the secular, noble lifestyle to which she was accustomed. However, none of these references to other sources dominates the text. It is an original piece of work and lacks many of the hagiographical *topoi* that appear in other texts translated in this volume.

Manuscripts and editions

The codex containing the earliest known copy of Ludwig's *gesta* is the second of a three-volume set of manuscripts known as the Arnstein Passional, which was compiled during the 1170s.[12] The collection contains an enormous number of saints' lives, organized by their feast days; the second volume alone contains more than 100 hagiographi-cal works on almost 200 folios.[13] The text concerning Ludwig was added in a blank space at the end, in a hand from the early thirteenth century. Since the manuscript otherwise contains the lives of saints, Ludwig's biography is not entirely appropriate, but such additions were not uncommon.[14] It is a text of local interest, included in order to

---

10 For more on the motivations behind the writing of monastic narratives like this one, see the general introduction.

11 Widmann suggests this possibility in his edition of the text: 'Die Lebensbeschreibung des Grafen Ludwig von Arnstein', 250.

12 London, British Library, Harley 2801.

13 Krings, *Das Prämonstratenserstift Arnstein*, 235–7.

14 Cf. *The life of an unnamed* magistra *of Admont*, also translated in this volume.

preserve the memory of a key – if not necessarily saintly – member of the religious community. The text survives in other manuscripts as well, all of them produced after 1400, and was printed several times between the seventeenth and nineteenth centuries. Despite this enduring popularity, and its obvious importance for regional history, the text was not included in the *Monumenta Germaniae Historica*. The best and most recent edition dates from 1883 and was printed in the rather obscure *Annalen des Vereins für Nassauische Alterthumskunde und Geschichts-forschung*.[15] There, the Latin edition is printed alongside a later, loose German translation of the text drawn from an early sixteenth-century manuscript.

Notes on this translation

The 1883 Latin edition has formed the basis for this translation, but I have also consulted the oldest, thirteenth-century manuscript version of the work in preparing my text. Simon Widmann, the editor of the 1883 edition, identified many of the source allusions in the *gesta*, but I have added others that he did not identify. On the basis of the manuscript, I have included chapter numbers, in brackets, to indicate where the scribe marked breaks in the text through rubricated initials. For the proper identification of the numerous people and places appearing in this work, I have relied on Bruno Krings' monumental 1990 study of the Premonstratensian house at Arnstein during the Middle Ages.[16]

The anonymous author of this text was not as skilled a writer as he thought he was. His numerous attempts at grand, rhetorical flourishes frequently fall flat, and the language of the text is consistently over-wrought. His lengthy reflection on the significance of Ludwig's triple roles as count, founder and *conversus* is one of the few places where his writing rises to the occasion and hits its mark. Despite the difficulties of the text's language, I have sought to preserve the author's style as best as possible in this translation, in order to stay faithful to the original and to offer it as a contrast to the other works in this volume. This text is not easy, but it rewards close reading.

---

15 'Die Lebensbeschreibung des Grafen Ludwig von Arnstein.'
16 Krings, *Das Prämonstratenserstift Arnstein.*

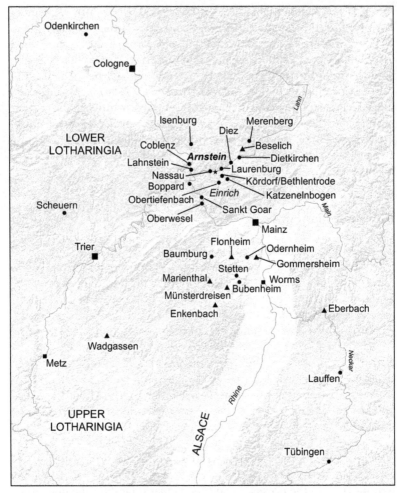

5 Arnstein and its environs (note: due to space limitations, not every location in the text has been included here)

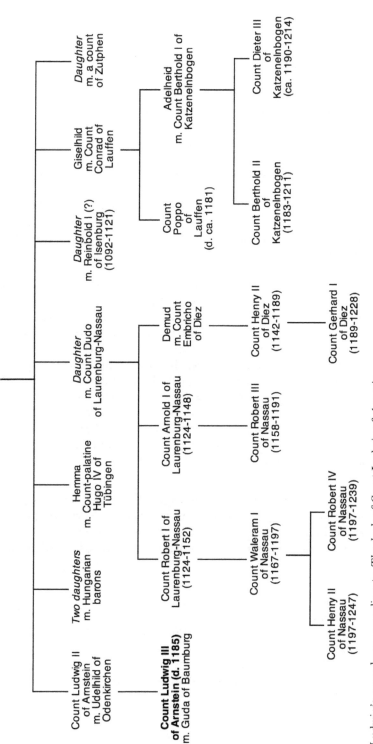

Ludwig's genealogy, according to *The deeds of Count Ludwig of Arnstein*

TRANSLATION

Here begins the prologue of the deeds of Count Ludwig, our founder.

Among all the various manifestations of worldly things and the curious pursuits of fickle intellect, by which human need is born along on the uncertain footsteps of this life, nothing is more precious than time. Once it has slipped away, by whatever progress or course, it cannot be regained with wealth of silver or gold or with any hard work. Weighing this carefully, very many men of past times – who were keen in intellect, strong in knowledge, and exalted in life and morals – brought the deeds of illustrious men to our times by their brilliant speech, leaving behind the lessons of their teaching for the memories of future generations, *like a* special *kind of mirror.*[1]

Filled with confidence by this, I will write (if not in golden letters, at least in ugly ones) about Count Ludwig, a man virtuous in all ways. I, who am cast down in life, lacking in grace, uncultivated in speech and poor in intellect, will write about his parents, birth, advancement in monastic profession and happy death in Christ. I am not concerned about the darts of detractors, because he is happy *whom no stork pecks from behind.*[2] For they will say that unpolished speech dishonours such distinguished material. To whom the Poet responds, not I: *It's possible to take some steps forward, even if we're not allowed to go any further.*[3] Nevertheless, the sweetness of honey is accustomed to being encased in a fragile reed and in an earthen vase,[4] and fire to being procured from hard flint.[5] Nor do the thick clouds that frequently surround and block the sun diminish its brightness.

[1] In a castle, which has been called Arnstein from ancient times until today, there was a count named Ludwig [II].[6] He was as famous for the long line of his ancestors as he was renowned for the marks of his own integrity and virtue. He had seven sisters, beloved virgins of

---

1 Gregory the Great, *Moralia in Iob*, II.1.

2 Persius, *Satires*, I.58.

3 Horace, *Epistles*, I.1.32. (*Satires and Epistles*, 66).

4 Cf. 2 Corinthians 4:7.

5 Cf. Virgil, *Aeneid*, VI.471.

6 Count Ludwig II of Arnstein was the father of Ludwig III, the subject of this text. He is named in sources between the years 1095 and 1110. See Krings, *Das Prä-monstratenserstift Arnstein*, 5.

elegant appearance, in whom there reflected a collective moral fitness *like* in *a kind of mirror.*[7] That same place [i.e., Arnstein] was three miles from the Rhine, toward the east, located on a mountain ridge above the Lahn River and surrounded on all sides by steep and high slopes.[8] On one side it had the Dörsbach, a stream well-stocked with fish and employed for some adopted functions, like mills and other uses. Moreover, at that time, the renowned place was so inaccessible and fortified that a single, very narrow path offered a difficult approach from only one side of the mountain, and this same approach was blocked with iron bars when needed.

At that time, the said count, who was prudent and circumspect in all sorts of matters, was concerned – above all else – with his sisters' honour and the next generation [of his lineage]. He desired to bind each one in marriage to a man whose origins befit the splendour of her noble light and the grace of her youthful form. Divine goodness favoured a beneficial result for his honourable wishes. For two of his sisters were married to two illustrious barons of the Hungarians no less solemnly than they had been nobly betrothed.[9] The third passed into the loving embrace of the count-palatine of Tübingen; her brother honourably presented her to this count at Sankt Goar, and the count-palatine received her ostentatiously with 200 *milites* and a great deal of splendour.[10]

A fourth, betrothed to the count of Nassau, bore Robert and Arnold as well as a daughter, Demud.[11] Count Arnold was the father of Count Robert, a war-like man, who died as a pilgrim in the lands across the

---

7 Cf. above, n. 1.

8 Three medieval German miles (*miliariis*) was the equivalent of approximately 20 kilometers, or 12 modern miles. As the crow flies, Arnstein is approximately 11 modern miles east of the Rhine.

9 The identities of these Hungarian noblemen are unknown.

10 Count-palatine Hugo IV of Tübingen married the daughter Hemma. For the term *milites*, see the general introduction.

11 This is probably Count Dudo of Laurenburg, who married a daughter whose name is unknown. He was an ancestor of the later line of the counts of Nassau and a neighbour of the counts of Arnstein. The author pauses in his narrative to give a detailed description of the descendants of this fourth sister, because many of them were prominent nobles in the region around Arnstein. Moreover, by the time the author was writing, this sister's descendants had inherited many of the Arnstein lineage's lands and rights. Many of these descendants were also probably patrons, or potential patrons, of the monastery during the author's own lifetime. See the family tree for the genealogy laid out here.

sea on the expedition of Emperor Frederick [I].[12] [The other] Robert, Arnold's brother, was the father of Count Waleram, whose sons are Henry and Robert, now counts; their mother was named Kunigunde.[13] Their [i.e., Arnold and Robert's] sister, Demud, was married to Embricho, who was the father of Count Henry, the father of Count Gerhard of Diez.[14]

The fifth was betrothed to the count of Lauffen.[15] She was the mother of Count Poppo and of his sister, Adelheid, to whom Counts Berthold and Dieter of Katzenelnbogen were born.[16] The sixth begot the Isenburg family.[17] The seventh sister crossed into the county of Zutphen.[18]

[2] The aforementioned count [i.e., Ludwig II] had a wife by the name of Udelhild, who was of old and illustrious blood – according to this world.[19] She did not dishonour the loving embraces of such a great man, and all of the morals and grace that the sun had sent in advance to her ancestors, who were of innate integrity, would also rise in the renown of her future offspring. What more is there? A son, elegant in appearance, was born to them, and – by divine providence – only this one, on whom would be poured forth both his father's name and the inheritance of the entire county.[20] For what Christ had foreseen to be united before the earthly times of his servants could not later be broken apart piece by piece.

---

12 Count Arnold I of Laurenburg-Nassau (1124–48) and his son Count Robert III of Nassau (1158–91), the latter of whom died on the Third Crusade led by Emperor Frederick I Barbarossa. This Count Robert (Rupert) played a prominent role on the crusade, according to various sources translated in *The crusade of Frederick Barbarossa*.

13 Count Robert I of Laurenburg-Nassau (1124–52) and his son Count Waleram I of Nassau, who probably died in 1197. Waleram's sons by his wife Kunigunde, Henry II and Robert IV, jointly held the county of Nassau until 1230, when Robert joined the Teutonic Order.

14 Count Embricho of Diez; Count Henry II of Diez (1142–89); and Count Gerhard I of Diez (1189–1228).

15 This sister's name was Giselhild. She married Count Conrad of Lauffen.

16 Count Poppo of Lauffen died c. 1181. Adelheid married Count Berthold I of Katzenelnbogen. Count Berthold II of Katzenelnbogen (1183–1211) and Count Dieter III of Katzenelnbogen (c. 1190–c. 1214) were their sons.

17 This daughter, whose name is unknown, probably married Reinbold of Isenburg.

18 The county of Zutphen was located to the north-west of Arnstein in the modern-day Netherlands. There was a short-lived line of counts of Zutphen during the late eleventh and early twelfth centuries, but it is unclear if this sister married a member of this lineage.

19 She is known as Udelhild of Odenkirchen in modern scholarship.

20 i.e., Count Ludwig III of Arnstein, the subject of this text.

Then, the little boy was handed over to a wet-nurse to be raised. Like a heavenly pearl, he was entrusted to her very carefully, and he – who would be *a chosen vessel*[21] – was filled every day with successes. The solicitous wet-nurse also exercised the utmost possible care, and from the beginning of his infancy he drank virtue with her milk. So that I may hasten through this quickly: a certain likeness of his future integrity beautified his tender years, such that he (who was playing in such youthful bloom) could already be directed easily toward what he would promise in manhood.

Meanwhile, the days rolled by, and he soon entered his adolescent years.[22] Because the end comes – *the end of all flesh comes*[23] – his father completed the days of his life. On the fifth Kalends of June [28 May], in accordance with *dust to dust*,[24] this brief visitor went out from this shipwreck of the world[25] and was buried in the church of the blessed virgin Margaret.[26] But his mother lived on for a long time after her son's conversion to the religious life. When the earth forced this small piece of itself, this particle of the world, to yield toward evening,[27] she lost her strength on her estate called Odenkirchen, and she concluded her final day on the third Nones of July [5 July]. She rests in the cathedral at Cologne.[28]

[3] Their son, Ludwig [III], successor and heir to such great parents, took on the responsibility for domestic affairs as a new overseer. Intellectually, he became a man, and he judged with a reasoning mind what had to be done and put in order. Shrewd in intellect, smooth in speech, generous in support, lavish in the example of his honesty, he refused

---

21 Acts of the Apostles 9:15.

22 In the medieval period, *adolescentia* was generally understood to begin at the age of fourteen for boys.

23 Genesis 6:13.

24 Genesis 3:19.

25 Cf. Gregory the Great, *Moralia in Iob*, Epistola ad Leandrum, 1.

26 His exact year of death is unknown. He last appears in a source in 1110 (Krings, *Das Prämonstratenserstift Arnstein*, 5). The nineteenth-century editor of the text, Widmann, argues for 1112 on the basis of later evidence ('Die Lebensbeschreibung des Grafen Ludwig von Arnstein', 248), but this cannot be verified by twelfth-century sources. The church of St. Margaret, where he was buried, was located at the base of the castle-hill in Arnstein.

27 Cf. *The life of Saint Epiphanius by Ennodius*, 46–7, ch. 37.

28 She died sometime after the year 1158, possibly as a canoness in Cologne. See Krings, *Das Prämonstratenserstift Arnstein*, 6.

everyone's devotion to him, especially that of his own men. He loved
his ministerials as companions.[29] They pressed him greatly with advice
about marriage and the conjugal bond, because the matter's utility
demanded it. But first he put his hand to strong things,[30] and with his
friends assuming the many costs, he was honourably girded with the
belt of knighthood. After the customary tournaments of worldly men,
he anticipated the approach of his legal marriage.

After this, owing to the helpful advice his friends offered, and to the
serious embassies sent by the count of Baumburg on the matter, he
took as his wife the daughter of that man, a virgin by the name of
Guda, who was presented with much pomp, as was proper.[31]

She remained barren for a long time. Because her infertility denied
them hope for a child, they came to be afflicted with a most ardent
contrition of spirit and implored the Lord's mercy with all their prayers
for a successor to such a great inheritance. But for a long time, divine
providence resisted their countless petitions, since it was He who was
arranging to inherit through his servants by right of affinity.[32] But
why? Were they cheated of their desire? By no means! How were they
not? Listen! *Rejoice, O barren one who does not bear, break forth and cry
aloud, you who do not give birth, because*[33] *your sons will* certainly *come from
afar, and your daughters will be carried on the hip. Lift up your eyes all
around, and see; they all gather together, they come to you.*[34] The days will
come when you, rejoicing mother of so many children, will sing: *Behold,
I and my children, whom* God *gave to me!*[35]

[4] O Muses, who have employed listless breezes until now,
    Blow, I beg, upon the surface of the sea for the rising sails,[36]
so that the structure of the work that follows may rest upon this

---

29 For ministerials, see the general introduction.

30 Cf. Proverbs 31:19 and Ovid, *Metamorphoses*, XIII.170.

31 Count Emicho of Schmidtburg, Kyrburg and Flonheim, whose lineage began to
    appear with the toponym 'of Baumburg' in the second half of the twelfth century,
    was probably her father. See Krings, *Das Prämonstratenserstift Arnstein*, 49.

32 Cf. above and *The life of Mechthild of Diessen*, ch. 21, p. 205.

33 Galatians 4:27.

34 Isaiah 60:4.

35 Isaiah 8:18.

36 There is no known source for these lines of verse. The nineteenth-century editor
    of the text, Widmann, suggests they may have been written by the author of the
    gesta ('Die Lebensbeschreibung des Grafen Ludwig von Arnstein', 250).

foundation, howsoever it was laid, and the accomplishments to be praised may always gild the quill pen of the uncultured writer of such renowned material.

[5] The castle of the aforesaid count can be called Arnstein in the vernacular and Lapis-Aquile (Eagle's Stone) in the Latin language. It was *the howling waste of the wilderness,*[37] ready for its prey,[38] suitable for plundering, and was a stone of stumbling and a rock of offence[39] for its inhabitants. Since they were not sufficiently content with their wages[40] and possessed too little of their own property, they seized everyone else's. The poor and the destitute sweated on land and sea for their excessive needs, and

The tireless trader rushes to furthest India.[41]

Consequently, these true soldiers of Pharaoh[42] carried both the wealth of the shipping lane and the spoils of the whole province to this place. Truly, according to the book: *The rock is refuge for the hedgehogs,*[43] for the prickly ones were covered all over with the sharp points of their sins.[44] Moreover, just as the sickness of the head runs down into the arms and legs, so too, to be sure, did the filth and vices of the limbs repeatedly disturb the virtue of the head. For the count, although he in no way at all needed spoils of this kind, nevertheless was made a party to the action by his consent. He, by being silent, and they, his men, by oppressing the poor, struck hard against the anger of the stern

---

37 Deuteronomy 32:10. See *The life of Bishop Otto of Bamberg,* III.1, p. 135 for this same biblical passage. This same phrase is also used to describe Admont's location in *The life of an unnamed magistra of Admont,* ch. 3, p. 157. It is a phrase often employed for monasteries, so its use here implies that Arnstein was well-suited to become a monastic house after Ludwig's conversion.

38 Cf. Psalm 16:12.

39 Cf. Isaiah 8:14.

40 Cf. Luke 3:14.

41 Horace, *Epistles,* I.1.45 (cf. *Satires and Epistles,* 66).

42 Cf. Exodus 14:28.

43 Psalm 103:18.

44 In the medieval bestiary tradition, hedgehogs are frequently symbols of greed and avarice, and their quills represent man's sins or the devil's snares. See *Bestiary,* 112–3. All of this is meant to convey the wickedness of the count's men who resided in the castle.

protector (although he bore it calmly). But how did it end? The word
of the Lord to you, O prince.[45] *Though you soar like the eagle and make
your nest* above the stars of heaven, *from there I will bring you down,
declares the Lord.*[46] When? The grace of the Holy Spirit does not know
how to act slowly.

[6] Therefore, God sent the spirit of his son into the count's heart,
and he changed into another man. He cast his thought on the Lord,
saying with the Psalmist: *'Who will give me wings like a dove, and I will
fly and be at rest? Behold, I have gone far off, fleeing,'*[47] and he was made
like the eagle[48] by a wonderful gift of God, who *calls those things that are
not, as those that are.*[49] God was now *enticing his young to fly,*[50] both by
word and example, so that what had been *the stench of death bringing
death* for that man consenting to wicked deeds might also be *the fragrance
of life bringing life.*[51]

The count thought to make a house of prayer there, where wild goats
once danced and the sirens answered in their temples of pleasure.[52]
But because this required his wife's agreement, he was (according
to Solomon) running about, making haste, stirring up his friend,[53]
so that, just as they were *two in one flesh,*[54] one spirit might unite
them in God. *Who shall find a strong woman? Far away, at the farthest
reaches, is her value.*[55] She [i.e., Guda] resisted and cried out in protest;
like the asp, she stopped up her ears to his salutary counsels.[56] But
because the unbelieving woman is often made holy by the believing

45 Cf. 2 Kings 9:5.

46 Obadiah 1:4.

47 Psalm 54:7–8.

48 Deuteronomy 32:11.

49 Romans 4:17.

50 Deuteronomy 32:11.

51 2 Corinthians 2:16.

52 Cf. Isaiah 13:21–22.

53 Cf. Proverbs 6:3.

54 Genesis 2:24.

55 Proverbs 31:10. See *The life of Mechthild of Diessen*, ch. 9, p. 181, for another use of
    this same biblical quotation. The second half of this quotation is more commonly
    translated as *She is far more precious than jewels*, but I have chosen a translation that
    follows the Latin more closely.

56 Cf. Psalm 57:5 and *Bestiary*, 188.

57 Cf. 1 Corinthians 7:14.

man[57] (and the reverse), she was finally subdued by frequent admonitions and offered herself *to the prize of the heavenly calling*[58] with most willing consent. Truly, *this is the change of the right hand of the Most High.*[59] Truly,

Divine power plays in human affairs.[60]

[7] Therefore, giving thanks to God, from whom comes *every good gift and every perfect gift,*[61] he handed over his heart for *watching early,*[62] so that the Lord might drop his hope's anchor in a safe place – lest the instability of the human heart change the still tender first fruits, or the venomous craftiness of the ancient serpent weaken them. For he feared what the weeping prophet once said: *His foes have become his masters.*[63] And Solomon: *Son, when you come to the service of God, prepare your soul for temptation.*[64] *When you come,* he said, because the craftiness of the tempter opposes the princes and always sets itself against the heads of warriors. While placed at this pivotal moment between hope and fear, the Lord's new athlete was wavering. Founding Zion with sapphires,[65] God, who knows all things before they are done (since he knew beforehand from eternity),[66] brought the grace of that man's spirit to perfection at the time he wished.

[8] At that time, there was a certain Otto, a deacon in rank, very rich in estates, descended from the noble and generous stock of the Saxons, and a relative of the celebrated count [i.e., Ludwig III].[67] For the love of Jesus Christ he had renounced his abundant estates and most splendid patrimony and had founded in these days a church called Gottesgnaden. It followed the Rule of the blessed Augustine and the early church, and it followed the model and way of life of the lord Archbishop Norbert

---

58 Philippians 3:14.

59 Psalm 76:11.

60 Ovid, *Ex Ponto,* IV.3.49.

61 James 1:17.

62 Ecclesiasticus 39:6.

63 Lamentations 1:5.

64 Cf. Ecclesiasticus 2:1.

65 Cf. Isaiah 54:11.

66 Cf. Acts of the Apostles 26:5.

67 Count Otto of Röblingen (1131–64), founder of Gottesgnaden. See Krings, *Das Prämonstratenserstift Arnstein,* 23–5.

of Magdeburg.[68] Because his memory comes to mind, we will make a digression from the present little work and insert what we consider necessary.

[9] In the year of the Lord 1119[69] Norbert of blessed memory, the thirteenth archbishop of Magdeburg, came to Prémontré and accepted a way of life, which he received not from man nor through man.[70] It was confirmed by apostolic decrees, and he handed it down to be observed by the brothers, just as it is preserved uniformly in the churches of the same order. He remained in this way of life on his archiepiscopal seat, without blemish, until in the year of grace 1130, that man, certain of the crown of justice, ended the course of his life blessedly.[71] Buried with due honour, he rests in the church of blessed Mary in Magdeburg.

Now let us return to the things already begun. The aforementioned Otto, because he was very rich, improved the church of the blessed Victor the Martyr from the Theban legion, which he had built on the River Saale, with such great gifts that you would say that this church is deservedly called Gottesgnaden [i.e., God's grace]: both for the great abundance of those things meant for the brothers' use, and for the agreeable pleasantness of the place.

[10] The count [i.e., Ludwig III], having heard rumours of this sort about Otto, went to him without delay, as if summoned by some sort of divine revelation. He was received honourably, and he laid bare the treasure chamber of his heart to his friend and revealed the whole secret of his breast.[72] Not without fruit. For Otto promised, in order to carry out what Ludwig had conceived in his mind, that he would send him the tender sprouts of his own community. With how much reverence and love was the count regarded while he stayed among them? Let the feather be silent, where the whole workshop of mental affection speaks.

---

68 Archbishop Norbert of Magdeburg (1126–34) was the founder of the Premonstrat-
    ensian order before becoming archbishop. He is also mentioned in *The life of Bishop
    Otto of Bamberg*, III.4, p. 138.

69 1120 according to other texts: *Norbert and early Norbertine spirituality*, 11 (the same
    book also includes translations of the earliest *vitae* for Norbert).

70 Cf. Galatians 1:1. This sentence is misleading; Norbert became archbishop of
    Magdeburg in 1126, several years after he founded Prémontré.

71 Norbert died in 1134.

72 Cf. Luke 6:45 and Ecclesiasticus 27:17.

Twelve canons from Gottesgnaden and just as many *conversi* brothers followed in his footsteps on his return, having gone forth from the spiritual heights of the holy profession ready to build the foundations on *Jesus Christ himself, the chief cornerstone.*[73] They brought with them in carts and carriages the Scriptures and ecclesiastical books and not a few furnishings.[74] They came, I say, *fellow citizens with the saints and members of the household of God,*[75] carrying peace, illuminating the fatherland with a certain angelic refinement, and sending forth the radiance of their intellect by their way of life. There was among them a teacher (*scolasticus*) from the church of St Maurice in Magdeburg, Godfrey of celebrated memory, a man of singular grace and merit, whom the other brothers followed as if he were some kind of celestial beam of light. Then, the will and plan of the count beloved to God was made known by a celebrated speech; then, the storeroom of the holy spirit infused everyone's noses with what until then had been shut away, and the alabaster box of his heart, broken open, perfumed the entire region,[76] such that many were saying, *Draw me: we will run after you to the smell of your ointments.*[77]

[11] In the year of the Lord's Incarnation 1139, Count Ludwig, with his venerable wife Guda, gave himself over by his own free will into the hands of the lord Godfrey *scolasticus* and the brothers of Gottesgnaden – along with all of his possessions and his castle Arnstein located in the diocese of Trier – for the praise of omnipotent God the Father and the Son and the Holy Spirit in honour of the glorious and pure virgin Mary and the excellent confessor Nicholas.[78] His chaplain and scribe Markward too, and his steward Swiker as well, and five other *milites*, abandoning the secular world, assumed the religious life of holy profession with him. Their father in Christ, the aforesaid Godfrey, was solemnly

---

73 Ephesians 2:20.

74 Melville, *The world of medieval monasticism*, 160–1, discusses the process of founding new Premonstratensian houses.

75 Ephesians 2:19.

76 Cf. Mark 14:3.

77 Song of Songs 1:3.

78 As the text makes clearer below, the church is dedicated to the sainted Pope Nicholas I (858–67). The earliest papal privilege for the monastery was issued by Pope Innocent II in 1142: *Urkundenbuch des Prämonstratensersklosters Arnstein*, 1–3, nr. 1. King Conrad III confirmed the monastery's foundation in a privilege from the year 1145: *MGH DD K. III*, 228–30, nr. 127.

ordained at this time at a general synod by the venerable Albero, archbishop of Trier and legate of the apostolic see in the German kingdom.[79] Happy is the day that brought joy to the angels of God on account of repentant sinners[80] and brought to men an example of worldly contempt so worthy of imitation. That happy day, I say, bestowed with much happiness, begins to dawn as often as the sinner becomes inflamed with heavenly desires by their example; it makes visible outside, in works, what the unction of the Holy Spirit teaches in the heart. *Unless you be converted*, said the Saviour, *and become as small children, you shall not enter into the kingdom of Heaven.*[81] He does not seek those who are like small children in their stature but in their humility; to these the son of God, who was small and humble in our world, promised the kingdom of Heaven.

[12] First of all, a special house was prepared for the lady countess Guda on the left side of the mountain, where having changed her way of life, she was permanently enclosed, never going out.[82] She atoned for the luxuries she had enjoyed in her earlier life, and the many plates of food, by being frugal with her very harsh fare. Through a small window she frequently listened to the divine offices, intent on the Psalms and prayers. And so, the wheel of her birth turned blessedly; she migrated from the world on the sixteenth Kalends of September [17 August],[83] and she was buried with veneration before the altar of St Nicholas in the sanctuary of the church.

[13] The count held the right of patronage for seventy-two churches; all of them belonged by filial right to the church of St Margaret.[84] Also under his jurisdiction were: Boppard, Oberwesel, the village of Sankt Goar, Lahnstein (both of them),[85] Coblenz and very many

---

79 Abbot Godfrey of Arnstein (1139–51) was ordained by Archbishop Albero of Trier (1131–52). For this archbishop, see *A warrior bishop of the twelfth century.*

80 Cf. Luke 15:7 and 15:10.

81 Matthew 18:3.

82 i.e., she became an anchoress, or recluse.

83 She died sometime after the year 1156. See Krings, *Das Prämonstratenserstift Arnstein,* 100.

84 St Margaret had been built in Arnstein prior to Ludwig III's foundation of the monastery. It was a parish church by 1139, and by 1156 it had come under the control of the monastery. See Krings, *Das Prämonstratenserstift Arnstein,* 377.

85 i.e., Oberlahnstein and Niederlahnstein, on either side of the Lahn River where it flows into the Rhine.

other villages in the Rhine Region, and the whole province called Einrich.[86] He looked on all these things like they were filth; he preferred better property in Heaven. He resigned his county to the lords of Isenburg. Afterwards, they sold it to the lords of Nassau and Katzenelnbogen.

In addition, these are the alods[87] he assigned for the use of those brothers serving God: Bubenheim (which is in the district of Worms) with its church, tithes and men and its fixed revenues, with full liberty of all kinds;[88] thirty *mansi*[89] in the village of Niederwiesen on the other side of the Rhine; eight *mansi* in the village of Attenhausen; four *mansi* in Weltrod; the village of Gosmerod with every right, and the court of Köberle; one *mansus* in Bremberg; the manor Hollerich with every right; also Salscheid with every tithe; three *mansi* in Singhofen; vineyards, fields and forests at Neef and Bremm with the tithes; a court and vineyards in Kamp; a court and vineyards in Niederlahnstein; the church of St Margaret; moreover, the manor Seelbach and the church at Kördorf with every right and in its entirety, namely with all its men and tithes. The venerable lord Albero, archbishop of Trier and legate of the papal see, gave these things to the count and to the brothers of Arnstein by a perpetual donation for the salvation of his soul and those of his successors, and he confirmed this with privileges.[90]

Also, Hartrad of Merenberg and his wife Irmengard, with the consent of their children and heirs, delegated in perpetuity to the church of the blessed Nicholas in Arnstein, in the hope of eternal life, the church in Obertiefenbach in Einrich – with its men, and the entire tithe of the village, and all its appurtenances both in fields and in meadows. They also delegated the entire tithe from Bettendorf, half of the tithe from Scheuern, the forest called Kammerforst, and the whole wood called Brustensbach except for eight trees. All of these things are described more fully in the church's privileges.[91]

---

86 The county of Einrich was one of Ludwig's chief holdings.

87 An alod was a property that a landholder possessed with full rights.

88 For the significance of tithes in this period, see Eldevik, *Episcopal power*.

89 A *mansus* was a measurement of land.

90 A privilege of Archbishop Albero of Trier does not survive. The earliest archiepiscopal privilege for Arnstein was issued by Archbishop Hillin of Trier in 1156: *Urkundenbuch des Prämonstratensersklosters Arnstein*, 5–7, nr. 3.

91 *Urkundenbuch des Prämonstratensersklosters Arnstein*, 7–9, nr. 4 (1163).

Moreover, in the aforesaid churches, namely of the blessed Margaret, Kördorf, and Obertiefenbach, no ecclesiastical person but the abbot of Arnstein will hold spiritual rights and will preside over an assembly whenever he should wish and it should seem proper to him. No advocate or secular person will hold any right, but whosoever will be the archbishop of the church of Trier will defend these churches for the sake of his soul's salvation, perpetually protecting them from trouble caused by those acting unjustly.[92] Moreover, in the aforesaid archbishopric, whatever moveable goods happen to be transferred from one place to another for the brothers' use, those things will be free from every transport duty and every tax.[93]

[14] The venerable father Godfrey, zealous in his charity, was vigilant concerning the dutiful protection of the Lord's flock. He strove to bring back the money entrusted to him with a profit by doubling his master's income.[94] Hence, using gold, silver and precious stones to build upon the foundation, which is Christ,[95] he thereafter raised *the high walls of the temple, enlarging the entrance of the house and the court* in the construction of the physical building.[96] For he had foresight in his counsel, he worked hard, he was sweet in learning and he was of remarkable humility and abstinence – as came to us in truthful reports from his contemporaries.

While he was standing immoveable in these watchtowers of perfection, it happened that Duke Frederick [II] of Swabia, father of the Frederick who was afterwards emperor of the Romans,[97] passed one time with his men by the church called Münsterdreisen near the stream Pfrimm. Also in his entourage was Count Ludwig [of Arnstein], who was a relative of the same duke and a very close friend.[98] The aforesaid duke gazed upon the place, which had already been instituted twice for divine service, namely once with canonesses and once with regular canons;[99]

---

92 Church advocates were local nobles responsible for defending a religious house's properties and, in some cases, for judging capital offences on the religious house's estates.

93 Cf. Archbishop Hillin's privilege of 1156: *Urkundenbuch des Prämonstratensersklosters Arnstein*, 5–7, nr. 3.

94 Cf. Matthew 25:14–30 for the parable alluded to here.

95 Cf. 1 Corinthians 3:11–12.

96 Ecclesiasticus 50:2 and 50:5.

97 Duke Frederick II of Swabia (d. 1147), father of Emperor Frederick I Barbarossa.

98 It is unclear how they were related to one another.

99 For this community's history, see Krings, *Das Prämonstratenserstift Arnstein*, 88.

but it had fallen away completely from all discipline, such that hunting dogs were running around in the church's sanctuary.[100] And Frederick, saying in accordance with the prophet, '*For foxes roam around on Mount Zion, because it lies in ruins*',[101] was moved from his innermost heart. Inflamed with zeal for God's love, he handed over that same place, with ownership of all its goods, to the beloved count and *conversus*,[102] begging and pleading in equal measure that the count – for the hope of heavenly rewards – arrange for the proper observance of monastic piety in that place.

Ludwig accepted the place joyfully and with great enthusiasm. He took counsel with his brothers and chose six canons of proven conduct from Gottesgnaden, joining them with other suitable people whom father Godfrey had assigned for this work. He placed at their head the count's chaplain, Markward, who had by this time ascended from the veil of tears.[103] Supported in the house of the Lord by the improvement of his virtues, he shouted out the Gradual Psalms,[104] inwardly rejoicing. In the year of grace 1145 this man came to the monastery with the assigned brothers in order to improve the vineyard of the Lord of Hosts. However, what kind of life he would lead in Christ, how fruitful his vine would become and the way he would live his days both for himself and for the Lord's household: we leave his successors to proclaim and praise these things – lest a different conversation should distract us from our subject matter.

[15] Later, the celebrated count, who was already living his life entirely in Christ, having forgotten those things that are behind (in accordance with the apostle),[105] extended himself toward the foremost gifts of divine promise through the steps of the virtues. Those holy women (*sanctimoniales*), who had previously resided at Bethlentrode and later Stetten, in whose company were daughters of noble *milites* from Einrich, submitted to the service of the Lord through the example of the lady Countess

---

100 See similar critiques of monasteries in need of reform in *The deeds of Margrave Wiprecht of Groitzsch*, p. 76 and *The life of Mechthild of Diessen*, p. 178.

101 Lamentations 5:18.

102 For the term *conversus*, see the introduction to this text.

103 Cf. Psalm 83:7.

104 A term for Psalms 119–33.

105 Cf. Philippians 3:13.

Guda. Ludwig transferred them to the Valley of St Mary [Marienthal].[106] Afterwards, he removed some of them to the convent of ladies called Enkenbach.[107]

[16] After the passing of those days, because *for those loving God all things work together for good*,[108] certain ministerials of the church of blessed Stephen of Metz many times offered their houses, fields and meadows in the village of Gommersheim, in the diocese of Mainz near Odernheim, in praise of God for the remission of their sins to the said count with abundant prayers. They did this, because he frequently passed by them when journeying to his alod of Bubenheim, and they considered him distinguished in reputation and most proper in conduct. And so, he did not waste the reverence they had for God; he constructed there, on the stream Selz, an oratory in honour of the mother of God and the blessed John the Evangelist for the holy women (*sanctimoniales*) whom he had gathered together there. Whoever should read this little work should know, moreover, that the same place is completely free from every secular advocate and every right of the parish of Odernheim – except the tithe, which it is obligated to surrender to the lords of Metz.[109]

[17] Meanwhile, the close-knit and blessed community of brothers at Arnstein fervently built the house of the Lord with daily exercises and exertions – and with manual labour, which everyone accomplished both together as a group and separately as individuals. It is easy to imagine what kind of disciplined, internal harmony there was. No one was idle in leisure there; no one was feigning labour, on account of the teaching that *the goal of our instruction* is connected to the chain of mutual *charity*.[110] Indeed, their hearts were humbled in their labours.[111] They found daily

---

106 Ludwig probably established the house of Premonstratensian canonesses at Marienthal around the year 1145. See Krings, *Das Prämonstratenserstift Arnstein*, 92–3.

107 The date of Ludwig's founding of the house of Premonstratensian canonesses at Enkenbach is unknown. See Krings, *Das Prämonstratenserstift Arnstein*, 93.

108 Romans 8:28.

109 The date of Ludwig's founding of the house of Premonstratensian canonesses at Gommersheim is unknown, but it was probably established between 1145 and 1151. See Krings, *Das Prämonstratenserstift Arnstein*, 93–5. For the term advocate, see above, n. 92.

110 1 Timothy 1:5. For the importance of monastic work more generally, see *RB 1980: the rule of St Benedict*, 248, ch. 48.

111 Cf. Psalm 106:12.

martyrdom, humility of mind and suffering of the flesh in the frequent endurance of poverty. Some set to work on the castle walls that had to be broken down; others set to work on the open spaces that had to be made level; others hauled the beams and posts for the buildings; and others cut through the projecting part of the cliff face, the height of which (as it is told) reached what is now the top of the church. Who is capable of naming the many labours of God's servants? Who is capable of estimating the sweat? Only the giver of gifts knows, who repaid a great many of them: 'henceforth,' the Spirit said to them, 'let them rest from their labours'.[112]

[18] At that time, in the twelfth year since he had been appointed to oversee the Lord's household, the troubles of the flesh became burdensome for father Godfrey of living memory. He died blessedly on the fourth Ides of October [12 October], on the journey to Prémontré, and was buried at Wadgassen.[113] Afterwards, his bones were honourably transferred to his own church [i.e., at Arnstein] and placed before the altar of the blessed apostles Peter and Paul with due honour.

[19] After his passing, Eustachius succeeded to the office of abbot. He was a man of strength and singular grace, and so the care of the Lord's sheepfold and the management of temporal affairs were deservedly entrusted to him.[114] In his times, a certain priest by the name of Godfrey gave the brothers of Arnstein a church called Beselich, which he had built in the parish of Dietkirchen with the consent of the lord Archdeacon Alexander of Trier, together with all the appurtenances of animals and crops located on the estate. He gave this in the hope of eternal salvation, so that the brothers might attend to the solemnities of the Mass for him in that same place in perpetuity. The brothers also oversaw a convent of holy women (sanctimoniales) in that place and dedicated the first fruits from the income of their good works to the Lord of Hosts.[115] The lords of Katzenelnbogen were at that time the advocates of this place, but for the love of Jesus Christ and his virgin

---

112 Revelation 14:13.

113 12 October 1151. Wadgassen near Saarbrücken, another Premonstratensian house. See Krings, *Das Prämonstratenserstift Arnstein*, 50–1.

114 Abbot Eustachius of Arnstein (1151–80).

115 For the donation of the church, see *Urkundenbuch des Prämonstratensersklosters Arnstein*, 7–9, nr. 4 (1163). For the religious community, see Krings, *Das Prämonstratenserstift Arnstein*, 95–8.

mother they renounced entirely their advocacy with every right.[116]
They handed it over in perpetual liberty into the hands of the aforesaid
brothers and the *conversus* count with the whole of everything that
exists on the estate. Hillin, at that time archbishop of Trier and legate
of the apostolic see, received that place under his protection and that
of his successors, to be defended by their special grace, after the said
Archdeacon Alexander had already resigned fully his right to these
things. And it was established and confirmed by privileges, for the
greater and perpetual stability of this act, that the said church be held
to pay annually to the archbishop of the church of Trier a gold *denarius*
or twelve silver *denarii* of the money of Coblenz.[117]

[20] But now, let us return to him, on whose account all this material
had its beginning, explaining to the reader what we promised about
his way of life and his passing. You have heard, reader, in the above
sections – if it has not vanished from memory – a few words about the
man's ancestors, his entry [into the spiritual life] and his progress as
well. Listen now and marvel with us, so that we may at least marvel
at those things we are unable to imitate. For we do not yet have hands
turned on a lathe, nor yet full of hyacinths,[118] so that they may be
extended for almsgiving with the example of light and, in the manner
of a lathe, may be most ready for producing works, howsoever subtle,
for love of the Lord. Hear 'count', hear 'founder' and hear *'conversus'* as
well. I marvel that these three descriptive nouns came together in one
man. Surely, according to Solomon, *a threefold cord is not easily broken.*[119]

When you hear 'count', pay no attention to his family tree, because
God has chosen the foolish and base things of the world.[120] Rather,
marvel at the triumphant despiser of temporal things. For he had
contempt for his name and his ancestry and worldly riches and honours,
so that naked he might follow the naked Christ. In order to escape the
punishments of the rich man dressed in purple,[121] he denied – on top

---

116 See *Urkundenbuch des Prämonstratensersklosters Arnstein*, 7–9, nr. 4 (1163). For the
terms advocate/advocacy, see n. 92 above.

117 See *Urkundenbuch des Prämonstratensersklosters Arnstein*, 7–9, nr. 4 (1163). A *denarius*
was a type of coin.

118 Cf. Song of Songs 5:14.

119 Ecclesiastes 4:12.

120 Cf. 1 Corinthians 1:27–28.

121 Cf. Luke 16:19–31.

of everything else – even himself, because that is most difficult. Did he not leave behind a great many things for Christ? He did! But what? The soft thigh on his wife's body. He *who leaves behind wife and children* among other things, said the Saviour, *will receive a hundredfold.*[122] Now, this hundredfold grows infinitely, because an infinite number of rewards grows and multiplies. But perhaps someone will say that this [i.e., marriage] could not be a hindrance to his salvation. Let that person hear what the excuse-maker said in the Gospels: *I have just married a wife, and therefore I cannot come.*[123]

When you hear 'founder', reflect on the provider of future goods, when Christ, becoming high priest, entered one time into the holies by his own blood.[124] He who sleeps in the summer will beg in the winter.[125] Therefore, he provided for tomorrow,[126] while he is named in the office of divine worship today. He provided the same worshippers with support for the present life. He provided for tomorrow, because he left behind as many sureties to his salvation as he will have future heirs to his patrimony. He founded it [i.e., the religious house at Arnstein] himself – and indeed, he fertilized it with his zeal for the holy profession. He founded others by the example of his virtue, and for that reason he deserved to be built upon the foundation of the church.[127]

When you hear '*conversus*', understand *a pursuer of good works.*[128] For he preferred to be connected in mind, deed and habit to the eternal bridegroom, who is in Heaven; even then, he did not conform to this world but was reformed in the spirit of his mind.[129] For, having converted and become like a little child, he who was previously a standard-bearer leading the way chose to be cast down in the house of God through the path of humility, because, as a certain one said, *the world conforms to the example of a king,*[130] and one is taught better by life than by word.[131]

---

122 Matthew 19:29.

123 Luke 14:20.

124 Cf. Hebrews 9:11–12.

125 Cf. Proverbs 6:6–11.

126 Cf. Ecclesiastes 4:13.

127 Cf. Ephesians 2:20.

128 Titus 2:14.

129 Cf. Romans 12:2.

130 Claudian, *Claudian's panegyric on the fourth consulate of Honorius*, 46–7, lines 299–300.

131 A variation on a Latin proverb: *Exemplo melius quam verbo quisque docetur.* Werner, *Lateinische Sprichwörter*, 50.

What am I going to say about his charity, about his compassion, he who in all ways was overflowing always from his heart with mercy? Very often, he went out in the icy cold, unprotected by the furs and shirts with which the cold limbs of widows were made warm. The voices of the poor, which frequently reached the ears of the infinite one, bear witness to this. He often handed them nourishment secretly and a covering for the shoulders furtively. In this virtue he was not inferior to Martin, who gave half his cloak, while Ludwig frequently gave the whole garment.[132]

[21] At this time, Abbot Eustachius of happy memory, after he had served vigorously as soldier for twenty-nine years in the castles of the Lord, was freed from the prison of the flesh by God, around whom the spirits of the dead live, and delivered his soul.[133] Richolf succeeded him, whose many marks of probity may be found in his management of the house of God.[134]

In Richolf's sixth year, the venerable count and *conversus* [i.e., Ludwig], as was often his habit, made his rounds with the abbot's permission to visit the churches he had founded and their estates. And when he had come to the convent of the ladies at Gommersheim, he was robbed of the strength of his body and sensed that the separation of death was approaching. Untroubled about his reward, he desired to be unloosed and to be with Christ. And so, wracked with fever for several days, he was instructed solemnly in the church's heavenly mysteries by Abbot Burchard of Münsterdreisen, Provost Werembold of Flonheim, Godfrey (the prior of the aforesaid place [i.e., Gommersheim]), and by many other priests who had flocked together.[135] His whole self burned with desire for the heavenly. Saying farewell to everyone on the eighth Kalends of November [25 October],[136] with the angels rejoicing, he sent his whole spirit across to Christ for the blessed rewards he deserved. For his funeral rites, the entire neighbourhood flocked together to weep for the man they had known. They prayed that he would recommend them to the Lord – nearly as much as they desired to recommend his own blessed spirit to God.

---

132 Cf. Sulpicius Severus, *Vita sancti Martini*, 3.2 (*The life of Saint Martin*, 7).

133 Eustachius died in 1180.

134 Abbot Richolf of Arnstein (1180–96).

135 Flonheim was a house of Augustinian canons; unlike Münsterdreisen and Gommersheim, Ludwig had not played a role in its foundation.

136 25 October 1185.

Thereafter, he lay for two nights' time at Gommersheim, on the third night at Eberbach, on the fourth at the church in Kördorf, and on the fifth at the church of St Margaret; each time, he was rendered favourable to the father of souls by many sweet odours of prayer, with solemn Masses. At last, on the sixth day, with the counts of Nassau, Katzenelnbogen and Diez and the lords of Isenburg carrying his bier,[137] he was laid to rest at his church of Arnstein with great lamentation. How many tears, how many sighs and how many gatherings of both sexes there were in that place is much easier to guess than to write. He was buried in front of the altar of the blessed Pope Nicholas, patron of the same church, on the day of the commemoration of the souls of all the faithful [2 November], in the year of grace 1185, in the forty-seventh year since the foundation of the said church, under Abbot Richolf.

[22] Receive now, reader, this short and simple text I have written, no match for the virtues of such a great man, a text which the sin of boasting did not knowingly spoil in the witness; rather, only a disregard for buried material led to that which may be seen. Let those who wish to do so alter and correct it out of charity; for it will not cry out in protest at the polishing it now awaits from the pen of a more learned talent. Brothers and lords, give – give, I pray – kindness and what you ought to give to such great ashes. Direct your attention vigilantly, I beg, lest you possess for nothing the sought-after land, lest from where you stand to gain grace and merit, you hereafter stand to gain sufferings and punishments.

The eye of the pious Pope Nicholas follows you, and pursues you, and enters through all the narrow spaces of places; it penetrates hidden lairs, it probes concealed places, it sees even if it does not want to be seen by you. Therefore, let us not be ungrateful on account of his kindness, so that his prayer may protect us. But *let us all hear together the conclusion of the discourse. Fear God and keep his commandments; this is the whole duty of man.*[138] *This is the whole duty of man*: that is, through this will he be perfected. Our Lord Jesus Christ, who invited us, leads to this perfection and the crown of the kingdom after the death of the flesh. Amen.

Here ends the little work on the deeds of Count Ludwig, our founder.

---

137 All of these families were introduced in the opening genealogy.
138 Ecclesiastes 12:12–13.

Epitaph[139]

Not death but life gathered this flower; the narrow tomb offers
    sorrow,
Not some clump of earth, but the spring rose, offers hope of life.
Behold the angel, who with the full majesty of God
Keeps this place of rest under its wings.[140]
The year revolves as one thousand with one hundred and eighty-five.
In life the excellent Count Ludwig gathers the stars.

139 I have not included here a second epitaph, for Abbot Godfrey, which also appears
    at the end of the text in the earliest manuscript.
140 The nineteenth-century editor of the text, Widmann, suggests this is a description
    of Ludwig's tomb ('Die Lebensbeschreibung des Grafen Ludwig von Arnstein',
    266).

BIBLIOGRAPHY

Unpublished sources

Leipzig, Universitätsbibliothek Leipzig, Ms 1325. Digitized manuscript available at: http://www.manuscripta-mediaevalia.de/#|4.

London, British Library, Harley 2801.

Munich, Bayerische Staatsbibliothek, Clm 1076. Digitized manuscript available at: http://www.digitale-sammlungen.de/.

Primary sources

The 1106 continuation of Frutolf's chronicle. In *Chronicles of the Investiture Contest,* 138–86.

The 1125 continuation of Frutolf's chronicle. In *Chronicles of the Investiture Contest,* 261–85.

Adam of Bremen. *History of the archbishops of Hamburg-Bremen.* Trans. Francis Joseph Tschan. New York: Columbia University Press, 1959.

Ambrose. *Über die Jungfrauen (De Virginibus).* Trans. Peter Dückers. *Fontes Christiani* 81. Turnhout: Brepols, 2009.

Annales Patherbrunnenses. Eine verlorene Quellenschrift des zwölften Jahrhunderts aus bruchstücken wiederhergestellt. Ed. Paul Scheffer-Boichorst. Innsbruck, 1870.

Annales Pegavienses et Bosovienses. Ed. Georg Heinrich Pertz. In *MGH SS* 16, 232–270. Hanover: Hahn, 1859.

Annales Sancti Petri Erphesfurdenses. Ed. Georg Heinrich Pertz. In *MGH SS* 16, 15–25. Hanover: Hahn, 1859.

Annalista Saxo. Ed. Georg Waitz. In *MGH SS* 6, 542–777. Hanover: Hahn, 1844.

The annals of Lampert of Hersfeld. Trans. I. S. Robinson. Manchester: Manchester University Press, 2015.

The anonymous imperial chronicle. In *Chronicles of the Investiture Contest,* 187–218.

Augustine of Hippo. *Letters,* vol. 5. Trans. Wilfrid Parsons. *The fathers of the church: writings of Saint Augustine* 32. New York, 1956.

— *Letters*. Trans. Roland Teske. *The works of Saint Augustine*, part II, vol. 4. New York: New City Press, 2005.

Barbarossa in Italy. Trans. Thomas Carson. New York: Italica Press, 1994.

Beowulf: A new verse translation. Trans. Seamus Heaney. New York and London: Norton, 2000.

Bernold of St Blasien. *Chronicle*. In *Eleventh-century Germany*, 245–337.

Berthold of Reichenau. *Chronicle: the second version*. In *Eleventh-century Germany*, 108–244.

Bestiary: being an English version of the Bodleian Library, MS Bodley 764. Trans. Richard Barber. Woodbridge: Boydell, 1993.

Boethius. *The consolation of philosophy*. Trans. Richard Green. New York and London: Macmillan, 1962.

Bruno of Merseburg. *Brunonis Saxonicum Bellum [Brunos Sachsenkrieg]*. In *Quellen zur Geschichte Kaiser Heinrichs IV*, 191–405. Trans. Franz-Josef Schmale. *Ausgewählte Quellen zur deutschen Geschichte des Mittelalters, Freiherr-vom-Stein Gedächtnisausgabe* 12. Darmstadt: Wissenschaftliche Buchgesellschaft, 1963.

Charlemagne and Louis the Pious: the lives by Einhard, Notker, Ermoldus, Thegan, and the Astronomer. Trans. Thomas F. X. Noble. University Park, PA: Pennsylvania State University Press, 2009.

The chronicle of Henry of Livonia. Trans. James A. Brundage. New York: Columbia University Press, 2003.

Chronicles of the Investiture Contest: Frutolf of Michelsberg and his continuators: selected sources. Trans. T. J. H. McCarthy. Manchester and New York: Manchester University Press, 2014.

Cicero. *De Inventione*. In *Cicero*, trans. H. M. Hubbell, 1–346. Cambridge, MA: Harvard University Press, 1949; repr. 1960.

Claudian. *Claudian's panegyric on the fourth consulate of Honorius*. Trans. William Barr. Liverpool: Cairns, 1981.

Codex Diplomaticus Saxoniae Regiae, part I, section A, vol. 2: *Urkunden der Markgrafen von Meissen und Landgrafen von Thüringen, 1100–1195*. Ed. Otto Posse. Leipzig: Giesecke & Devrient, 1889.

Conrad of Scheyern. *Chronicon Schirense*. Ed. Philipp Jaffé. In *MGH SS* 17, 615–28. Hanover: Hahn, 1861.

Corpus Orationum, vol. 3. Eds E. Moeller, J.-M. Clément and B. Coppieters 't Wallant. *Corpus Christianorum Series Latina*, 160 B. Turnhout: Brepols, 1993.

Cosmas of Prague. *The chronicle of the Czechs*. Trans. Lisa Wolverton. Washington, DC: Catholic University of America Press, 2009.

Cronica S. Petri Erfordensis moderna. Ed. Oswald Holder-Egger. In *MGH SSrG* 42, 117–369. Hanover and Leipzig: Hahn, 1899.

The crusade of Frederick Barbarossa: the history of the expedition of the Emperor Frederick and related texts. Trans. Graham A. Loud. Farnham and Burlington: Ashgate, 2010.

Decretales Pseudo-Isidorianae et Capitula Angilrammi. Ed. Paul Hinschius. Leipzig: Bernhard Tauchnitz, 1863.

The deeds of Pope Innocent III by an anonymous author. Trans. James M. Powell. Washington, DC: Catholic University of America Press, 2004.

Dobereiner, Philipp. *History der heyligen Junckfrawen Mechtildis († 1160).* Introduced by Hans Pörnbacher. Amsterdam and Utrecht: APA-Holland University Press, 2002; orig. Munich, 1574.

The donation of Constantine (Constitutum Constantini). In Johannes Fried, *Donation of Constantine and Constitutum Constantini: the misinterpretation of a fiction and its original meaning,* 129–45. Berlin and New York: Walter de Gruyter, 2007.

Donizo of Canossa. *Donizonis Vita Mathildis.* Ed. Ludwig Bethmann. In *MGH SS* 12, 348–409. Hanover: Hahn, 1856.

Ebo of Michelsberg. *Das Leben des Bischofs und Bekenners Otto.* In *Heiligenleben zur deutsch-slawischen Geschichte,* 192–271.

Eidelberg, Shlomo, ed. and trans. *The Jews and the crusaders: the Hebrew chronicles of the First and Second Crusades.* Madison, WI: University of Wisconsin Press, 1977.

Einhard. *The life of Charlemagne.* In Einhard and Notker the Stammerer, *Two lives of Charlemagne.* Trans. David Ganz. 1–44. London: Penguin, 2008.

— *Vita Karoli Magni.* Ed. Oswald Holder-Egger. *MGH SSrG* 25. Hanover and Leipzig: Hahn, 1911.

Ekkehard of Aura. *Chronicle, book 5.* In *Chronicles of the Investiture Contest,* 219–53.

Eleventh-century Germany: the Swabian chronicles. Trans. I. S. Robinson. Manchester and New York: Manchester University Press, 2008.

Elisabeth of Schönau: the complete works. Trans. Anne L. Clark. New York and Mahwah, NJ: Paulist Press, 2000.

Engelhard of Langheim. *Vita B. Mathildis Virginis.* Ed. Gottfried Henschen. In *Acta Sanctorum,* 7 May, 436–49. Paris and Rome: Victor Palmé, 1866.

Ennodius. *The life of Saint Epiphanius by Ennodius.* Ed. and trans. Genevieve Marie Cook. Washington, DC: Catholic University of America Press, 1942.

Frutolf of Michelsberg, *Chronicle.* In *Chronicles of the Investiture Contest,* 85–137.

Frutolfs und Ekkehards Chroniken und die Anonyme Kaiserchronik. Trans. Franz-Josef Schmale and Irene Schmale-Ott. *Ausgewählte Quellen zur deutschen Geschichte des Mittelalters, Freiherr-vom-Stein Gedächtnisausgabe* 15. Darmstadt: Wissenschaftliche Buchgesellschaft, 1972.

Germania Pontificia, vol. I. Ed. Albert Brackmann. Berlin: Weidmann, 1911.

— vol. III, part 3. Ed. Albert Brackmann. Berlin: Weidmann, 1935.

Gesta Archiepiscoporum Magdeburgensium. Ed. Wilhelm Schum. In *MGH SS* 14, 361–486. Hanover: Hahn, 1883.

The 'Gesta Normannorum ducum' of William of Jumièges, Orderic Vitalis, and Robert of Torigni, 2 vols. Ed. and trans. Elisabeth van Houts. Oxford: Clarendon Press, 1992–95.

Gregory of Tours. *De virtutibus b. Martini*. Ed. Bruno Krusch. *MGH Scriptores rerum Merovingicarum*, vol. I, part 2, 134–211. Hanover: Hahn, 1885; repr. 1969.

— *The miracles of the Bishop St. Martin*. In Raymond Van Dam, *Saints and their miracles in late antique Gaul*, 199–303. Princeton, NJ: Princeton University Press, 1993.

Gregory the Great. *Homiliae in Hiezechihelem prophetam*. Ed. Marcus Adriaen. *Corpus Christianorum Series Latina* 142. Turnhout: Brepols, 1971.

— *Moralia in Iob*. 3 vols. Ed. Marcus Adriaen. *Corpus Christianorum Series Latina* 143. Turnhout: Brepols, 1979.

Heiligenleben zur deutsch-slawischen Geschichte: Adalbert von Prag und Otto von Bamberg. Trans. Jerzy Strzelczyk and Lorenz Weinrich. *Ausgewählte Quellen zur deutschen Geschichte des Mittelalters, Freiherr-vom-Stein Gedächtnisausgabe* 23. Darmstadt: Wissenschaftliche Buchgesellschaft, 2005.

Helmold of Bosau. *The chronicle of the Slavs*. Trans. Francis Joseph Tschan. New York: Columbia University Press, 1935.

Herbord of Michelsberg. *Leben und Werke des seligen Bamberger Bischofs Otto*. In *Heiligenleben zur deutsch-slawischen Geschichte*, 272–493.

Hildegard of Bingen. *The letters of Hildegard of Bingen*, 3 vols. Trans. Joseph L. Baird and Radd K. Ehrman. New York and Oxford: Oxford University Press, 1994–2004.

— *Scivias*. Trans. Columba Hart and Jane Bishop. New York and Mahwah, NJ: Paulist Press, 1990.

The histories of a medieval German city, Worms c. 1000–c. 1300: translation and commentary. Trans. David S. Bachrach. Farnham and Burlington: Ashgate, 2014.

History and politics in late Carolingian and Ottonian Europe: the chronicle of Regino of Prüm and Adalbert of Magdeburg. Trans. Simon MacLean. Manchester and New York: Manchester University Press, 2009.

Horace. *Satires and Epistles*. Trans. John Davie. Oxford: Oxford University Press, 2011.

Imperial lives and letters of the eleventh century. Trans. Theodor E. Mommsen and Karl F. Morrison. New York: Columbia University Press, 1962.

Isidore of Seville. *Isidori Hispalensis Episcopi Etymologiarum sive Originum Libri XX*. Ed. W. M. Lindsay. Oxford: Clarendon, 1911.

Jerome. *Sancti Eusebii Hieronymi Epistulae*, 3 vols. Ed. Isidore Hilberg. *Corpus Scriptorum Ecclesiasticorum Latinorum* 54–6. Vienna and Leipzig: F. Tempsky and G. Freytag, 1910–18.

Jutta and Hildegard: the biographical sources. Trans. Anna Silvas. University Park, PA: Pennsylvania State University Press, 1999.

'Die Lebensbeschreibung des Grafen Ludwig von Arnstein'. Ed. Simon Widmann. *Annalen des Vereins für Nassauische Alterthumskunde und Geschichtsforschung* 18 (1883–84): 244–66.

Letter of Bishop Eberhard of Bamberg to Gerhoh of Reichersberg (Eberhardi episcopi Babenbergensis ad Gerhoham praepositum Reicherspergensem epistola). In J.-P. Migne, ed., *Patrologia latina* 193, 524A–529B. Paris, 1854.

The life of Emperor Henry IV. In *Imperial lives and letters of the eleventh century,* 101–37.

The life of Godfrey of Cappenberg. In *Norbert and Early Norbertine Spirituality,* 85–119.

The life of Otto, apostle of Pomerania (1060–1139), by Ebo and Herbordus. Trans. Charles H. Robinson. London and New York: Macmillan, 1920.

Liudprand of Cremona. *The complete works of Liudprand of Cremona.* Trans. Paolo Squatriti. Washington, DC: Catholic University of America Press, 2007.

Lucan. *The civil war (Pharsalia).* Trans. J. D. Duff. Cambridge, MA: Harvard University Press, 1928; repr. 1997.

Medieval hagiography: an anthology. Ed. Thomas Head. New York: Garland, 2000.

Miller, Maureen. *Power and the holy in the age of the Investiture Conflict: a brief history with documents.* Boston and New York: Bedford/St. Martin's, 2005.

Norbert and early Norbertine spirituality. Trans. Theodore J. Antry and Carol Neel. New York and Mahwah, NJ: Paulist Press, 2007.

Notker the Stammerer. *The deeds of Charlemagne.* In Einhard and Notker the Stammerer, *Two lives of Charlemagne,* trans. David Ganz, 45–116. London: Penguin, 2008.

Otto of Freising. *The two cities: a chronicle of universal history to the year 1146 A.D.* Trans. Charles Christopher Mierow. New York: Columbia University Press, 1928; repr. 2002.

Otto of Freising and Rahewin. *The deeds of Frederick Barbarossa.* Trans. Charles Christopher Mierow. New York: Columbia University Press, 1953; repr. 2004.

Ottonian Germany: the chronicon of Thietmar of Merseburg. Trans. David Warner. Manchester and New York: Manchester University Press, 2001.

Ovid. *Ex Ponto.* In *Ovid,* trans. Arthur Leslie Wheeler; revised by G. P. Goold, 263–489. Cambridge, MA: Harvard University Press, 1924; repr. 1988.

— *Metamorphoses,* 2 vols. Trans. Frank Justus Miller; revised by G. P. Goold. Cambridge, MA: Harvard University Press, 1916; repr. 1958.

The papal reform of the eleventh century: lives of Pope Leo IX and Pope Gregory VII. Trans. I. S. Robinson. Manchester and New York: Manchester University Press, 2004.

Passio Thiemonis. Ed. Wilhelm Wattenbach. In *MGH SS* 11, 51–62. Hanover: Hahn, 1854.

Paul the Deacon. *Historia Romana.* Ed. Hans Droysen. *MGH SSrG* 49. Berlin: Weidmann, 1879.

Persius. *Satires.* In *Juvenal and Persius*, ed. and trans. Susanna Morton Braund, 41–125. Cambridge, MA: Harvard University Press, 2004.

Die Prüfeninger Vita Bischof Ottos I. von Bamberg nach der Fassung des Großen Österreichischen Legendars. Ed. Jürgen Petersohn. MGH SSrG 71. Hanover: Hahn, 1999.

Queenship and sanctity: the lives of Mathilda and the epitaph of Adelheid. Trans. Sean Gilsdorf. Washington, DC: Catholic University of America Press, 2004.

RB 1980: the rule of St Benedict in Latin and English with notes. Ed. Timothy Fry. Collegeville, MN: The Liturgical Press, 1981.

Die Regesten der Bischöfe von Passau, vol. 1. Ed. Egon Boshof. Munich: C. H. Beck, 1992.

Relatio de piis operibus Ottonis episcopi Bambergensis. Ed. Oswald Holder-Egger. In *MGH SS* 15:2, 1151–66. Hanover: Hahn, 1888.

Richard of St. Victor. *The twelve patriarchs (Benjamin minor).* In *Richard of St Victor*, trans. Grover A. Zinn, 51–147. New York: Paulist Press, 1979.

Saints and cities in medieval Italy. Trans. Diana Webb. Manchester and New York: Manchester University Press, 2007.

Sallust. *The War with Catiline.* In *Sallust*, trans. J. C. Rolfe, 1–129. Cambridge, MA: Harvard University Press, 1971; repr. 2013.

— *The War with Jugurtha.* In *Sallust*, trans. J. C. Rolfe, 131–381. Cambridge, MA: Harvard University Press, 1971; repr. 2013.

Seneca. *Ad Lucilium Epistolae morales*, 3 vols. Trans. Richard M. Gummere. Cambridge, MA: Harvard University Press, 1917–25.

Soldiers of Christ: saints and saints' lives from late antiquity and the early middle ages. Eds Thomas F. X. Noble and Thomas Head. University Park, PA: Pennsylvania State University Press, 1995.

Suetonius. *Lives of the Caesars.* Trans. Catharine Edwards. *Oxford World's Classics.* Oxford: Oxford University Press, 2008.

Sulpicius Severus. *Dialogus Primus.* In Sulpicius Severus, *Libri qui supersunt (Opera omnia)*, ed. Karl Halm, *Corpus Scriptorum Ecclesiasticorum Latinorum* 1, 152–80. Vienna, 1866.

— *Dialogus Tertius.* In Sulpicius Severus, *Libri qui supersunt (Opera omnia)*, ed. Karl Halm, *Corpus Scriptorum Ecclesiasticorum Latinorum* 1, 198–216. Vienna, 1866.

— *Epistula Tertia.* In Sulpicius Severus, *Libri qui supersunt (Opera omnia)*, ed. Karl Halm, *Corpus Scriptorum Ecclesiasticorum Latinorum* 1, 146–51. Vienna, 1866.

— *The First Dialogue.* Trans. Bernard M. Peebles. In *The Fathers of the Church*, vol. 7, 161–99. Washington, DC: Catholic University of America Press, 1949.

— *The Letter to Bassula (Epist. 3).* Trans. Bernard M. Peebles. In *The Fathers of the Church*, vol. 7, 153–9. Washington, DC: Catholic University of America Press, 1949.

— *The life of Saint Martin of Tours.* Trans. F. R. Hoare. In *Soldiers of Christ,* 1–29.

— *The Third Dialogue.* Trans. Bernard M. Peebles. In *The Fathers of the Church,* vol. 7, 225–51. Washington, DC: Catholic University of America Press, 1949.

— *Vita Sancti Martini.* In Sulpicius Severus, *Libri qui supersunt (Opera omnia),* ed. Karl Halm, *Corpus Scriptorum Ecclesiasticorum Latinorum* 1, 107–37. Vienna, 1866.

Die Traditionen und Urkunden des Stiftes Diessen 1114–1362. Ed. Waldemar Schlögl. *Quellen und Erörterungen zur bayerischen Geschichte, Neue Folge* 22:1. Munich: C. H. Beck, 1967.

Die Urkunden Friedrichs I. Ed. Heinrich Appelt. *Monumenta Germaniae Historica. Die Urkunden der deutschen Könige und Kaiser* 10, 5 vols. Hanover: Hahn, 1975–90.

Die Urkunden Heinrichs IV. Eds Dietrich von Gladiss and Alfred Gawlik. *Monumenta Germaniae Historica. Die Urkunden der deutschen Könige und Kaiser* 6, 3 vols. Berlin: Weidmann, 1941–78.

Die Urkunden Heinrichs V. und der Königin Mathilde. Ed. Matthias Thiel. *Monumenta Germaniae Historica. Die Urkunden der deutschen Könige und Kaiser* 7. Online edition: www.mgh.de/ddhv/ (accessed 2 August 2016)

Die Urkunden Konrads III. und seines Sohnes Heinrich. Ed. Friedrich Hausmann. *Monumenta Germaniae Historica. Die Urkunden der deutschen Könige und Kaiser* 9. Vienna, Cologne & Graz: Hermann Böhlaus Nachf., 1969.

Die Urkunden Lothars III. und der Kaiserin Richenza. Ed. Emil von Ottenthal and Hans Hirsch. *Monumenta Germaniae Historica. Die Urkunden der deutschen Könige und Kaiser* 8. Berlin: Weidmann, 1927.

Urkundenbuch des Prämonstratensersklosters Arnstein an der Lahn. Ed. Karl Herquet. Wiesbaden: Limbarth, 1883.

Virgil. *The Aeneid.* Trans. Robert Fitzgerald. New York: Vintage Books, 1990.

— *Aeneid,* 2 vols. Trans. H. Rushton Fairclough; revised by G. P. Goold. Cambridge, MA: Harvard University Press, 1918; repr. 1999.

Vita Burchardi [The life of Bishop Burchard of Worms]. In *The histories of a medieval German city, Worms c. 1000–c. 1300,* 29–60.

Vita Sancti Eckenberti [The life of Saint Eckenbert]. In *The histories of a medieval German city, Worms c. 1000–c. 1300,* 61–79.

'Vita, ut videtur, cuiusdam magistrae monialium Admuntensium in Styria saeculo XII'. *Analecta Bollandiana* 12 (1893): 359–66.

Warfare and politics in medieval Germany, ca. 1000: on the variety of our times by Alpert of Metz. Trans. David S. Bachrach. Toronto: Pontifical Institute of Mediaeval Studies, 2012.

A warrior bishop of the twelfth century: the deeds of Albero of Trier, by Balderich. Trans. Brian A. Pavlac. Toronto: Pontifical Institute of Mediaeval Studies, 2008.

Widukind of Corvey. *Deeds of the Saxons.* Trans. Bernard S. Bachrach and David S. Bachrach. Washington, DC: The Catholic University of America Press, 2014.

William of Malmesbury. *The deeds of the bishops of England (Gesta Pontificum Anglorum) of William of Malmesbury*. Trans. David Preest. Woodbridge: Boydell, 2002.

— *The history of the English kings (Gesta Regum Anglorum)*, vol. 1. Ed. and trans. R. A. B. Mynors, R. M. Thomson and M. Winterbottom. Oxford: Clarendon Press, 1998.

Wipo. *The deeds of Conrad II*. In *Imperial lives and letters of the eleventh century*, 52–100.

Secondary sources

Ackley, Joseph Salvatore. 'Re-approaching the Western medieval church treasury inventory, c.800–1250'. *Journal of Art Historiography* 11 (December 2014): https://arthistoriography.files.wordpress.com/2014/11/ackley.pdf.

Ahlfeld, Richard. 'Das Chronicon Gozecense'. *Deutsches Archiv für Erforschung des Mittelalters* 11 (1954–55): 74–100.

Althoff, Gerd. *Family, friends and followers: political and social bonds in early medieval Europe*. Trans. Christopher Carroll. Cambridge: Cambridge University Press, 2004.

Arnold, Benjamin. *German knighthood 1050–1300*. Oxford: Clarendon Press, 1985.

— *Medieval Germany, 500–1300: a political interpretation*. Toronto and Buffalo: University of Toronto Press, 1997.

— *Power and property in medieval Germany: economic and social change c. 900–1300*. Oxford: Oxford University Press, 2004.

— *Princes and territories in medieval Germany*. Cambridge: Cambridge University Press, 1991.

— 'The Western Empire, 1125–1197'. In *The new Cambridge medieval history*, vol. 4:2, eds David Luscombe and Jonathan Riley-Smith, 384–421. Cambridge: Cambridge University Press, 2004.

Bachrach, David S. '*Milites* and warfare in pre-crusade Germany'. *War in History* 22 (2015): 298–343.

Backmund, Norbert. *Die Chorherrenorden und ihre Stifter in Bayern: Augustinerchorherren, Prämonstratenser, Chorherren v. Hl. Geist, Antoniter*. Passau: Neue-Presse-Verlag, 1966.

Bartlett, Robert. 'The conversion of a pagan society in the middle ages'. *History: the quarterly journal of the Historical Association* 70 (1985): 185–201.

— *Why can the dead do such great things? Saints and worshippers from the martyrs to the Reformation*. Princeton, NJ and Oxford: Princeton University Press, 2013.

Beach, Alison I. 'Voices from a distant land: fragments of a twelfth-century nuns' letter collection'. *Speculum* 77 (2002): 34–54.

— *Women as scribes: book production and monastic reform in twelfth-century Bavaria.* Cambridge: Cambridge University Press, 2004.

— ed. *Manuscripts and monastic culture: reform and renewal in twelfth-century Germany.* Turnhout: Brepols, 2007.

Benson, Robert L. *The bishop-elect: a study in medieval ecclesiastical office.* Princeton, NJ: Princeton University Press, 1968.

Blumenthal, Uta-Renate. *The Investiture Controversy: church and monarchy from the ninth to the twelfth century.* Philadelphia, PA: University of Pennsylvania Press, 1988.

Borgolte, Michael. 'Stiftergedenken in Kloster Dießen: Ein Beitrag zur Kritik bayerischer Traditionsbücher'. *Frühmittelalterliche Studien* 24 (1990): 235–89.

Brown, Elizabeth A. R. 'The tyranny of a construct: feudalism and historians of medieval Europe'. *American Historical Review* 79 (1974): 1063–88.

Bruce, Scott G. *Silence and sign language in medieval monasticism: the Cluniac tradition, c. 900–1200.* Cambridge and New York: Cambridge University Press, 2007.

Christiansen, Eric. *The northern crusades: the Baltic and the Catholic frontier, 1100–1525.* Minneapolis, MN: University of Minnesota Press, 1980.

Classen, Peter. *Gerhoch von Reichersberg: eine Biographie mit einem Anhang über die Quellen, ihre handschriftliche Überlieferung und ihre Chronologie.* Wiesbaden: F. Steiner, 1960.

Constable, Giles. *The reformation of the twelfth century.* Cambridge: Cambridge University Press, 1996.

Cowdrey, H. E. J. *The Cluniacs and the Gregorian Reform.* Oxford: Clarendon, 1970.

Crusius, Irene. '... *ut nulla fere provincia sit in partibus Occidentis, ubi ejusdem religionis congregations non inveniantur* ... Prämonstratenser als Forschungsaufgabe'. In Crusius and Flachenecker, eds, *Studien zum Prämonstratenser,* 11–32.

— ed. *Studien zum Kanonissenstift.* Veröffentlichungen des Max-Planck-Instituts für Geschichte 167. Göttingen: Vandenhoeck & Ruprecht, 2001.

Crusius, Irene and Helmut Flachenecker, eds. *Studien zum Prämonstratenserorden.* Veröffentlichungen des Max-Planck-Instituts für Geschichte 185. Göttingen: Vandenhoeck & Ruprecht, 2003.

Dale, Johanna. 'Inauguration and political liturgy in the Hohenstaufen Empire, 1138–1215'. *German History* 34 (2016): 191–213.

Delehaye, Hippolyte. *The legends of the saints.* Trans. Donald Attwater. New York: Fordham University Press, 1962; orig. Brussels, 1905.

Dendorfer, Jürgen and Roman Deutinger, eds. *Das Lehnswesen im Hochmittelalter: Forschungskonstrukte–Quellenbefunde–Deutungsrelevanz.* Ostfildern: Jan Thorbecke Verlag, 2010.

Eldevik, John. 'Driving the chariot of the Lord: Siegfried I of Mainz (1060–1084) and episcopal identity in an age of transition'. In *The bishop reformed: studies of episcopal power and culture in the central middle ages,* eds John S. Ott and Anna Trumbore Jones, 161–88. Aldershot and Burlington: Ashgate, 2007.

— *Episcopal power and ecclesiastical reform in the German Empire: tithes, lordship, and community, 950–1150.* Cambridge: Cambridge University Press, 2012.

Elliott, Dyan. *Spiritual marriage: sexual abstinence in medieval wedlock.* Princeton, NJ: Princeton University Press, 1993.

Fassler, Margot. *Music in the medieval West.* New York and London: Norton, 2014.

Freed, John B. *The counts of Falkenstein: noble self-consciousness in twelfth-century Germany.* Philadelphia, PA: American Philosophical Society, 1984.

— *Frederick Barbarossa: the prince and the myth.* New Haven, CT and London: Yale University Press, 2016.

— 'German source collections: the archdiocese of Salzburg as a case study'. In *Medieval women and the sources of medieval history,* ed. Joel T. Rosenthal, 80–121. Athens, GA and London: University of Georgia Press, 1990.

— 'Medieval German social history: generalizations and particularism'. *Central European History* 25 (1992): 1–26.

— *Noble bondsmen: ministerial marriages in the archdiocese of Salzburg, 1100–1343.* Ithaca, NY and London: Cornell University Press, 1995.

— 'Nobles, ministerials and knights in the archdiocese of Salzburg'. *Speculum* 62 (1987): 575–611.

— 'Reflections on the medieval German nobility'. *American Historical Review* 91 (1986): 553–75.

Fuhrmann, Horst. *Germany in the high middle ages c. 1050–1200.* Trans. Timothy Reuter. Cambridge: Cambridge University Press, 1986.

Goldberg, Eric J. *Struggle for empire: kingship and conflict under Louis the German, 817–876.* Ithaca, NY and London: Cornell University Press, 2006.

Griffiths, Fiona J. 'Women and reform in the central middle ages'. In *The Oxford handbook of women and gender in medieval Europe,* eds Judith M. Bennett and Ruth Mazo Karras, 447–63. Oxford: Oxford University Press, 2013.

Haverkamp, Alfred. *Medieval Germany, 1056–1273.* Trans. Helga Braun and Richard Mortimer. 2nd edn. Oxford: Oxford University Press, 1988.

Hechberger, Werner. *Adel im fränkisch-deutschen Mittelalter: Zur Anatomie eines Forschungsproblems.* Ostfildern: Jan Thorbecke Verlag, 2005.

Henderson, Alfred. *Latin proverbs and quotations.* London, 1869.

Howe, John. *Before the Gregorian Reform: the Latin church at the turn of the first millennium.* Ithaca, NY and London: Cornell University Press, 2016.

— 'The nobility's reform of the medieval church'. *American Historical Review* 93 (1988): 317–39.

Jaeger, C. Stephen. *The origins of courtliness: civilizing trends and the formation of courtly ideals, 939–1210.* Philadelphia, PA: University of Pennsylvania Press, 1985.

Jakobs, Hermann. *Die Hirsauer: Ihre Ausbreitung und Rechtsstellung im Zeitalter des Investiturstreites*. Cologne: Böhlau, 1961.

Kaeuper, Richard W. *Medieval chivalry*. Cambridge: Cambridge University Press, 2016.

Klebel, Ernst. 'Bamberger Besitz in Österreich und Bayern'. *Jahrbuch für fränkische Landesforschung* 11/12 (1953): 207–20.

Krings, Bruno. *Das Prämonstratenserstift Arnstein a. d. Lahn im Mittelalter (1139–1527)*. Wiesbaden: Selbstverlag der Historischen Kommission für Nassau, 1990.

— 'Die Prämonstratenser und ihr weiblicher Zweig'. In Crusius and Flachenecker, eds, *Studien zum Prämonstratenser*, 75–105.

Leciejewicz, Lech. 'Die Entstehung der Stadt Szczecin im Rahmen der frühen Stadtentwicklung an der südlichen Ostseeküste'. In *Vor- und frühformen der europäischen Stadt im Mittelalter*, eds Herbert Jankuhn, Walter Schlesinger and Heiko Steuer, vol. 2, 209–30. Göttingen: Vandenhoeck & Ruprecht, 1974.

Lutter, Christina. *Geschlecht & Wissen, Norm & Praxis, Lesen & Schreiben: Monastische Reformgemeinschaften im 12. Jahrhundert*. Veröffentlichungen des Instituts für Österreichische Geschichtsforschung 43. Vienna and Munich: R. Oldenbourg Verlag, 2005.

— 'Normative ideals, social practice, and doing community in high medieval Central European reform movements'. In *Between community and seclusion: defining the religious life in the South Asian traditions, in Buddhism, and in Eastern and Western Christianity*, eds Gert Melville and Katrin Rösler. Berlin: Lit Verlag (forthcoming).

Lyon, Jonathan R. 'Cooperation, compromise and conflict avoidance: family relationships in the house of Andechs, ca. 1100–1204'. PhD diss., University of Notre Dame, 2004.

— 'The letters of Princess Sophia of Hungary, a nun at Admont'. In *Writing Medieval Women's Lives*, eds Charlotte Newman Goldy and Amy Livingstone, 51–68. New York: Palgrave Macmillan, 2012.

— 'Noble lineages, *Hausklöster*, and monastic advocacy in the twelfth century: the Garsten Vogtweistum in its dynastic context'. *Mitteilungen des Instituts für Österreichische Geschichtsforschung* (2015): 1–29.

— *Princely brothers and sisters: the sibling bond in German politics, 1100–1250*. Ithaca, NY and London: Cornell University Press, 2013.

Melville, Gert. *The world of medieval monasticism*. Trans. James D. Mixson. Collegeville, MN: Liturgical Press, 2016.

Miklosich, Franz. *Etymologisches Wörterbuch der slavischen Sprachen*. Vienna: Wilhelm Braumüller, 1886.

Miller, Maureen. *Clothing the clergy: virtue and power in medieval Europe, c. 800–1200*. Ithaca, NY and London: Cornell University Press, 2014.

Mortimer, Richard. 'Knights and knighthood in Germany in the central middle ages'. In *The ideals and practice of medieval knighthood*, eds Christopher Harper-Bill and Ruth Harvey, 86–103. Woodbridge: Boydell, 1986.

Moszyński, Leszek. *Die vorchristliche Religion der Slaven im Lichte der slavischen Sprachwissenschaft*. Cologne: Böhlau, 1992.

Newman, Martha G. 'Real men and imaginary women: Engelhard of Langheim considers a woman in disguise'. *Speculum* 78 (2003): 1184–1213.

Ó Riain, Diarmuid. 'The *Magnum Legendarium Austriacum*: a new investigation of one of medieval Europe's richest hagiographical collections'. *Analecta Bollandiana* 133 (2015): 87–165.

Patze, Hans. 'Die Pegauer Annalen, die Königserhebung Wratislaws von Böhmen und die Anfänge der Stadt Pegau'. *Jahrbuch für die Geschichte Mittel- und Ostdeutschlands* 12 (1963): 1–62.

Patzold, Steffen. *Das Lehnswesen*. Munich: C. H. Beck, 2012.

Paul, Nicholas. *To follow in their footsteps: the crusades and family memory in the high Middle Ages*. Ithaca, NY and London: Cornell University Press, 2012.

Peter, Tylo. 'Aufregung und Wirren um die *Annales Pegavienses*'. *Heimatblätter des Bornaer Landes* 12 (2006): 2–13.

Petersohn, Jürgen. 'Otto von Bamberg und seine Biographen: Grundformen und Entwicklung des Ottobildes im hohen und späten Mittelalter'. *Zeitschrift für bayerische Landesgeschichte* 43 (1980): 3–27.

—— *Der südliche Ostseeraum im kirchlich-politischen Kräftespiel des Reichs, Polens und Dänemarks vom 10. bis 13. Jahrhundert*. Cologne and Vienna: Böhlau, 1979.

Phillips, Jonathan. *The Second Crusade: extending the frontiers of Christendom*. New Haven, CT and London: Yale University Press, 2007.

Reuter, Timothy. 'The medieval nobility in twentieth-century historiography'. In *Companion to historiography*, ed. Michael Bentley, 177–202. London and New York: Routledge, 1997.

—— 'Past, present and no future in the twelfth-century Regnum Teutonicum'. In *The perception of the past in twelfth-century Europe*, ed. Paul Magdalino, 15–36. London: Hambledon Press, 1992.

Reynolds, Susan. *Fiefs and vassals: the medieval evidence reinterpreted*. Oxford: Oxford University Press, 1994.

Robinson, I. S. *Henry IV of Germany, 1056–1106*. Cambridge: Cambridge University Press, 1999.

—— 'Reform and the church, 1073–1122'. In *The new Cambridge medieval history*, vol. 4:1, eds David Luscombe and Jonathan Riley-Smith, 268–334. Cambridge: Cambridge University Press, 2004.

Rossignol, Sébastien. 'Bilingualism in medieval Europe: Germans and Slavs in Helmold of Bosau's *Chronicle*'. *Central European History* 47 (2014): 523–43.

Schmid, Karl. 'Adel und Reform in Schwaben'. In *Investiturstreit und Reichsverfassung*, ed. Josef Fleckenstein, 295–319. Sigmaringen: Jan Thorbecke Verlag, 1973. Reprinted in Karl Schmid, *Gebetsgedenken und adliges Selbstverständnis im Mittelalter: Ausgewählte Beiträge* (Sigmaringen: Jan Thorbecke Verlag, 1983), 337–59.

Schneidmüller, Bernd. 'Die einzigartig geliebte Stadt – Heinrich II. und Bamberg'. In *Kaiser Heinrich II. 1002–1024*, eds Josef Kirmeier, Bernd Schneidmüller, Stefan Weinfurter and Evamaria Brockhoff, 30–51. Augsburg: J. P. Himmer, 2002.

—— 'Rule by consensus: forms and concepts of political order in the European middle ages'. *The Medieval History Journal* 16:2 (2013): 449–71.

Schulenburg, Jane Tibbetts. 'Saints' lives as a source for the history of women, 500–1100'. In *Medieval women and the sources of medieval history*, ed. Joel T. Rosenthal, 285–320. Athens, GA and London: University of Georgia Press, 1990.

Seitz, Reinhard W. 'Zur Person der Gisela, "Gräfin von Schwabegg", Stifterin des Frauenklosters Edelstetten'. *Archivalische Zeitschrift, Neue Folge* 80 (1997): 360–73.

Sot, Michel. *Gesta episcoporum, gesta abbatum.* Typologie des sources du Moyen Age occidental 37. Turnhout: Brepols, 1981.

Stieldorf, Andrea. *Marken und Markgrafen: Studien zur Grenzsicherung durch die fränkisch-deutschen Herrscher.* Hanover: Hahnsche Buchhandlung, 2012.

Tellenbach, Gerd. *The church in Western Europe from the tenth to the early twelfth century.* Trans. Timothy Reuter. Cambridge: Cambridge University Press, 1993.

Vanderputten, Steven. *Monastic reform as process: realities and representations in medieval Flanders, 900–1100.* Ithaca, NY and London: Cornell University Press, 2013.

Van Engen, John. *Rupert of Deutz.* Berkeley, CA: University of California Press, 1983.

Venarde, Bruce L. *Women's monasticism and medieval society: nunneries in France and England, 890–1215.* Ithaca, NY and London: Cornell University Press, 1997.

Vogtherr, Thomas. 'Pegau'. In *Die Mönchsklöster der Benediktiner in Mecklenburg-Vorpommern, Sachsen-Anhalt, Thüringen und Sachsen*, vol. 2, eds Christof Römer and Monika Lücke, 1195–1224. St. Ottilien: EOS Verlag, 2012.

—— 'Wiprecht von Groitzsch: Bemerkungen zur Figur des sozialen Aufsteigers im hohen Mittelalter'. In *Figuren und Strukturen: Historische Essays für Hartmut Zwahr zum 65. Geburtstag*, eds Manfred Hettling, Uwe Schirmer and Susanne Schötz, 157–69. Munich: K. G. Saur, 2002.

—— 'Wiprecht von Groitzsch und das Jakobspatrozinium des Klosters Pegau. Ein Beitrag zur Kritik der Pegauer Annalen'. *Neues Archiv für Sächsische Geschichte* 72 (2001): 35–54.

Wattenbach, Wilhelm. *Deutschlands Geschichtsquellen im Mittelalter bis zur Mitte des dreizehnten Jahrhunderts*, 2 vols. Berlin: Wilhelm Hertz, 1885–86.

Weiler, Björn. 'Suitability and right: imperial succession and the norms of politics in early Staufen Germany'. In *Making and breaking the rules: succession in medieval Europe, c. 1000–c. 1600*, eds Frédérique Lachaud and Michael Penman, 71–86. Turnhout: Brepols, 2008.

Weinfurter, Stefan. *The Salian century: main currents in an age of transition.* Trans. Barbara M. Bowlus. Philadelphia, PA: University of Pennsylvania Press, 1999.

Weller, Tobias. *Die Heiratspolitik des deutschen Hochadels im 12. Jahrhundert.* Cologne, Weimar and Vienna: Böhlau Verlag, 2004.

Werner, Jakob and Peter Flury. *Lateinische Sprichwörter und Sinnsprüche des Mittelalters.* Heidelberg: Carl Winter Universitätsverlag, 1966.

Wickham, Chris. *Medieval Rome: stability and crisis of a city, 900–1150.* Oxford: Oxford University Press, 2015.

Wolbrink, Shelley Amiste. 'Women in the Premonstratensian Order of north-western Germany, 1120–1250'. *The Catholic Historical Review* 89 (2003): 387–408.

Wüst, Wolfgang. 'Die Schwabegger (898?–1167) und die Eberstaller (1113–1330): Schwäbische Edelfreie zwischen Ministerialität, Vasallität und Nobilität'. In *Hochmittelalterliche Adelsfamilien in Altbayern, Franken und Schwaben,* eds Ferdinand Kramer and Wilhelm Störmer, 433–47. Munich: Kommission für bayerische Landesgeschichte, 2005.

INDEX

Note: italicized page numbers refer to the maps and genealogies; 'n.' after a page reference indicates the number of a note on that page.